WHERE TO WATCH BIRDS IN CATALONIA

WHERE TO WATCH BIRDS IN CATALONIA

Josep del Hoyo
Jordi Sargatal
and
Oriol Alamany
Martí Boada
Toni Curcó
Joan Estrada
Ferran Gonzalez
Alex de Juan
Miquel Macias
Xavier Marco
Albert Martínez
Anna Motis
Jaume Orta
Joan Vazquez

Foreword by
Herbert Axell

Lynx Edicions

First edition: september 1989

© **Lynx Promocions, S.A.**, Avinguda Diagonal, 477, planta 19. 08036-Barcelona

The specific contributions of each author were as follows:
Oriol Alamany (chapter 11); *Martí Boada* (chapter 4); *Toni Curcó* (chapter 9); *Joan Estrada* (chapters 5 and 9); *Ferran Gonzalez* (chapter 14); *Josep Del Hoyo* (Introduction, chapters 2, 9 and 10, Specialities and Appendices); *Alex de Juan* (chapter 13); *Miquel Macias* (chapter 5); *Xavier Marco* (chapter 10); *Albert Martínez* (chapter 7); *Anna Motis* (chapters 5, 6, 8 and 12); *Jaume Orta* (chapters 5, 6, 8 and 12); *Jordi Sargatal* (Introduction, chapters 1, 2 and 3, Specialities and Appendices); *Joan Vazquez* (chapter 10).

Editing coordination: *Josep del Hoyo* and *Jordi Sargatal*.

Cover Design: *Oriol Alamany*.

Cover photographs (from left to right and from top to bottom): Roller, White Stork at the nest, Hoopoe, Rock Thrush, Red-crested Pochard and adult Bearded Vulture with young on the nest: © *Oriol Alamany*.

Drawings: *Jordi Mateos*.

Maps: *Mònica Martinoy*.

Interior design and computerized layout: *Josep del Hoyo* and *Xavier Ruiz*.

English translation: *Toni Strubell*.

Printed by *Maestrax, S.A.*, Sant Guillem, 23. 08000-Barcelona

D.L.: B-38592-89

ISBN: 84-87334-00-8

INDEX

FOREWORD

As in all developed countries, the distribution of birds in modern Catalonia (where they are, of what species, how many, which breed, which winter or pass through) is predominantly the result of agricultural and industrial development. Everywhere, man's use of natural resources, which he has considered to exist only for his own benefit, so abuses bird habitats that the existence of more than one tenth of the World's remaining 9000 species is seriously threatened. In Europe alone, many millions of the survivors are killed every year for sport or to provide epicurean delicacies.

The situation is no less true in Catalonia than anywhere else. When the Spanish State's coastline was up for grabs by developers during the Franco regime, new urbanizations arose and spread at the expense of birds that had long depended on this lovely coast for nesting sites or winter quarters or refuelling stops on the great seasonal migrations between Europe and Africa. Quickly the Catalan Costa Brava became the target area for millions of other migrants as north European sunseekers took over every sandy shore and their accomodation was provided wherever building was possible, including some of the wild, heather-clad tops of intervening parts of the rugged coast that gave this beautiful area its name.

Then, with the Spanish State's entry into the European Community, with the consequent availability of grants to "improve" land in Mediterranean countries which had been considered of little importance to agriculture, avian populations continued to suffer as more parts of wilderness areas were lost -and the EEC's food surplus grew.

But now, in first-World countries at least, we are becoming frightened of the damage we are doing to the gene-pool of plants and insects which not only sustain birds but help maintain a sanitary environment for humans too. "Green" movements are burgeoning and are no longer thought of as environmentalist cranks but have increasing political clout and may not be ignored by the people who govern our lives.

The authors of this book are very successfully green. As founders of Catalonia's Organization for the Defence of the National Heritage (DEPANA), their prime objective has been to save bird habitats and reduce bird slaughter. In this they have been lucky in having a sympathetic government.

Newly self-governing again, the Generalitat de Catalunya (Catalan Government) was conscious of the threat to their country's natural heritage resulting from an expanding economy, headlong urbanization and agricultural development.

In the Empordà region, just south of the border where the Pyrenees mountains fall into the Mediterranean with dramatic abandon, lie the only coastal wetlands remaining between France's Camargue and the River Ebre's delta. Ninth in importance in the Spanish State, these marshes have long been a stop-over feeding site and wintering area for birds. But they were owned by a development consortium who were about to convert their property into an extension of a new holiday town. However, when the conservationists protested, the Generalitat listened and acted. They bought the whole 525 hectares of saltmarsh for 1,500 million pesetas, at £5,874 per acre, making a record investment in the future of their country's wildlife heritage and a courageous step for which the Catalan Government deserved worldwide acclaim.

Catalonia is one quarter the size of England. It has a greater variety of wildlife habitats which range from the new Aiguamolls de l'Empordà Nature Park, where birdwatching is easy from trails and hides, to the awesome alps reached by steep tracks out of Andorra to the vast lagoons and mud flats of the Ebre Delta. This guide covers some 40 itineraries in the best 15 zones of this dramatically-varied area and tells birdwatchers how best to get to them and from which points to watch without causing disturbance. To avoid birdwatchers wandering around vast dusty steppes of thistles and dried grasses, tips are given as to where to sit and be able to sort out Thekla, Crested and Skylarks while also enjoying good views of Short-toed and Dupont's Larks. It gives advice on the best vantage points for seeing Bearded Vulture, Bonelli's Eagle, Griffon and Egyptian Vultures, Little Bustard, a big variety of heron species, Flamingo, White Stork, Pratincole, Audouin's, Mediterranean and Slender-billed Gulls, Pin-tailed and Black-bellied Sandgrouse, Great Spotted Cuckoo, Roller, Bee-eater, Wallcreeper, Penduline Tit and many more birds of this rich sector of the Mediterranean basin which rarely, if ever, come much further north.

All of the sites described are of critical importance to birds which breed in Britain and NW Europe and migrate through or winter in the NE corner of the Iberian Peninsula. Most are safeguarded by local conservationists and a helpful Government prepared to cope with the ever-growing problem of balancing the pressures of industry and lucrative tourism - which increasingly includes birdwatchers - with the need to protect natural resources.

Incongruously, after what we have done to them, birds now need people - they need the money which birdwatchers are prepared to pay as subscriptions to protection societies who can then buy land, or influence government bodies to acquire land, which can be managed as nature reserves and provide facilities for observation without disturbance. This guide serves that objective.

Herbert Axell

INTRODUCTION

Birdwatching is a hobby that is becoming more and more popular in many countries of the world, especially in Europe and North America. In Great Britain, for example, hundreds of thousands of people, belonging to many different societies, spend a great deal of their spare time enjoying birds, identifying them, watching them with their binoculars, photographing them or studying their biology and behaviour.

The fact that more people are interested in watching birds than in watching fishes, amphibians, reptiles, mammals or plants has a straightforward explanation. There are plenty of different species of birds to be found almost anywhere; birds are very colourful and have varying forms; they can also be easily seen when they fly. On any single walk in the country, more different species of birds will be seen (without too much effort) than any other group of vertebrates.

The combination of these factors has given European and North American bird study and protection societies in Europe and North America a large amount of members. These societies tend to be very powerful, and for this reason they have normally been at the head of the nature conservation movement. This is the case, for example, of the Royal Society for the Protection of Birds (RSPB) in Great Britain, and the Audubon Society in North America, to mention but two of these societies.

Sooner or later, this same process was bound to occur in Catalonia too. Indeed, over the course of the last few years, the number of people who have taken up birdwatching has grown considerably. When this boom occured, many of us were worried about the negative effect this might have on the birds and on the conservation of nature areas. This kind of activity inevitably needs control, as well as the widespread adoption of codes of behaviour that ensure the priority of safety, and peace and quiet for the birds (and the environment in general) over the fancies of the birdwatcher. However, as time goes by, it has become increasingly clear that the danger naturalists could have represented is not very acute, especially when compared with many other human activities that progressively alter or destroy large areas of our natural heritage. It has furthermore become clear that the existence of more and more people with an increasing awareness of the need for nature conservation is vital in bringing the authorities round to a more conservationist position, or, at least in counteracting pressure of a contrary nature coming from many other sectors. The positive effect that has been achieved is not only applicable to people from one country in particular, but may also be applied in an international context. The presence of foreign visitors primarily attracted by the birds of the country may well play an important role in the conservation of nature there.

The prime objective of this book is to provide a useful instrument for all those people who wish to watch birds in Catalonia. In the different itineraries supplied, a very thorough picture of the wide range of this country's varied habitats (that range from peaks above 3000 metres high to the coast, with many intermediary habitats) and its varied birdlife may be had.

In this book, birdwatchers will find a whole series of itineraries as well as advice that will make their stay in Catalonia highly productive. There is information on the most interesting sites and details are given on how to find the most characteristic Mediterranean species, which are probably the major attraction for birdwatchers.

Catalonia is a country (at the moment it is a self-governing community within the Spanish State) with an advanced cultural and economic level. This factor does not mean that the birdlife is poor, but rather adds extra interest to the trip both for the birdwatcher and for accompanying friends or family (who may not be particularly keen birdwatchers). For instance, the book tells you how you can be watching Bonelli's Eagle at 7 o'clock on a summer afternoon, and be in your seat for one of the season's operas at Barcelona's El Liceu Opera House in the evening; or how you may visit a Romanesque church in the Pyrenees with the added thrill of seeing a Bearded Vulture fly over the valley; or how to see Roman and Greek ruins, hot in pursuit of warblers, and Black-eared and Black Wheatears; or how to enjoy one of the many tasty Catalan dishes with one eye on the Purple Heron that is to be seen through the restaurant window. If you prefer getting a good sun tan on one of the long beaches or in one of the small coves on the Catalan coast, you can also make it compatible with sightings of Audouin's Gull, Slender-billed Gull and terns off the beach, or rock-loving birds in the coves.

The characteristics of Catalan birdlife

From a biogeographical point of view, Catalonia and Andorra (the geographical area covered in this book) belong to the Palearctic region, which includes all Europe, non-tropical Asia and North Africa. Within the Palearctic region, Catalonia and Andorra are in the Mediterranean subregion.

A remarkable feature about Catalan birdlife is the large number of species it embraces. Up until the present day, 380 species have been recorded in Catalonia and Andorra. When compared with the figures for the Iberian Pensinsula (400) and the whole Palearctic region (761), this figure is high in proportion with the territory's surface area.

The reason for this high number of species is the country's geographical situation and the variety of habitats. Its position on the western coast of the Mediterranean basin (an area which is important for western European bird migration) makes Catalonia an inevitable migratory corridor for many species. The variety of biotopes means that birds associated with very different habitats can be seen in a relatively small area. In Catalonia and Andorra, there are Boreal-Alpine habitats on peaks over the 2300 or 2500 metre mark; Euro-Siberian habitats, such as Subalpine coniferous forests or humid mountain habitats with meadows and deciduous trees; and Mediterranean habitats, with a wide variety of possibilities ranging from ilex woods to scrub and steppe etc.. There are also large wetland areas such as the Delta of the river Ebre, the Aiguamolls de l'Empordà and the Delta of the river Llobregat. The coastline is also very varied, with areas of differing morphologies and compositions.

Of the 380 species of birds that have been seen in Catalonia and Andorra, 221 breed (some very locally or in an irregular fashion). Of these breeding species, 74 are summer vistors and the remaining 147 are present throughout the year. A further 43 species that breed further north are strictly wintering species (many of which are very abundant). All these species benefit from the mild weather and the food supplied by numerous plants that flower and produce fruit in the western Mediterranean in winter. During migration, a further 37 species (which neither breed nor winter in the country) can be seen on passage with varying degrees of frequency. The remaining 79 species can be considered to be vagrants, that is to say, species which have been recorded less than 10 times in the area.

The state of conservation

Despite the variety of habitats we have referred to just now, it must be remembered that the area we are dealing with is highly developed, as is the rest of Europe. It is for this reason that many habitats have now been destroyed or harmed, and many species have also become rare or extinct. Examples of this would be the loss of large areas of steppe habitat in Catalonia, a phenomenon that has led to the decrease in Montagu's Harrier and Black-bellied Sandgrouse numbers; bad forestry management has led to the same effect on Black Woodpecker, and the drying up of marshes can be associated with the disappearance of Marbled Teal and the current rarity of Bittern.

Fortunately, in the last few years (especially since the return of democracy), there has been a significant upsurge of feeling about the environment and conservation both in Catalonia and in Spain. This increased concern has had a positive effect on the Administration and has led to the creation of a network of nature reserves. Although limited both in area and in effective possibilities, this is a step in the right direction. Most of the itineraries described in this book are in protected areas, be they Parks or Nature Reserves.

The choice of the itineraries

As we have just stated, most of the itineraries described here are in protected nature areas, or in areas that are about to be protected. This factor is by no means a coincidence, and can be explained by two factors. Firstly, protected areas are normally to be counted among the more interesting areas of the country (that is why they are protected) and this statement also holds for the birdlife they harbour. Secondly, Natural Parks and areas which have some kind of protection tend to have a certain degree of surveillance and management, and this makes them less vulnerable to the presence of visitors than areas

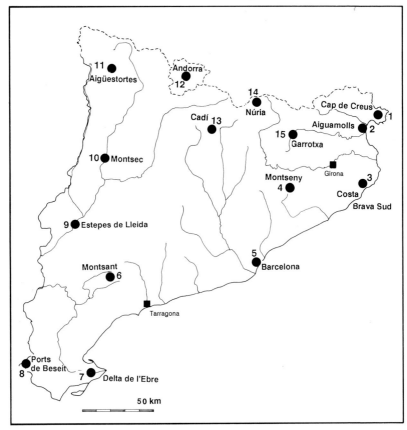

that have no control whatsoever. However, it was necessary to include some areas that are not as yet protected so as to guarantee that all the characteristic habitats in our country were covered by itineraries. This was obviously one of the factors that most affected the choice of itinerary areas. In any case, this selection was always made bearing in mind the need to make compatible the possibility of seeing the more interesting birds (which are often the rarer ones) with the basic precept that lays down that no harm shall be done to the environment.

This book is the result of 14 ornithologists' work. Each one of them is an expert on the area he/she is describing. The experience that has been accumulated over the course of many visits to a particular site has been summarized in a clear and methodical way in the space of a few pages. It is as if each reader were being given all the answers to the questions he/she would be making about a particular site, by one of its leading experts. What the area is like, how to get there, what birds are to be seen, which site is best for each species, and even where to sleep and eat or which interesting places (apart from ornithological sites) there are in the area.

The fact that the book has a long list of co-authors (a factor that in our opinion adds interest to the book) would explain the possible differences in treatment that may be encountered from one chapter to another. These differences, that in no way affect the efficiency of the book (prior to publication, the work was carefully edited and homogenized), were respected insofar as they conserve the particular style of each author.

Planning the itineraries

At the beginning of each chapter, there is a summary with general information about the area and at the beginning of each itinerary, there is a brief explanation. These two sections will give the basic information to enable you to plan each outing.

The distribution and number of the itineraries was decided in a clockwise fashion, taking Cap de Creus as a starting point (it is the area nearest to the El Portús frontier, where the majority of European tourists enter the country). Needless to say, though, the order of the outings can be selected at will by the reader of this book according to his/her own particular convenience.

Theoretically you could cover all the itineraries described in this handbook in 28 days (taking travelling time between the different zones into account) if you did so at a good pace, almost without pause between one itinerary and the next. We do not advise anyone to try this out, however, because it would be more like a rally than a birdwatching trip! If you have five weeks, however, you will be able to cover all the itineraries without too much trouble.

It may also be worth selecting the itineraries according to your fancy because some areas have a lot in common with others, although all areas have elements that make them worthwhile.

If you only have a short time for your trip to Catalonia, or a short time available for birdwatching, you may choose one of two options: to cover only a few of the itineraries in depth, or to have an overall view of as many of them as possible. If you choose this latter option, it may help you to have a list of those itineraries that will give you the most representative view of an area's birdlife: 1A, 2A, 2B, 3A, 3C, 4B, 5B, 6A, 7B, 7C, 8A, 9C, 10A, 11A, 12A, 13A, 14C and 15B. (This selection in no way questions the interest of the other itineraries).

Although you will find information about each area in the introductory summaries, we now include a list of areas with a brief definition for the benefit of those foreign visitors who are not acquainted with the geography of Catalonia:

1.- Cap de Creus. Coastal Mediterranean mountain area on a cape.

2.- Aiguamolls de l'Empordà. Coastal wetland area.

3.- Southern Costa Brava. Coastal mountain areas, offshore islands and wetland areas.

4.- Montseny. Humid mountain area.

5.- Barcelona and its surrounding area. Urban and Mediterranean mountain areas.

6.- Montsant-Siurana. Mediterranean mountain areas.

7.- Delta of the river Ebre. Coastal wetland area.

8.- Ports de Tortosa-Beceit. Inland Mediterranean mountain areas.

9.- Lleida steppes. Dry agricultural and inland steppe areas.

10.- Montsec. Inland Mediterranean mountain areas.

11.- Aigüestortes-Sant Maurici. Pyrenean high mountain areas.

12.- Andorra. Pyrenean high mountain areas.

13.- Cadí-Moixeró. High mountain areas in the Pyrenean foothills.

14.- Freser-Setcases and Núria. Pyrenean high mountain areas.

15.- Garrotxa volcanic area and Puigsacalm. Volcanic and humid mountain areas.

Layout of the handbook

This handbook comprises an introduction, fifteen chapters (dealing with one particular area each), a chapter with information on the more interesting species, and a list of Catalan birds with a key to their degree of rarity in all the areas covered in the book.

The fifteen chapters on the natural areas are divided into six sections: data summary, description and habitat, how to visit the area, birdwatching, board and lodging and other places of interest.

In the **data summary** there is a brief description of the area as well as other items of information: geographical situation, the surface area, the kind of protection (if any) the area enjoys, the kinds of habitat in the area and other information that will enable you to get an overall picture of the area you are interested in. There is also a list of interesting species, divided into as many as four sections, according to the seasons of the year they can be seen in the area. These lists indicate the most representative, spectacular and rare species that are normally to be found in the particular area.

In **description and habitat**, there is a general description of the area, and the principal ecosystems in the area are listed. The variation in birdlife between the respective ecosystems is made clear. The basic concepts given in this section will enable you to get to grips with the itineraries, and will make it easier to understand them in a more practical fashion.

In **how to visit the area** you are generally informed about how to reach the starting point for the itinerary (or itineraries) in the area, or the name of the town you are advised to adopt as your base during your stay. You are also given advice on how to organize your visit, which the best itineraries are (in the various seasons) for those who do not have much time, which order the itineraries can be covered in or what the best time of day for the visit is, bearing in mind factors such as the situation of the sun or the activity of the species you wish to see, and any other information that may help to improve your visit. Although information on how to reach the area on public transport is given, it must be pointed out that the itineraries are preferably, and sometimes obligatorily, to be covered by car.

In **birdwatching**, the longest and most important section, there is a description of between two and four itineraries in the area. The quality and characteristics of the itineraries in each chapter have been chosen so that the more outstanding and varied habitats of the area in question are covered. This facilitates the observation of as many species of birds as possible. In this guidebook, we have opted for the close description of each itinerary rather than giving a general idea of the area (that would perhaps have allowed birdwatchers to cover the itineraries with greater "freedom"!). We believe that if you are not acquainted with the area, you might miss some of the better sites. On the other hand, there is nothing to stop you using the information we supply as a basis for a more independent visit, especially if you have the time. For this reason, both the itineraries covered by car and those covered on foot give full details on how to follow the roads, tracks and paths, as well as on the places where it is worth stopping off to birdwatch. The wealth of details on routes, diversions, optional ways and stopping places may well cause a certain degree of confusion, especially on the longer and more complicated itineraries. We therefore recommend you to read the chapter and study the maps before you venture out. In this way, you will be able to get acquainted with the main landmarks along the way. If you do your homework, we feel sure that you will have no difficulty following the itineraries without getting lost!

You must bear in mind that the information regarding the state of a few of the tracks and the official kilometre gauging may have dated since the time the book was published. Changes of this nature, which were foreseeable at that same period (such as the forthcoming paving of a road or the change in the identification number of roads etc.), have been included in the text, but it is highly probable that in time, new changes will be occuring.

As regards birdwatching, references are made along the way to the most interesting birds to be seen, although they can also be seen on many other stretches or points on the itinerary. If the species in question have a clear status (being sedentary, summer or winter visitors in the whole area of Catalonia), this factor is not always recorded so as not to encumber the text with unnecessary details). It is normally a well-known fact which can also be checked in the species check-list. The status of the species is given in a systematic fashion when it is less well known, as for example in the case of species that live in different areas at different times of year according to the itinerary you are on. The times of day you are most likely to see a species are also given, as well as any factor that may facilitate its observation.

Although birds are the principal interest in this book, other interesting species of flora and fauna, which you may encounter along the way, are also mentioned. The more obvious changes in vegetation are pointed out in the itinerary description section, especially when they may affect the birdlife. Explanations and advice for the observation of other vertebrates are also given for those species that are of interest to the average naturalist, and for those species that are especially common and visible at one particular spot (although they might not be particularly spectacular or interesting species).

In **board and lodging**, particular information is given about the different possibilities for solving these vital necessities! In areas where there are not many facilities for tourists, the majority (maybe even all) of the local hotels and restaurants are listed. In more frequented areas, we only mention the hotels and restaurants that are placed nearest the itinerary areas or are recommendable for some specific reason (pleasant and peaceful places to sleep, hotels situated near areas of interest, local culinary specialities or especially good cooking at a particular place). An attempt has been made to cover the different needs and to offer choices for different budgets, degrees of comfort and types of lodging, with special refernces to camping sites and free camping areas.

In **other places of interest** you will find a short list of interesting sites in the vicinity. They are normally historic or artistic monuments, fine buildings or unusually attractive villages or particularly interesting or original museums that can help to give you a more detailed picture of the history and culture of Catalonia. In this way, you can take advantage of trips (which have generally been motivated by the birds or by nature) to get to know other places of special interest on or near the itineraries. You can thus combine naturalist experiences with others of a more general and cultural kind. The places listed and the indications given are necessarily short because of lack of space. Those interested, however, will be able to get additional information in any of the guidebooks there are on the subject without any difficulty. It must also be remembered that the density of monuments and other sites of cultural interest, in our country's different areas, is very uneven, and this may explain the considerable difference in the amount of information offered per chapter.

After the fifteen chapters dedicated to the itineraries, you will find another chapter called **specialities** in which specific information is given on the fifty species most birdwatchers are keenest to see, be it for their interest, their beauty or their rarity. Both the number (it could have been longer or shorter) and the choice of species were decided at random, in a subjective fashion. We hope that our selection will largely coincide with that of the majority of readers! However, one factor that was borne in mind is the difficulty the observation of the species entails, especially if your chances of spotting it improve with the supply of additional information. The best itineraries for each selected species are given, along with details about specific spots you are likely to see them. Advice and extra details, which may enable you to spot the bird and to distinguish it from other species, are also supplied. The names of the birds are given in English, Latin and Catalan.

In the **list of birds**, you will be able to check the status of Catalonia's species in each of the book's 15 nature areas in a rapid and easy way (all the information is on the same page). Apart from the English, Catalan and Latin names for each bird, there is also information about its status in the country as a whole, with explanatory notes for difficult species or birds that have a different status in different areas of Catalonia. Under each of the columns for the 15 nature areas involved, the area's species are marked with a symbol that indicates the frequency with which they can be seen. This symbol refers primarily to the chances you have of coming across the bird (either visually or hearing its call) rather than to its effective population in the area. The symbols used in the text are:

Status:
P: present all the year round.
S: summer visitor.
W: winter visitor.
m: on migration only.

Frequency:
V : very common. You will see or hear it at least 8 out of every 10 times you visit suitable habitats on the itinerary (at the correct time of year for the species in question).
Q: quite common. You will see or hear it between 4 and 7 out of every 10 times you visit the area under the conditions mentioned above.
u: uncommon. You will see or hear it 3 (or even less) out of every 10 times you visit the area under the conditions mentioned above. They are generally species that are present (at the right time of year) but that are difficult to see or hear because they are rare or shy (Bittern would be a good example), or else rare but regular migrants that are seen yearly.
o: Occasional. Birds that turn up sporadically (though not exceptionally) and that are unlikely to be encountered on a single visit. It may also refer to migrants or wintering birds which are not seen yearly. However, it does not include species that are accidentals in the natural area in question.

To make things simpler, the list does not include species that are regarded to be accidentals (less than 10 sightings) in Catalonia. Their presence bears no direct relationship with the nature areas described in the book. In any case, were an accidental species to be seen, it may be useful to know if it has already been recorded in Catalonia. Appendix A lists all the species of this kind that have been recorded (prior to this book's going to print).

Finally, before the index, you will find the following **appendices**: A) list of accidental species in Catalonia; B) list of mammals, reptiles and amphibians of Catalonia; C) instructions for visiting and taking photographs in reserve areas; and D) useful addresses.

Advice and precautions to be taken into consideration

- **Vehicle**. A lot of the itineraries are on unpaved tracks, some of which are in middling condition. But all the itineraries have been selected so that they can be covered in a normal car, though at times patience will be necessary. You are advised to start out with a full petrol tank, especially on the longer and more complex itineraries. In winter you must also take chains and use anti-freeze, as temperatures may descend to -20 º C.

- Equipment. The vital equipment you will need to go birdwatching are a field guide and some binoculars. Binoculars should have a magnification factor of between 7 and 12, but remember that the more powerful they are, the less clear vision will be. For birdwatching in forested areas, 7 or 8 x 40 binoculars should do nicely. On more open ground, 12 x 50 would be more recommendable. One of the best types of binoculars for all-round birdwatching are the 10 x 50s. You are not advised to use binoculars with a magnification factor of over 12 because the image will become blurred. For birdwatching in wetlands and for the scanning of great rock faces, a telescope with a magnification factor between 20 and 60 is very handy. You must always use a tripod.

As regards clothing, try and keep it as discreet as possible. Bear in mind that in mountain areas sudden storms are quite common, even in the middle of summer. Footwear must be sturdy in rocky and mountain areas. In marshy areas, Wellington boots can be quite handy, especially in wet weather.

- Maps. There are diagrams for all the itineraries described in the book. They include landmarks and the paths you are to follow. They are quite schematic and are not a substitute for other more detailed maps you may need for some of the more complicated itineraries. You are therefore advised to get hold of a good road map (there are many on the market). For the itineraries on foot (especially in mountain areas), more detailed maps (such as those published by Alpina or the Army Cartographic Service) should be very useful.

- High mountain areas. Several itineraries (basically those in Aigüestortes-Sant Maurici, Andorra, Cadí-Moixeró and Núria, chapters 11 - 14) are in high mountain areas. In these areas you must always follow the precautions associated with mountainous zones and bear in mind that your equipment (especially in winter), degree of fitness and experience may help you to avoid unfortunate accidents. Watch out for gales, avalanches (that may occur in spring), heavy snowfall (that may cut you off) and ice, that is often concealed beneath a thin layer of snow. In thunder storms (that may occur in summer), do remember to keep clear of trees and try to head for lower ground.

- Adders. Poisonous snakes are common on almost all the mountain itineraries described in this book. To avoid accidents, mind where you place your hands, where you sit and where you lie down. If you come across a snake, the best thing to do is to leave it alone.

-**Mosquitoes**. When you visit marshland areas in spring, summer and autumn, be sure to take some mosquito repellent with you because they can sometimes be very tiresome!

Acknowledgements

In a guidebook such as this, which covers a large part of Catalonia, the data and records supplied over the years by a large number of birdwatchers are very important as a basis for the information being offered. For this reason it would be impossible to name all the people who in one way or another helped to make this book what it is. However, we do want to express our thanks to the following naturalists for their invaluable help resolving problems raised during the course of the preparation of this book: Raul Aymí, Joan Barat, Bernat Garrigós, Francesc Llimona, Rosa Llinàs, Ramon Mascort, Eloïsa Matheu, Xavier Parellada, Miquel Rafa, José Luis Romero and Deli Saavedra. We would also like to thank Xavier Batllori, author of the report on the birdlife in Barcelona's gardens (1987) that was used in the preparation of the itinerary in Barcelona's city parks.

1

CAP DE CREUS

The cape known as "Cap de Creus" is to the north of the Costa Brava. It is a rocky and mountainous peninsula (highest peak, Sant Salvador, 670 metres), being the most easterly point of the Iberian Peninsula. It is a good site for migrant passerines and seabirds.

It is still mainly unspoilt, although human activity has indeed left its mark. The area is protected by a preliminary conservation plan, and will in time become a Nature Park.

Surface area: about 15,000 hectares.

Habitats: rocky shoreline and islands, scrub, small cork oak and pine woods, streams and ponds, vineyards and olive groves.

Interesting species:
- *Present all the year round*: Cory's Shearwater, Manx Shearwater, Bonelli's Eagle, Peregrine Falcon, Red-legged Partridge, Thekla's Lark, Dartford Warbler, Sardinian Warbler, Blue Rock Thrush, Rock Bunting, Black Wheatear, Crag Martin.
- *Summer visitors*: Alpine Swift, Pallid Swift, Red-rumped Swallow, Spectacled Warbler, Subalpine Warbler, Orphean Warbler, Rock Thrush, Black-eared Wheatear.
- *Winter visitors*: Gannet, Great Skua, Alpine Accentor, Wallcreeper.
- *Migrants*: Seabirds, aquatic species and passerines in general.

Description and habitat

A distinction must be made between the Cap de Creus Peninsula and the Cap de Creus itself. The Cap de Creus peninsula would comprise all the coves and capes between Llançà and Roses, as well as the valleys and hills there are inland, including the Serra de Verdera. However, when referring to the Cap de Creus, the tip of the peninsula is what is meant.

The Cap de Creus peninsula or massif is the last section of the Pyrenees before they plunge down into the sea, the Cap de Creus being the most easterly point of the Iberian Peninsula. Its position jutting out into the sea makes it a good site for spotting birds which migrate along the coast such as several aquatic species and seabirds, as well as a good assembly site for many species of passerines and raptors.

The Cap de Creus massif was created by the action of a series of marginal faults bordering on a subsidence trough which began to take on this form after the period of geological stress that followed the appearance of the Pyrenean folds in the Miocene period.

From a geological point of view, the Cap de Creus peninsula has a silicic composition and is lacking in carbonates. Metamorphic rocks abound, and it is indeed considered to be one of the best sites in Catalonia for this kind of mineral. The geological landscape has remarkable folds and eroded forms, with sculptured rocks of great beauty at several different sites. The extraction of rock for gardening and aquarium decoration was beginning to become a problem, and it is now a practice which is completely forbidden and punishable by law.

When describing the vegetation of the Cap de Creus, the effect of several factors, some natural, others caused by human action, has to be borne in mind. Among the natural factors, the following are significant: the rocky substratum, the influence of brine on areas beside the sea, and the force of the *Tramuntana* wind (from the north), which in places completely shapes the vegetation, as may be seen in the forms taken on by sheltered and south-facing bushes and trees on the more prominent points of the massif.

Human impact accounts for the initial deforestation that the need for wood, agricultural land and pastures led to. Also significant is the damage caused by the regular burning of pastures by the shepherds.

A long time ago, as history and the place names would seem to suggest, the Cap de Creus peninsula had been densely wooded with cork oak, ilex and oak. The very name "Port de la Selva" (Port of the Forest) is a clue to the presence of woods in days gone by. Indeed it is said that the people of Port de la Selva and Cadaqués found it less difficult to go to the Balearic islands by sea than to Figueres (the county capital) overland. This was no doubt due to the almost impenetrable nature of the woods that covered those mountains.

Little by little, first of all to obtain wood for ship-building (later on for railway sleepers) and after to prepare land for pastures, vineyards and olive groves (endless terraces with stone walls still cover large areas of the mountains), the landscape has taken on today's appearance: small patches of woodland, large areas of scrub and ever-increasing zones of bare rock.

Unfortunately, the Cap de Creus mountains are still apt to burn too frequently, and there is at least one major fire a year. This prevents the vegetation from recovering and leads to increasing loss of topsoil. Most fires are intentionally lit to improve and enlarge pastures for Pyrenean cattle wintering in the area. Some cattle farmers fail to see that by doing this, the area will not be able to accommodate as much cattle, and that there are other ways of ensuring pastures without destroying natural resources.

There are six main types of habitat to be found on the Cap de Creus peninsula. The **rocky coastal areas**, made up of outcrops and off-shore islands, all of which are very much exposed to the salinity of the sea. Typical plants are Samphire, *Armeria ruscinonensis*, a plant which is endemic to this coast, and *Astragalus massiliensis*, all of which grow in sheltered spots.

The majority of **inland scrub areas** are made up of rockrose and heather, plants that are typical of silicic coastal areas, with broom, Lentiscus and aromatic plants such as rosemary, lavender and thyme also occurring. After fires have affected an area, a carpet of grass appears followed by the new shoots of bushes. It is possible to know how long a specific area has not suffered a fire by the state of growth and composition of the bushes.

In other areas which have not been so badly affected by fire, small pine plantations, as well as patches of ilex and cork oak **woodland**, tend to appear. The cork oak is fire-resistant because of the layer of cork covering its trunk and main branches. It is well adapted to dry climates and Mediterranean areas where fires happen often.

The massif has many large rocky areas, although **cliffs** as such are only present at a limited number of sites on the coast (for instance, Cap Norfeu) or inland (Serra de Verdera).

Most valleys in the massif have seasonal **torrents**, although some have running streams all the year round. There are also several **ponds** on the higher ground (at La Birba and near the tip of the Cape) or at the mouths of the streams (Jóncols and Taballera coves).

In the massif, the **plantations** are mainly vineyards and olive groves, and at certain points - especially in the valleys - there are small vegetable and cereal plots. The vineyards and olive groves are receding because it is difficult to use machinery on such steep slopes.

In general, it may be said that the cryptogamous plants - lichens, mosses etc. - are very well represented on the Cap de Creus. For instance, 128 different species of moss have so far been found, of which 15 do not occur elsewhere in Catalonia. The interest of the Cap de Creus may also be applicable to two other fields that are mentioned in passing: the scientific interest and beauty of the sea floor, and the interesting historical and archaeological remains (for instance, Sant Pere de Roda monastery and the Creu d'en Cobertella dolmen).

How to visit the area

A whole day will be necessary for itinerary 1A and half a day for itinerary 1B. Itinerary 1A begins at Vilajuïga and 1B at Roses. You are advised to begin itinerary 1A on the first day and to sleep at Cadaqués. On the second day, take a look around Cadaqués, or even take another look at the interesting area near the cape itself. Then you can go on to Roses and do itinerary 1B in the afternoon.

If you arrive on the evening before your excursion day (for instance, on a Friday evening if you are to follow the itineraries over the weekend), you may care to stay at Roses both nights (a good idea for those who have a lot of luggage and do not want to be carrying it around for the whole excursion).

To reach Vilajuïga or Roses, the instructions depend on which road you are coming on. If you are coming from France by way of El Portús-La Jonquera (you must leave the motorway at this latter town), you are advised to take the turning on your left to Capmany, Garriguella, Vilajuïga and Roses, 7 kms after La Jonquera. The road goes through an interesting area of olive groves, vineyards and cork oak woods. In the breeding season both Red-rumped Swallow and Lesser Grey Shrike may be seen in this area. This road leads to Vilajuïga or Roses, depending on the itinerary you have chosen.

Bird-watching

1A. Itinerary in the Verdera range and Cap de Creus

Starting point: Vilajuïga **End of the itinerary**: Cadaqués **Time needed**: one day **Means of transport**: by car and on foot

The itinerary begins at the village of Vilajuïga. The starting point (kilometre 0) will be on the Garriguella-Roses road, at the crossroads with the road leading to the village, where the Sant Pere de Rodes monastery signpost is. After 300 metres, you must turn right following the signposts leading to Sant Pere de Rodes monastery (8 kms).

After leaving the village, the road soon starts to climb up the mountain. The first stretch of road passes through an area of olive groves on the left. There is a seasonal stream here that is well worth taking a look at as it is a special habitat which occasionally attracts interesting species such as the Orphean Warbler in the breeding season. At the foot of this mountain range the odd pair of Mistle Thrush will be found breeding in the lusher vegetation.

After **1.6 km** of your itinerary, you may care to stop the car and take a stroll beside the torrent and through the olive groves, where you will come across odd clumps of cork oak and oak trees. This is a good spot for wintering thrushes and starlings, species which thrive on the abundant olives scattered on the ground. Blackcaps and Sardinian Warblers are also attracted by the olive groves. Winter populations of finches are also noteworthy. They come in search of olives and gramineae seeds, which abound because herbicides are not usually used in the olive groves.

Once you have left the lower part of the valley, the vegetation begins to change because of the effect of successive fires. Here and there, you will come across burnt areas with odd charred cork oaks. As you proceed upwards, the areas of rockrose and heather become more common. It is here that several species of warbler breed: the Spectacled Warbler in the grassier areas with scattered bushes; the Subalpine and Dartford Warblers in thicker scrubland and the Sardinian Warbler in the areas with more undergrowth. In the clearer patches with bare rock, you may see the Black-eared Wheatear in Spring and Summer, and the Thekla Lark all the year round.

In recently burnt areas, the first birds to move in are those that prefer open ground such as Rock and Ortolan Bunting and finches such as Goldfinch, Linnet and Greenfinch, as well as Wood Lark, Tawny Pipit, Black-eared and Black Wheatear. As the vegetation begins to grow again, the warblers gradually move back into these areas.

After **5.6 kms.**, you will come to a pine plantation where Serin and Goldfinch are to be seen, as well as other passerines during migration.

After this point, the road continues on up, and the wide Empordà plain opens up to our right. On days when the Tramuntana wind blows the view will be excellent, although the same will not be said for the bird-watching.

After **8.7 kms.** you will come to a turning to Port de la Selva. You will be taking this road later, but for the moment go on until you reach the Sant Pere de Rodes monastery car-park. You may care to climb up to Sant Salvador castle. Take care because there are two car parks, one near the monastery, and another very much closer to the road leading to Port de la Selva. You should go to the former (**km 9.**3), unless it is full up, in which case it will have to be the latter.

From the first car park you continue on foot (a 5 minute walk) as far as Sant Pere de Rodes monastery. It was founded in the XIIth century by Benedictine monks and is considered to be one of the finest Romanesque monuments of its period. The monastery, that witnessed the events that took place in the Empordà in the Middle Ages, would be able to give us a description of the evolution of the habitats that surround it, were it able to speak. It has no doubt contemplated the change in habitat from thick forest to the scrub and rock that is dominant today. The visiting hours for the monastery are from 9 am to 12.45 pm and from 2 pm to 4.45 pm in winter and from 9 am to 13.45 pm and from 4pm to 7.45 pm between Easter and the end of September. The visit is well worth it, both for the monastery itself and for the pair of Blue Rock Thrush breeding in one of the towers.

Before or after visiting the monastery, you may care to climb up to Sant Salvador. It will take you between one hour and one hour and a half at a birdwatcher's gait. It is quite a climb but the path is well marked out and not too steep. The species you may see are interesting and on clear days the view of the Pyrenees, the rest of the Cap de Creus massif and the Empordà plain is breathtaking.

The higher you climb, the more apparent the signs of fire become. You will soon be seeing bare rock, a good habitat for the Black Wheatear and the Blue Rock Thrush throughout the year, and for the Rock Thrush in summer. In the breeding season, all the scrub warblers are to be seen, as well as the three European species of Swift and the Crag Martin, which can also be seen in winter.

From the top of Sant Salvador, you are sure to see the Kestrel and may be lucky enough to see a Peregrine swooping after an unsuspecting Wood Pigeon, or a Bonelli's Eagle soaring along the edge of the ridge. In migration, many other species of raptor may be seen on their way north in Spring and south in Autumn.

One species which is almost always present in winter, and can be seen on Sant Salvador, is the Alpine Accentor. You should look out for it perching on the stone walls or large rocks, very often in small flocks. If you do not spot any here do not lose heart, but scan all areas with large boulders around the monastery, since it has also been seen right beside the car park and at the site where the road to Port de la Selva passes beneath the monastery.

Once you have seen the local species as well as the views of the mountains and the plain (from here several other itinerary areas described in this book are to be seen: the Aiguamolls de l'Empordà (itin. 2) at our feet, the

Garrotxa (itin. 15) in the middle distance and the Pyrenees (itins. 11, 12, 13, 14) in the far distance), you should make your way down to Sant Pere de Rodes. From there drive towards Port de la Selva. From the car park to the point where you turn to the right it is about 600 metres (you will have reached km. **9.9 km** of the itinerary by this stage).

The road down the mountain is wide and in good condition, and goes through areas of scrub and a few fields of cereals which are specially planted by the Port de la Selva hunters to provide food for partridges, which may often be seen on or beside the road. Thekla Lark are also very common here. In the breeding season it is not uncommon to see plenty of warblers flying about or flitting from bush to bush, and Black-eared Wheatear singing from prominent vantage points.

After **19 km** you will arrive at Port de la Selva. Before entering the town you cross a stream. During migration,it is not a rare occurence to see waders or even the odd heron resting here. Beside the stream, there is an area of vegetable gardens with bamboo fences separating the plots. In migration, and especially when the *Tramuntana* wind is blowing, many birds will be found sheltering here. It is also worth having a look at the small bay where seabirds tend to take refuge especially during gales.

You may stop for lunch in Port de la Selva, or motor on to Cadaqués (11 kilometres further on). If you want to picnic, the best thing would be to stop somewhere between the monastery and Port de la Selva and enjoy the view, or else at the beach. In Port de la Selva and Cadaqués there are no suitable places for picnics.

To get to Cadaqués you must take a road to your right at the entrance of the village. You climb up to Perafita pass (km 26), an area which has suffered numerous fires, and from here you make your way down to Cadaqués, which is 5 kms away. Be careful on the way down because the bends are quite treacherous!

Once you reach the **30 km** mark at the entrance to Cadaqués, you take a road to the left leading to Cap de Creus (9 kms further on). Between Cadaqués and Cap de Creus you will again be finding a landscape of olive groves, scattered pines and scrub. You may well put up the odd partridge or Thekla Lark along your way. As you are leaving Cadaqués, you go past the small bay of Port Lligat and the house where the artist Salvador Dalí lived for many years. The house stands out because of the original decoration of the roof, which appears to have huge eggs on it.

At the **35.5 km** mark, on a downward slope, there is a path to the left which after 200 metres brings you to Mas Rabassers de Baix (a restaurant). If you so wish, you may leave your car here and walk east along the path leading to Mas Rabassers de Dalt (a ruined farm) and further inland to La Birba.

A stroll in this area can result in good bird-watching during the migratory season, as many passerines tend to gather here: warblers, Ortolan Bunting, wheatears etc. The length of your walk will depend on the presence of migrants or the time you have available, and you can head back to the car when you please. However, if you wish to reach La Birba, it will take you about two hours. At this farm, it is worth taking a look at the flooded meadows in the wet season; take another quick look at the ruins of Mas Rabassers de Dalt (farm) to see if the Little Owl is around; at Rabassers de Baix, it is also worth seeing the small pond at the back of the house, behind a small hillock. Although this itinerary is best in migration time, good sightings of Black Wheatear are to be had, a species which is very common at this spot.

Black Wheatear

Back at the car once more, drive on to Cap de Creus (cape). At **km 37**, on the left, there is a turning to the Club Mediterranée, which you should not take. Keep on until you reach the lighthouse at **km 39** and leave the car in the small car park.

From here, looking to the east (if you have lost your sense of direction, the lighthouse weathercock may be of help) you will see a tower. This is the foghorn tower (it works on foggy days), and can be used as a point of reference when you descend into the gullies and rocky valleys at the tip of the cape. You are advised to descend towards the tower and to continue on to the right where the path to the tower begins. To observe seabird migration you may stand on the very tip of the cape, though you can also stay beside the foghorn tower if you do not want to walk so far. Wherever you choose to stand, the use of a telescope will greatly improve the bird-watching.

The rock structure is completely different in this area to that in the inland part you visited before. Here the shapes are more jagged and dramatic. Be careful not to fall!

Cap de Creus, the cape on which you are now standing, is as we have already said, the most easterly point of the Iberian Pensinsula and is a good spot for watching migratory birds: both land birds stopping over and seabirds, aquatic birds and raptors moving on. Successful bird-watching will be a question of luck, of course, and a day at the height of the migratory season may well produce no migrants at all! To see seabirds on migration, however, days of Llevant (easterly) wind are the best because birds normally migrating out at sea are blown towards the coast.

If your visit to the Cap de Creus is on a weekday, it is a good idea to be at the point at about 4 pm, because it is at this time, both in summer and in winter, that the trawlers return to Roses. They clean their nets on their way back discarding small and unmarketable fish. Many species of seabirds follow the boats for this reason, picking up what fish they may. In winter the main species are Herring and Black-headed Gull, though Kittiwake, Gannet, Razorbill, Cory's and Manx Shearwater, Sandwich Tern and the odd Great Skua are also to be seen. This latter species is likely to be in hot pursuit of other birds' prey. In summer, only Black-headed and Herring Gull remain, along with a few shearwaters. In the migratory season, the number of species of gull, tern and skua may well increase.

On the rocks at the tip of the Cap de Creus, Black Wheatear, Sardinian Warbler and Blue Rock Thrush are to be found all the year round, and the Rock Thrush joins them in summer. The Grey Wagtail is common in winter, and with a little bit of luck, you may see the Wallcreeper, a species which winters regularly in small numbers here, although it is difficult to see because of the great number of rocks it may be feeding on.

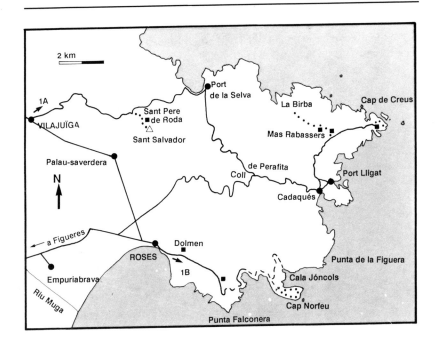

If you wait until sunset at Cap de Creus, the view and the bird-watching should be worthwhile, but you may feel the cold. If you want to warm up, you may care to take a *cremat*, a typical seaman's punch made with coffee and burnt rum, at one of the bars on Cadaqués beach, where this itinerary ends. Cheers!

1B. Cap Norfeu Itinerary

Starting point and end of the itinerary: Roses **Time needed**: half a day **Means of transport**: by car and on foot **Observations**: best in the afternoon

In Roses take the street called Gran Via Pau Casals, which you will find on the inland part of the city, to the turning leading to Cala Jóncols. The starting point (km 0) of the itinerary will be the foot of the hill, at a point where there is a sign to Cala Montjoi (7 kms away), Cala Palosa (9 kms away) and Cala Jóncols (12 kms away).

The tarmac road is narrow and climbs up through an area of terraces with occasional pine plantations and many olive groves, which are a good wintering area for thrushes and starlings. To the right there are large quarries, some of which are no longer exploited and have been taken over by Blue Rock Thrush, who find excellent - though somewhat artificial - cliffs for breeding here.

After **1.5 kms**, on a sharp right-hand bend, you will see a signpost on the left and a small area for parking (if full, there is another parking place back along the road) where you can leave your car to visit the Creu d'en Cobertella dolmen, the largest megalithic monument in Catalonia.

The walk up the path to the dolmen passes through an area of scrub and olive groves. It is a good spot for warblers, especially Blackcap and Dartford Warbler in winter, and Sardinian Warbler throughout the year, as well as other species of warblers and passerines during migration. You will take 45-60 minutes to complete this walk to the dolmen and its surrounding area.

Back at the car, follow the road upwards and at **km 1.7**, on the right, you will come across a farm surrounded by meadows where there are often cows pasturing. It is worth taking a look at this area during migration as interesting species tend to crop up here.

After the meadows, you will come to an area which is very much affected by the fires caused principally by the uncontrolled municipal incinerator of Roses, which also accounts for the large amount of plastic bags which the frequent Empordà winds scatter over the countryside.

After **3.6 kms** you will come to the Torre del Sastre (the tailor's tower) where it is worth taking a quick look, since Rock Sparrow have been seen at this spot and Common Starling breed there.

After **4 kms**, Cape Norfeu will be seen to the north. Take note of its structure and the tower there is at the top, because it will help you not to get lost when you are walking on the peninsula. A little further on, to the right, on a clear day you will get a good view of the Bay of Roses plain.

After **4.5 kms** you will come to a track to the right, which you must not take. If you were to follow it (it is in fact forbidden to do so), you would come to Punta Falconera (Falcon Point), a place with a very evocative name, one of the last breeding sites of the Lesser Kestrel in Catalonia.

After this turning, you will come across small clumps of pines on the right hand side of the road. They have miraculously survived the fires, thanks mainly to the action of the fire brigade operating from the road itself. On the right you can see small coves such as La Murtra and La Rostella. You will come across more and more pine woods where woodland species may be encountered: Blackbird and Great, Blue and Crested tits.

After **6.2 kms.**, on a bend, the cove Cala Montjoi suddenly comes into view. This pebble beach is in fact at the end of a valley that you will see spread out before you. It is easy to imagine how interesting this area must have been originally, before deforestation.

After **6.9 km** of the itinerary you will pass the "El Bulli" restaurant (cf. Board and lodging). If it is time for a meal, you will eat very well here, although it is not the cheapest of restaurants. Cheaper meals can be had at an improvised restaurant on the beach at Cala Montjoi.

After **7.3 kms** of the itinerary you will come to Cala Montjoi. The tarmac ends here, but a decent track continues along the coast. After a further kilometre there are a few fairly unspoilt coves such as La Palosa. There are a few clumps of cork oak on the mountains as you near Cap Norfeu.

Look out for Red-legged Partridge and Thekla Lark on the track, although they may also be seen in lesser numbers on the tarmac road beforehand.

When you reach **kilometre 10**, leave the car at a place where there is a path leading off to the right, and continue on foot. You could in fact have driven on for a further 600 metres, but it is not advisable to do so as there is no place to turn around.

The excursion will take about 4 or 5 hours. First make your way along the 600 metres of track and then continue along the path which leads to some intriguing constructions; they are shepherd huts with stone walls built in such a way as to take advantage of the overhanging rock for shelter. From here on, the path leads to a piece of higher ground where there are many paths - some of which have been made by the cattle - criss-crossing the peninsula. You are advised to go to the tip along the northern edge, which is the side you first come to, and to come back by way of the southern edge. The tower will at all times make an excellent point of reference.

As you wander through the scrub of Cap Norfeu, good bird-watching is to be had, especially in the migratory period, when a good number of passerines tend to stop over. You may see Woodchat Shrike, warblers of all descriptions, flycatchers, wheatears, Ortolan Bunting etc.

In the breeding season, Red-legged Partridge, Thekla Lark, Woodchat Shrike, Tawny Pipit, Nightingale, Stonechat, Black-eared Wheatear, Black Wheatear, Blue Rock Thrush, Sardinian Warbler, Subalpine Warbler, Dartford Warbler etc. are all present. In winter, apart from the resident species such as Blue Rock Thrush, Black Wheatear and some of the warblers, small flocks of Cirl Bunting, Goldfinch, Serin and Chaffinch, as well as the odd Black Redstart, can all be seen.

You may also sometimes see the odd pair of Raven, small flocks of Jackdaw and single Peregrine Falcon flying over. Kestrel will be seen more regularly as there are three or four pairs breeding on Cap Norfeu. Alas, there are no longer problems distinguishing between kestrels (Common and Lesser)! The last Lesser Kestrels disappeared from here in the mid eighties.

On days when the Llevant (easterly) wind is blowing or when the Roses fishing fleet is returning to port, almost the same birdlife as described for Cap de Creus can be seen at Cap Norfeu (cf. itinerary 1A). However, it is easier to see Shag here, especially immature birds, which are probably winter visitors from the Balearic Islands' colonies, although the presence of adults suggests that the odd pair may breed sporadically on the magnificent Norfeu cliffs.

At the very tip of the cape there is an island called "El Gat" (the cat) due to its shape, which is better appreciated when seen from the sea. A few pairs of Herring Gull breed here, and there is a mixed colony of all three European swifts (Alpine, Pallid and Common), as on other cliff faces on the peninsula. The Crag Martin also breeds here, being the only one of the four species to stay on in winter.

On a point further to the north of Norfeu called Punta Figuera, there is sometimes a Starling roost in winter. It is intriguing to watch the flight of the flocks, especially when the Peregrine Falcon is after them, as happens every afternoon when the roost is used.

To avoid getting lost, it is better not to stay on too late on the point. If you wish to observe the Starling roost, you may do so equally well from the shepherds' huts near the beginning of the itinerary, which are a stone's throw from the car.

If you have time after returning to the car, drive down the track to Cala Jóncols, one of the prettiest and most solitary coves in the area (there is a small hotel with a restaurant there which only opens in the summer).

Board and Lodging

The villages along the itineraries (Vilajuïga, Port de la Selva, Cadaqués and Roses) all have good restaurants. In Vilajuïga there are several good Catalan restaurants (Can Maricanes, Stop, Sant Pere). It is worth eating fish at restaurants in villages on the coast (Ca l'Erminda or the Hotel Comerç at Port de la Selva; La Galiota or Es Trull at Cadaqués; and Can Ramon, El Pescador, L'Antull or El Bulli at Roses).

Unless you have chosen to stay at Roses (2 nights) for reasons of convenience, you are advised to sleep in Cadaqués, where you are almost sure to find accommodation, unless you are visiting the area at the height of the season or on a long holiday weekend. There are plenty of hotels both in Cadaqués and in Roses, but you are advised to go either to the Hotel Port Lligat at Cadaqués, or the Almadrava Park and the Vistabella hotels at Roses because of their privileged setting.

The day you go on itinerary 1B, you will be passing a very famous restaurant, which is not expensive if you consider the quality it offers. It is El Bulli restaurant, at Cala Montjoi. In summer, you may also choose to eat at one of the provisional restaurants at Cala Montjoi itself, or at La Pelosa, or else at the restaurant at Cala Jóncols (to the north of Cap Norfeu).

Other places of interest

- Monastery of Sant Pere de Rodes. One of the finest Romanesque monuments in the world. Itinerary 1A covers the visit and informs you of the monastery's visiting hours.

- Creu d'en Cobertella dolmen. The largest megalithic monument in Catalonia. The location is given in itinerary 1B.

- Salvador Dalí's house at Port Lligat (Cadaqués). The interior and exterior of the house were decorated in a surrealistic style by the famous Catalan artist. The cove nearby is also a beautiful spot.

- Perrot-Moore European Graphic Art Museum (Cadaqués). A collection of XV-XXth century graphic art brought together by a former secretary of Salvador Dalí. Only open in summer.

2

AIGUAMOLLS DE L'EMPORDÀ NATURAL PARK

Situated at the northern end of the Costa Brava (Roses bay).

The second most important wetland area in Catalonia after the Ebre Delta. It is included on the Ramsar Convention list of sites of international importance.

Inaugural date: October 1983.

Area: 4,783.5 hectares (867.5 of which are Integral Nature Reserve Areas).

Address: Parc Natural dels Aiguamolls,
El Cortalet,
17486 Castelló d'Empúries,
Girona (Catalonia),
Spain.

Habitats: saltmarsh, freshwater marsh, coastal sandy areas, water meadows, riverside woodland and agricultural land.

Interesting species:
- *Present all the year round*: Little Egret, Cattle Egret, Bittern, White Stork (reintroduction project under way), Marsh Harrier, Red-legged Partridge, Stone Curlew, Purple Gallinule (reintroduction project under way), Hoopoe, Moustached Warbler, Cetti's Warbler, Fan-tailed Warbler, Sardinian Warbler and Penduline Tit.
- *Summer visitors*: Purple Heron, Night Heron, Little Bittern, Garganey, Short-toed Eagle, Black-winged Stilt, Kentish Plover, Great Spotted Cuckoo, Bee-eater, Golden Oriole, Lesser Grey Shrike.
- *Winter visitors*: Black-throated Diver, Curlew, Booted Eagle, wild-fowl, waders.
- *Migratory species*: Flamingo, Glossy Ibis, Red-footed Falcon, Eleanora's Falcon, waders, terns, Red-throated Pipit etc..

Description and habitat

The Aiguamolls de l'Empordà Natural Park is one of the best known and most significant natural areas in Catalonia. Its inauguration in 1983 was only made possible after a long and intensive defence campaign which began in 1976. The campaign managed to stop a development project which would have led to the construction of a residential marina area for 60,000 tourists in the saltmarsh area!

The Roses Bay plain, composed of silt deposited by the Muga, Fluvià and Ter rivers, has undergone great changes over the course of history. At the time the Greeks founded the nearby settlement of Empúries, it was a vast area of marshes. Now, however, it is a highly populated area with agricultural land, meadows and seaside resorts. Within the limits of the natural park (which has an overall area of 4,783 hectares) one may find the area's remaining marshland as well as other zones of natural interest such as beaches, meadows and traditional agricultural areas. Six different habitats can be found in the park: saltmarsh with brackish lagoons, freshwater marsh with lagoons, coastal sandy areas, *closes* or temporarily flooded water meadows, riverside woodland and agricultural areas.

The **saltmarsh area** is immediately behind the beach in the area between the mouths of the rivers Muga and Fluvià. It covers 532 hectares and accounts for one of the natural park's three Integral Reserve Areas. In the saltmarsh there are eight permanent lagoons which have the following names (from north to south): La Muga Vella, L'Estany d'en Túries, La Rogera, La Serpa, La Fonda, La Llarga, La Massona and L'Estany Sirvent. The degree of salinity of the waters in these lagoons is the result of the varying proportion of freshwater (from the hinterland) and sea water (entering the lagoon system during the easterly storms known as *llevantades*. The salinity readings for each lagoon depend on the distance of the lagoon to the intake points. This factor (along with the difference in depth of the lagoons) widens the range of habitats to a considerable extent as well as attracting more species to the area. The least saline of the lagoons is La Massona. It is the only one surrounded by a fairly broad reedbed, which attracts a good many reed-dwelling species. At the other end of the scale is La Rogera, which is the saltiest lagoon. It is by way of this lagoon that most of the sea water floods onto the saltmarsh. La Rogera is also shallower than the other lagoons. These characteristics help to explain the difference in the birdlife on this lagoon in relation, for example, to that of La Massona. The vegetation around the lagoons (with the exception of La Massona's reedbeds) consists of typical saltwort marsh which gradually mixes in with areas of rushes and occasional rows of tamarisk trees further inland.

The **freshwater marshes**, which make up another Integral Nature Reserve area, are what remain of the old Castelló lagoon. This lagoon had measured 8 kilometres in diameter in the XVIIth century. The freshwater marsh is situated inland and its waters are free of salt. The habitats, vegetation and birdlife are radically different from those in the saltmarsh area by the sea. The principal lagoons in the area are Vilahut, Mornau, Palau, Castelló and El Tec. In this area one may find bullrush beds, water meadows and other forms of aquatic vegetation such as crow-foot and irises.

The **coastal sandy areas** are present along the whole of the park's sea front. They are the last of the Costa Brava's unspoilt beaches. The stretch of sand that extends southwards (it is within the park boundaries) is intended to preserve a representative portion of this habitat. The least spoilt zone, where well-formed dunes are still to be found, is at the mouth of the river Muga, within the saltmarsh reserve area. The dune vegetation is well conserved and interesting dune fauna, such as the Large Psammodromus, can be seen here.

In the Empordà region, the typical meadows, that are surrounded or "enclosed" by rows of trees, are called *closes*. They are on the beds of the old lagoons and tend to flood in the wet season. They are used as pasture areas for cows and horses, and are very attractive for many species of birds and other fauna. The flooded water meadows are indeed a good source of food and the rows of trees give plenty of cover, shelter, vantage posts and nesting sites. Changes in agricultural policy brought about by Spain's joining the EEC have led to the consideration of these areas as being less profitable for pasturing than for the potential intensive cultivation of maize. This is obviously a threat to the conservation of this interesting habitat. The vegetation there is also interesting, with various noteworthy species of Gramineae and leguminous plants as well as typical riverside trees such as elm, ash, poplar and alder in the enclosure rows.

Apart from the trees around the *closes* or water meadows, there are further areas of **riverside woodland** habitat on the lower courses of the rivers Muga, Mugueta and Fluvià, as well as along the old river bed. The lower courses of rivers are normally in very fertile flood plains which are highly exploited, causing the transformation of their environment to be particularly dramatic. Nevertheless, the Aiguamolls Park has a small (though well con-served) area of riverside woodland on its third Integral Reserve Area, Car-amany Island. It covers 5.6 hectares and is situated on the Fluvià river between Sant Pere Pescador and the sea. It is covered with untended natural riverside woodland. The island is out of bounds, and hardly anyone ever ventures on to it. It is not only a site of botanical interest, but also an attractive sanctuary for various species of birds.

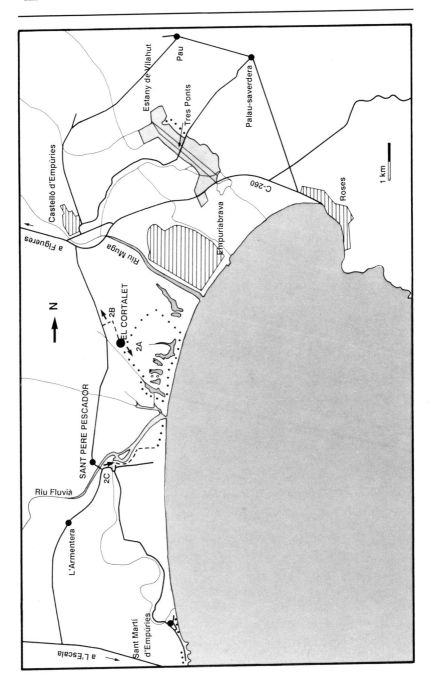

The **crops** to be found within the park limits have been undergoing changes as a result of the increase in the availability of irrigation water. Winter cereals (barley and wheat) have gradually been suplanted by maize, sorghum, sunflower and fruit orchards (mainly apple and apricot). These crops, which are over-sprayed with pesticides, do not favour the presence of breeding species. In late summer and autumn, however, the barley and maize fields become good feeding areas for Mallard. The fruit orchards are good wintering habitats for insectivorous birds and thrushes due to the great amount of rotten fruit (mainly apples) on the ground. The orchards are also good for hares, which use them as relatively safe breeding areas and as a good refuge during the hunting season, when they are a favourite prey.

The paddy fields are certainly the most productive agricultural area for water birds. The park management brought back rice-planting to the Alt Empordà *comarca* (county), where it had stopped in 1968. At the moment there are about 150 hectares of paddy fields. Practically no pesticides are used there, and they are kept flooded outside the rice-growing season (October-March) in order to provide a suitable habitat for wintering birds.

How to visit the park

To reach the park, the best idea is to head for Castelló d'Empúries. You must take the Figueres turning off the A-7 motorway or the N-2 national road, which both run between La Jonquera and Barcelona. It is not necessary to enter Figueres (unless you have a specific interest in doing so: > cf. Other places of interest), and you must follow signs to Roses, first along the Figueres by-pass and later on the C-260 road. Half way between Figueres and Roses (8 kilometres after leaving Figueres), you come to Castelló d'Empúries. If you are travelling by train, the nearest station to Castelló is Figueres. There is a regular bus service between the two towns (the Figueres bus station is right beside the train station).

Since the park has an Information Centre (El Cortalet), the best idea is to head straight there. Park maps, specific advice and general information brochures may be obtained here (in English, Catalan, German, French and Spanish) as well as a full check-list of interesting birds seen over the course of the previous few days. The "El Cortalet" Information centre is open all the year round from 9 am to 2 pm, and from 3 pm to 6 pm (from October to March) and from 4 pm to 7 pm (from April to September). In July, August and September, the Park organizes guided tours in different languages led by local naturalists.

To reach the Information Centre, you must take the road from Castelló d'Empúries to Sant Pere Pescador. Three kilometres after you have turned on to this road, and shortly after passing a petrol station on your right, you must take a gravel lane (sign-posted) for just over one kilometre. You will then arrive at the El Cortalet parking area.

Although other nature trails are being planned, at the time this book went to press, there was only one official nature trail in the park. It is referred to as nature trail or "itinerari" number 1. Following this trail you will get to know the saltmarsh Integral Reserve Area, although other habitats (water meadows, paddy fields and sandy coastal areas) can also be visited. Habitats such as freshwater marsh and waterside woodland, however, cannot be seen on this trail. We therefore supply details about other possible itineraries and more information which will permit you to visit sites that will give you a more complete range of this nature reserve's habitats. This will enable you to observe almost all the reserve's bird species.

The minimum amount of time needed for a visit of the reserve is one full day: a half day for the saltmarsh area (itinerary 2A) and a further half day for the freshwater marsh area (itinerary 2B). If you wish to visit all the habitats in an unhurried fashion, it is better to plan your visit over a two-day period. The second day can be dedicated to itinerary 2C. You will still have plenty of time for a visit to Vilahut lagoon in the evening. Observations may vary substantially from one day to the next. Itinerary 2C is far more interesting in winter, although birdwatching is by no means poor at other times of year. It will also permit you to see Caramany island and its rich riverside woodland area. In July and August, however, this itinerary will afford us little more than sights of motorboats and swimming costumes.

During the best birdwatching period (May, and April to a lesser extent), when all the breeding birds have arrived and there is still a heavy passage of migratory birds, it is worth staying on in the park because changes take place overnight and surprises (rare and accidental species, which are quite easily located by local birdwatchers) are more frequent.

Birdwatching

2A. Itinerary in the saltmarsh Reserve

Starting point and end of the itinerary: El Cortalet **Time needed**: 4-5 hours **Means of transport**: on foot **Observations**: best in the morning

The itinerary or nature trail begins right in front of El Cortalet Information Centre where there is a large shallow freshwater lagoon covering about 18 hectares. It is man-made, and was inaugurated in spring 1989. The idea is to maintain the water level throughout the year (except in July and

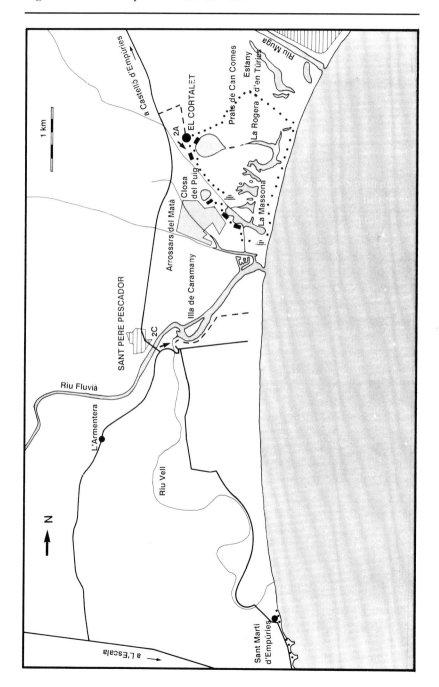

August). There is a hide right beside the Information Centre, and another hide will be built shortly after this book goes to print.

The itineray continues through an area of water meadows. If it is migration time, you must look out for the "little brown jobs" flitting around in the trees alongside the path. Not all of them will be Blackcap or Nightingale. At this time of year it is common to see Redstart, Melodious Warbler and Pied Flycatcher as well as different *Phylloscopus* and *Sylvia* warblers such as Whitethroat (very abundant on some days) or Subalpine Warbler.

About two hundred and fifty metres from the start you will come to a **raised hide** on your right. It is accessible from the path. From here you can see the breeding area for White Stork and Fallow Deer. The plan is to reintroduce Fallow Deer into the saltmarsh reserve in the future so that the sheep and horses (whose task it is to keep the area's vegetation down) may be substituted by deer. A pair of Roller are sure to be breeding in one of the rows of trees in the vicinity. They may possibly change their exact breeding site from year to year (keep your eyes open for Roller all along the edge of the trees). The bright flash of blue when it takes to the wing will soon give its presence away! Stop along the way at strategic points offering good views of the meadows and rows of trees. Other interesting birds such as Stone Curlew, Kestrel, Curlew, Green Woodpecker and Hoopoe will make your wait anything but boring. Hoopoe winter in the Empordà and it is possible to see this species even during the bitterest frosty periods in January and February.

Once you start walking again, you will soon come to a small **look-out point** (*Mirador*) on a small mound. From here it is possible to get a good view of most of the saltmarsh. In winter, and to a lesser extent in autumn, good numbers of wildfowl can be seen, and it is common to see flights of several hundred duck rise up in alarm as one of the park's abundant wintering Marsh Harrier (or rarer Hen Harrier) flies past. Wildfowl are probably the birds to have benefitted most from the area's protection and the creation of the Integral Reserve Areas in the park. This is primarily due to the ban on hunting. Winter counts in the months of January used to give an overall average of between 300 and 400 ducks before protection measures were introduced. Since then there has been a remarkable increase in wildfowl numbers. Over 7,000 were recorded in early 1989. The most typical species during the winter are Mallard (3,700), Teal (1,400), Wigeon (300) and Shoveler (250). Though less abundant on the reserve, Gadwall, Pochard, Tufted Duck, Shelduck and a small quantity of Grey Lag Geese (between 3 and 10 birds wintering), are also to be seen. From the *mirador* you may well see groups of Grey Heron, Little Egret or even Flamingo winging from one lagoon to the next.

You will cross a **bridge over the Corredor canal** at a point very close to the *mirador*. This canal supplies fresh water to the Massona lagoon at a point

Purple Heron

where there is a large reedbed. If you stand on (or near) the bridge at the crack of dawn (when birds are most active and visitors few), you are likely to spot the area's small reed-dwelling birds. Cetti's Warbler and Fan-tailed Warbler are abundant throughout the year. This is also one of the best sites for observing the interesting Moustached Warbler. In the breeding season, Reed Warbler and Great Reed Warbler can also be seen here in good numbers. Savi's Warbler, however, is a good deal rarer. A knowledge of the song of each of these species is useful when identifying these species. In this reed bed there are also several pairs of Little Bittern, one pair of Marsh Harrier and another of Bittern. This latter species, however, can be spotted more easily in the freshwater marsh.

After crossing the bridge, the trail continues for 100 metres, bordered by reeds and rows of trees where Penduline Tit might well be encountered. You will soon come to the **paddy fields**. This new habitat will supply good birdwatching at all times of year because the park management keeps them permanently flooded (except in February and March when the fields have to be prepared). A good many water birds are thus attracted here, especially herons, wildfowl, waders and gulls. During the breeding season there are small colonies of Black-winged Stilt, clutches of Mallard and abundant Blue-headed Wagtail nest here. Other species breeding nearby, including Purple Heron, Bittern and Marsh Harrier, come to the paddy fields to feed. The paddy fields are overrun with waders during spring passage, particularly in April and May, when the recently ploughed earth provides excellent, vegetation-free muddy areas. The most common species are Redshank, Wood Sandpiper, Ruff, Black-tailed Godwit and Snipe, although most European species of waders can also be seen here. On both migrations the commoner species of terns (Black, Whiskered, Common, Gull-billed etc.) can also be seen (watch out for White-winged Black tern in May and Caspian tern in late summer). Glossy Ibis, though rare, is an increasingly regular visitor, especially in October. In winter the flooded paddy fields are regularly visited by good numbers of Grey Heron, Little Egret and Cattle Egret. At night, and to a lesser extent in the evening, they are visited by wildfowl, although some of the more diurnal species, such as Grey Lag Goose and Shelduck, can be seen there in broad daylight.

Once you have reached the paddy fields, the trail continues to the left, but first it is worth making a small detour to the **Closa del Puig raised hide** on the right. From this hide the paddy fields can be seen on one side and there is a water meadow (where a scrape has been made) on the other side. At the far end of the meadow there is an isolated patch of riverside woodland where efforts are being made to encourage the establishment of a colony of tree-breeding herons. The central point of attention (apart from the small copse itself) is a semi-concealed cage containing herons born in captivity at Barcelona Zoo. The scrape is a favourite fishing spot for herons, and from April to September, it is quite common to see tortoises here.

Heading back to the main trail again, the path leads between the Massona lagoon reedbeds (on the left) and the paddy fields (on the right) to another **hide** known as the "**Gall Marí**" (in Catalan: Purple Gallinulule, a species that has been re-introduced and is easily seen here). It gives a good view of the Gall Marí (an artificial lagoon which links up with the Massona lagoon) and the canal which joins the Massona and La Llarga lagoon. The Gall Marí lagoon is also very good for waders in August and September when the water level is low. In winter it is good for wildfowl which can be seen on the lagoon during the day and flying down on to the adjacent paddy fields in the evening, encouraged by the approach of dark. The back of the hide faces west and the flights of duck gliding down on to the paddy fields can be observed against the sunset. On some days, flights of wildfowl against a crimson sky backdrop - and the sound of their whistling wings - provide the last breath-taking thrills of the day for those birdwatchers and nature lovers who do not mind making it back to El Cortalet or to the Mas El Matà car park under the mantle of darkness.

Leaving the paddy fields behind you, the trail crosses an area of bullrushes as far as the **El Matà hide**, which gives us a view of the El Matà lagoon and the inland half of the Massona lagoon. This is a good spot for observing migratory or wintering fishing birds such as grebes, Cormorant and Osprey (present for a few days each year). It is also a good spot for observing the passage of herons and raptors between the saltmarsh and the paddy fields, as well as wildfowl and Coot feeding. On winter evenings you can observe flocks of up to 20 Marsh Harrier gathering together nearby before retiring to their roosts. A close watch on the reedbeds and the bullrushes within view of the El Matà and Gall Marí hides may produce good views of Little Bittern, Kingfisher, rails and small reed-dwelling birds (their species will depend on the season).

After the El Matà hide, the trail borders the Massona canal which links this lagoon with the Sirvent lagoon. You must cross a bridge over this canal and head towards the sea before reaching the camping site. The trail continues through areas of brackish water meadows alongside the camping site until you reach the beach. On the last stretch you pass through an area of thinned-out reedbeds and saltwort marsh, which is normally flooded in winter. You may well see interesting small birds and rails here.

On arrival at the beach, you may climb up a **look-out tower** and spot wintering sea-birds such as Black-throated Diver (flocks of up to 40 in some winters) and Razorbill. Velvet Scoter, Common Scoter and Eider Duck are normally less common. On days when the *Tramuntana* (northerly) and

Llevantada (easterly) winds blow, Gannet, Manx and Cory's Shearwater seek shelter in the bay and can be seen from the beach. *Llevantada* gales, which are most spectacular, are often particularly violent at this point because of its position in the middle of the bay, causing waves to break with maximum force. From October to May there are frequently *Llevantada* storms which are strong enough to send waves crashing across the beach and spilling on to the saltmarsh, which soon becomes totally flooded. It is at this time that the flooded area of the *Aiguamolls* (Catalan: marsh) swells considerably, making the area more attractive for many wintering or migratory water birds.

After climbing down the look-out tower, you must follow the beach towards the north as far as the mouth of the Rogera lagoon. As you cover this stretch of beach, you will be able to make out the various lagoons inland. The lagoons are out of bounds to avoid disturbance to the birds. In winter, however, the flight of a Marsh Harrier over the lagoons is sure to put up hundreds of duck and other water birds for birdwatchers to see. In the breeding season you can see typical sand-dwelling species such as Kentish Plover (in large numbers) and Stone Curlew or Short-toed Lark (in lesser numbers) here. During migration this stretch often provides you with sights of rarities of all kinds, ranging from Short-eared Owl to the "little brown jobs" of all descriptions that dart about in the low vegetation. In winter you must also look out to see. The divers may not all be Black-throated!

At the **Rogera lagoon** there is a small screen hide which affords a good general view of the lagoon. Good birdwatching is to be had at this point at all times of year. The breeding birdlife is for the moment limited to a few species such as Kentish Plover, isolated pairs of Little Tern and Redshank. Hopefully the list of breeding species will increase as the conservation programme is made more efficient. Although not breeding, many other species, particularly in the heron and wader line, tend to stay on in this area during the summer period. During migration, the Rogera lagoon is excellent for waders and terns, and it is the site where Flamingo most often come to rest. In winter there are moments when the Rogera is literally swarming with ducks of various species. Black-necked Grebe and Cormorant are also seen swimming and fishing, often in good numbers. Little Egret and numerous Grey Heron seek their prey on the shores of the lake, alongside Curlew, Grey Plover and other waders. The lagoon is also the favourite spot for migrating Flamingo. On winter evenings, the beach beside the Rogera lagoon is a roost for up to a hundred Curlew and up to six thousand Black-headed Gull.

The following stage of the trail takes you past the Rogera lagoon and northwards along the beach as far as the signposts that indicate you are to cut inland across the saltmarsh. In spring, the beautiful song of the Skylark is to heard all the time.

After a while the saltwort gives way to brackish meadows (the **Can Comes meadows**) which may prove to be of great interest. This is one of the areas (along with the area near Vilahut lagoon) where one of the park's five pairs of Lesser Grey Shrike can be seen in the summer period. This shrike is one of the most interesting breeding species in the Aiguamolls Park because it only breeds at one other site in the whole of the Iberian Peninsula (cf. Itinerary 9A). It is also in this area that the majority of yearly sightings of Red-throated Pipit are made during migration (mainly in late April and early May, a time when they are very distinct in their summer plumage). Flocks of migrating Dotterel are a speciality at this spot, though the species is much less regular than the pipit. In winter you can see good numbers of Lapwing, Golden Plover and Stone Curlew alongside huge flights of larks and finches. Merlin and Peregrine Falcon are often seen in the vicinity of these flocks, on the look out for easy prey.

When the trail reaches a pebble track (the foundation of what was to have been the main access road into the holiday resort planned in the area), you must head south-westwards towards El Cortalet, bordering meadows and cultivated land which are rich in birdlife. You will pass a **ruined farm house** which is the set of one of the park's pairs of foxes. The dry inland area around the farm is where Red-legged Partridge and Woodchat Shrike are most easily seen.

The last part of the trail before you reach the finishing point at El Cortalet Information centre follows the northern edge of the El Cortalet artificial lagoon (flooded in spring 1989).

2B. Itinerary in the freshwater marsh Reserve: Tres Ponts (Three Bridges), Vilahut, Mornau water meadows

Starting point: El Cortalet **End of the itinerary**: Castelló d'Empúries **Time needed**: half a day
Means of transport: by car and on foot **Observations**: best in the afternoon

To reach this reserve, which is situated in the northern part of the park you drive from El Cortalet (central point for all itineraries) to Castelló d'Empúries (after **4 kilometres** you will reach the C-260 road. Turn left as if you wanted to go to Figueres, but turn right almost immediately over the bridge into Castelló d'Empúries). Drive straight on through the village until you reach a bridge over the small La Mugueta lagoon (one kilometre from the town, **km 5.6** on your overall itinerary that started at El Cortalet). It is worth stopping on the bridge (traffic permitting) to take a quick look at the lagoon. During the breeding season Mute Swan (feral), Little Grebe, Little Bittern and Penduline Tit are all to be seen here.

Turn left along a lane immediately after the bridge and after 400 metres (**km 6** on your itinerary) you must turn left again taking the second of two tracks (which are very close together). At this point it is also worth stopping to have a look at the Castelló Sewage works, a good spot for waders.

After 300 metres (**kilometre 6.3** of your itinerary) you will come to the Castelló d'Empúries - Palau-Savardera rural road. It winds its way through agricultural land within the park area, alongside the Mugueta river (a tributary of the Muga which supplies water to the lagoons in the "Three Bridges" area). When your itinerary has covered **9.3 kilometres**, the road reaches a clump of very high poplar trees right beside two identical farm buildings. It is a good stopping place, especially in the breeding and migratory seasons. Walk back

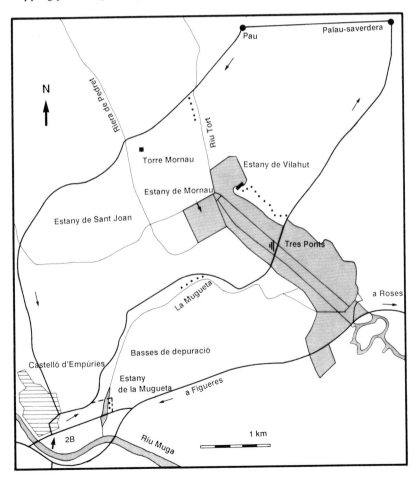

along the Mugueta river on a path which borders its left-hand bank. Here you will encounter a small -though very productive- sample of riverside woodland. Roller perched in the poplars or hunting in neighbouring fields are a common sight, and you may be lucky enough to catch sight of a Kingfisher darting over the waters of the Mugueta, and hear (or see) Penduline Tit in the willow trees on the river bank. During migration this area is excellent for migratory passerines.

Back on the Palau-Savardera road once again, you will come to the "Tres Ponts" (in reference to the three bridges which cross over the drainage canals in the marsh). Stop on the middle bridge (at **km 10.7** of your itinerary). In winter, good numbers of wildfowl can usually be seen on the canal. Raptors are sure to be hunting over the nearby reedbeds and bullrushes. In spring and summer, dawn and dusk at this spot will supply excellent views of the flight of many herons to and from their roosts and feeding grounds. Little Egret, Cattle Egret and Purple Heron will be the commonest species, but a little more patience is needed to spot Night Heron. Both patience and luck are essential to see Bittern. Nevertheless, this is the best spot in the whole park (and dare one say in all Catalonia?) to see this rare, declining and elusive species in flight, at dawn or dusk. The "Tres Ponts" is also a good place to hear Bittern booming from March to May. This sound has given rise to delightful legends in the Empordà area. By the way, please remember that it is forbidden to wander into the reserve or to follow the paths which border the canals.

After the last of the three bridges, you must keep going for 800 metres until you reach an overhead electric cable, supported by a pylon on the left-hand side of the road. A notice on the pylon indicates you have come to the Vilahut lagoon trail. Leave the car on the right-hand side of the road (you will have reached **km 11.5** by now), and walk along the path on the left, skirting the large iron gate. The Vilahut lagoon hide is about 800 metres away, and the path to get there is beautiful and interesting. You will go through an area of meadows and small clumps of oak trees on granite outcrops. During the breeding season, you are likely to see Roller and Lesser Grey Shrike on these trees, and on the electric cable which runs across the area. There is also a pair of Kestrel in the vicinity and in May it is here that the Red-footed Falcon is most often seen. Although considered to be a rare species, it is seen regularly, at times even in small flocks!

When you reach the fence which encloses Vilahut lagoon, you will find a large mass of granite on which a couple of fine cork oak trees have managed not only to survive, but to thrive! This is a good spot to get a first general view of the lagoon, or to wait for the last birdwatchers to leave the hide. In summer, a scan of the nearby mountains (Serra Verdera) and the meadows of the reserve

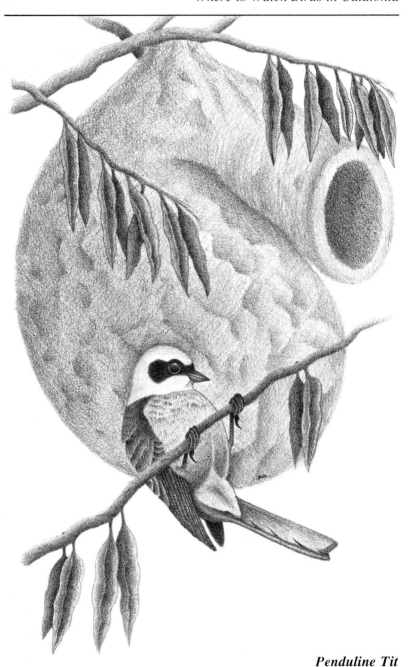

Penduline Tit

area may well supply you with a sight of hovering Short-toed Eagle, a species which hunts snakes in the grass.

If the water level is high, the Vilahut lagoon hide is excellent for birdwatching at all times of year. In winter, wildfowl numbers are impressive (especially Mallard and Teal) and Gadwall, Wigeon, Shoveler and occasional Pochard and Tufted Duck can be seen. Ferruginous Duck have also been seen on more than one occasion. In the breeding season, the hide gives excellent views of numerous breeding species such as Purple Heron, Bittern, Little Bittern, Marsh Harrier, Water Rail (Vilahut is one of the best places for observing this species), Moustached Warbler, and, when the water level so permits, Coot and Little Grebe. During migration, Vilahut lagoon is renown for the rarities that appear there. The species of water birds present here change daily, and it is the best spot in the park for rare accidentals. Reef Heron and Blue-winged Teal are but two examples of accidentals recorded on the lagoon in the last few years.

You return to the car along the same path. Thereafter, time-permitting, you may care to continue your birdwatching itinerary to the Mornau and Sant Joan *closes* (water meadows). You must follow the same road towards Palau-Savardera. After **km 13.8**, you pass a turning to Roses on your right (do not take it) and you come to an area of olive groves. In March and April, Great Spotted Cuckoo can be seen and heard in this area, along with Sardinian Warbler, which is a resident species. There are several good stopping places where you can try your luck.

Soon after you will reach the outskirts of the village called Palau, where you take the road to the left (mind the crossing) towards Pau. As you enter Pau (**km 17.5**), take the first sharp turning left on to a country lane. When you have reached **km 19.7**, you will come across a notice which indicates you are entering the park, and the bridge over the Tort river. After the bridge, there is a path to the left which you can walk along in the breeding season in the hope of getting sights of Roller and Lesser Grey Shrike.

If you now drive to Castelló d'Empúries, you will pass the Torre Mornau, a large-white building surrounded by an area of interesting and beautiful water meadows. This building was formerly a Spanish army cavalry barracks. When you reach **km 21.1**, the road fords the Pedret stream. In heavy rain, however, do not drive across the ford because it can be very dangerous. You will cross the Molí canal at **km 24.7**, and this is a good spot for scanning the nearby water meadows when they are flooded. During migration, good flights of Ruff, Black-tailed Godwit and other waders can be seen here.

At **km 25.8**, you will arrive in Castelló d'Empúries once again. Before calling it a day, you may care to make your way through the centre of town to the mill (Catalan: *molí*). Although it is one of the oldest factories in Catalonia, it is still in working order. If you ask the way, it will not be too difficult to find this interesting building behind the cathedral. There is a small colony of Collared Dove which has recently settled in this area. If you cannot see these birds, try your luck at the nearby washing-place -another beautiful spot where you can freshen up after such an exhausting day!

2C. Itinerary to Caramany island and Sant Pere Pescador

Starting point: Sant Pere Pescador **End of the itinerary**: l'Escala **Time needed**: 3-4 hours **Means of transport**: by car and on foot (optional) **Observations**: not very worthwhile in summer

You set out from El Cortalet towards Sant Pere Pescador (turn left at the tarmac road). Drive through Sant Pere Pescador, turning left towards the bridge over the Fluvià river. The centre of the bridge will be the starting point for this itinerary. Whether you are coming from El Cortalet, Castelló d'Empúries or Sant Pere Pescador, you will certainly have to cross this bridge. You must turn sharp left again immediately after the bridge. Six hundred metres further on you will come to a T-junction where you must take the left-hand turning to the beach. Turn off this road almost immediately (100 metres after the T-junction) and take a lane to the left on a bend where there is a "Parc Natural" notice. This lane is fine in all but the wettest weather, and follows a stretch of the river Fluvià on its right-hand bank, leading eventually to the sea. On the riverside stretch you will be able to see the whole of Caramany island on the other side of the main flow of the river. (Boating in the main stream and access on to the island are forbidden because Caramany island is the third of the Park's Integral Reserve Areas).

The best season for birdwatching here is winter. There are good numbers of wildfowl (especially diving ducks) as well as Coot and Cormorant in the river. The trees on the island are also used as roosts by herons, Jackdaw and a good number of Wood Pigeon and Stock Dove. Dusk can be quite spectacular here.

After **2 km** of the itinerary, the lane leads away form the river, crosses some apple orchards and heads towards a farm house (Catalan: *mas*). In the vicinity of the *mas* there are several rows of tamarisk trees and during migration many interesting birds are seen here. Further on, the lane can become quite treacherous in the wet season, and you might get bogged down. Be very careful and do not drive on if you are not sure of your ground!

Following the lane (on foot or by car) you will come to Sant Pere beach (at **km 2.9**). From the beach you can take a pleasant walk to the left as far as the mouth of the Fluvià river. The area around the mouth is good for wintering sea-birds such as divers, sea ducks and Razorbill, which are attracted by the nutrients in the river.

When you get back to the car, take the lane again, and when you reach "La Gaviota" camping site (**km 3.6**), take the tarmac road away from the beach. After **5.2 km** you will once again come to the T-junction where you must turn left towards the "Amfora", "Las Dunas" and "La Ballena Alegre" camping sites, and the village of Sant Martí d'Empúries. The road makes its way through large apple orchards (good passerine-watching in winter) and at **km 11** it borders an old dried-up lagoon which in the wet season is good for waders. At **km 12** you will reach Sant Martí d'Empúries, a tiny medieval walled village which is especially famous for the Greek and Roman ruins nearby.

Once you reach the town, drive to the church square and from there to the vantage point commanding a view of the sea. Seabirds can be observed from here, and it is also an ideal spot for getting the full thrill of a good easterly gale (Catalan: *Llevantada*) if you like that kind of sensation!

Those eager for more sea-watching are advised to take the road to L'Escala (southwards). It skirts the sea and passes through an area of sand dunes with small sheltered coves which are well worth a scan. Any one of them may harbour Red-throated Diver. Great Crested Grebe and Cormorant can also be seen there in winter. The road soon runs alongside the ruins of Empúries (cf. Other places of interest) and an area of fixed dunes where it is not unusual to hear the strident call of Great Spotted Cuckoo in spring. Short-toed Treecreeper, Sardinian Warbler and Collared Dove are also to be seen here, the doves being particularly conspicuous behind the Hotel Empúries. At **km 14** the itinerary comes to an end at L'Escala.

Board and lodging

If you are visiting the Aiguamolls area, there are two towns that you can use as a base: Castelló d'Empúries and Sant Pere Pescador. There are good board and lodging facilities (hotels, guest houses etc.) in both towns (Ca l'Anton, Can Canet and Empòrium at Castelló d'Empúries; El Pescador and El Collverd at Sant Pere Pescador), where you will be sure to find a room or a table at all times of year except in July and August (and special holidays), when swarms of tourists overrun the Empordà region.

Those wishing to taste the delicious Empordà cuisine can also motor across for meals at Palau-Savardera (Terra Nostra restaurant), Pau (Garimall restaurant) and Vilanova de la Muga (La Resclosa restaurant). Those wanting a more lavish meal can go to one of Catalonia's finest restaurants, "Hostal la Llar", on the Castelló d'Empúries-Roses road. (It is very close to the freshwater marsh reserve area). The Empordà is one of the finest "gourmet" *comarques* in Catalonia, and there are many fine restaurants in the area. Local Perelada wines and *cava* will also be a pleasant surprise for the uninitiated and Vilajuïga water will also be found to be refreshing.

Campers will find six camping sites within the park area (from north to south: Castell Mar, International Amberes, L'Estrella, Laguna, Almatà and El Rio).

Being a tourist area, there is a wide range of good hotels and other facilities for tourists at either end of the Roses bay (at Roses and at L'Escala).

Other places of interest

- Castelló d'Empúries cathedral. An interesting Gothic cathedral with Romanesque foundations. Concerts in summer on the splendid organ. Variable opening times. If closed, the parish priest can supply the key.

- Peralada castle. A beautiful castle that has been partially converted into a casino. It houses a fine arts collection, valuable books and manuscripts in its library, and has a magnificent garden. Summer music festival. On the outskirts of Perelada, 8 kms from Castelló. Open daily from 10 am to 7 pm.

- Empúries ruins. The finest and best conserved Greek and Roman ruins in Catalonia. One kilometre south of Sant Martí d'Empúries on the coastal road to L'Escala. Open daily from 10 am to 1 pm and from 3 pm to 5 pm, except on Mondays.

- Teatre-Museu Dalí (Dalí Museum). One of the best collections of this Catalan painter's work with some of his most famous works. Figueres city centre. Open daily from 11.30 am to 5.15 pm.

- Museu del Joguet (Toy Museum). A fascinating collection of antique and modern games and toys. On the Figueres "Rambla" (avenue). Weekdays from 10 am to 12.30 pm, and 4 pm to 7.30 pm. Weekends from 11 am to 1.30 pm.

3
COSTA BRAVA SUD

The coast between L'Escala and Blanes is known as the Costa Brava. Despite the harm done to the coast by tourist development, the area still has very interesting sites such as the Montgrí massif, the Medes Islands, the Baix Ter and Pals marshes and the Gavarres mountains, all of which are due to be converted into Nature Parks or Reserves. This area has been the subject of many ornithological publications, especially written by Britons, due to the large amount of visitors the area has received since the beginning of the tourist boom in Catalonia.

Habitats: sea cliffs, coastal islands, scrub, pine and cork oak woods, sand dunes, coastal marshes.

Interesting species:
- *Present all the year round*: Storm Petrel, Bonelli's Eagle, Peregrine Falcon, Eagle Owl, Reg-legged Partridge, Thekla'a Lark, Dartford Warbler, Cetti's Warbler, Moustached Warbler, Sardinian Warbler, Blue Rock Thrush, Black Wheatear, Crag Martin, Crested Tit, Penduline Tit and Rock Sparrow.
- *Summer visitors*: Night Heron, Little Egret, Cattle Egret, Little Bittern, Hobby, Herring Gull (large colony), Nightjar, Alpine Swift, Pallid Swift, Red-rumped Swallow, Rock Thrush, Spectacled Warbler, Subalpine Warbler, Orphean Warbler, Black-eared Wheatear, Great Reed Warbler, Bonelli's Warbler, Woodchat Shrike.
- *Winter visitors*: Black-throated Diver, Red-throated Diver, Gannet, wildfowl, Razorbill.
- *Migrants*: water birds, Eleanora's Falcon and passerines in general.

Description and habitat

The coastline of the Montgrí massif on the Costa Brava is completely different from that of the Cap de Creus (chapter 1). The limestone cliffs, such as those at Miradones, are almost three hundred feet high, and fall in a sheer drop into the sea. In this area, there are hardly any coves (only La Pedrosa and La Farriola), nor any inlets. There are only caves and cavities in the rocks caused by the erosion of the limestone. The white colour of the bare rock, which supports no vegetation, makes the landscape unmistakable and typical of limestone cliff areas.

South of the Montgrí massif, there is the flood plain of the rivers Ter and Daró. It is a depression with a very similar morphology to that of the Roses Bay flood plain, though it is more varied and smaller in size. As at Roses, there is a coastal strip of marshes with water meadows inland. The area has occasional hillocks here and there which are rarely over 150 feet high. Here, though, instead of a wide, open plain, the landscape is composed of small -and even tiny- compartments, such as the Torroella, Ullastret and Pals plains, which are boxed in between rows of low hills.

The Baix Ter plain is bordered on its south side by two old though not particularly high massifs which are very similar from the geological and geographical points of view. Nearer the coast is the Begur massif (Puig son Ric, 305 m), and further inland, the Gavarres (about 500 m high). These small ranges are separated by the so-called Palamós-Palafrugell corridor, along which runs the Albi river, and are the northernmost extremities of the Catalan Coastal Range (Serralada Litoral). They are made up of highly eroded materials (slate, limestone, granite) with very weathered forms, and rounded summits and slopes.

At several points, though, there seems to be a slight process of renewed geological activity, especially in those areas nearest the sea. One of these areas can indeed be seen in the Begur massif, in an area that is considered to be the heart of the Costa Brava, with its typical coves (Fornells, Aiguablava, Llafranc, Calella, etc.).

The section of Coastal Range known as the Gavarres tails off in the south at the Ridaura or d'Aro valley, a long and narrow depression crossing the range, beyond which the La Selva massif rises up, forming an area of granite summits, the most characteristic part of which is the Cadiretes range or *serra*.

Going back to the coastal area itself, it must be added that the true Costa Brava stretches from Begur to Blanes, and has characteristics that make it different from the coast of the Montgrí massif or the Cap de Creus. Granite is predominant here, with summits rising up to 500 m, with tectonic lines such as the Palafrugell and Aro Valley depressions, at the heads of which large beaches are to be found. In the remaining areas, the hills generally slope down gently to the sea, with minor valleys forming coves with tiny beaches, and are boxed in by rocky spurs. Between Tossa and Sant Feliu is the only section with granite cliffs, half cloaked in pine woods. This splendid section of cliffs reminds us of the Montgrí massif.

The Montgrí massif, in its inland rocky areas, is covered in scrub, having kermes oak as its predominant species. There are also shrubs associated with calcareous areas such as rosemary, heather and bloodroot, and a few stunted plantations of Aleppo and stone Pine. On the sand-covered valley floors, there is a fine stone Pine wood, which was planted with the express idea of stabilizing the inland dunes.

The Medes islands, a small archipelago made up of seven islands, is a site of great biological and ecological importance because of the wealth of species and habitats it supports. It is interesting both for scientific reasons and for the scenery. The vegetation and land fauna are worthy of study, though the submarine habitat around the islands is the factor that gives the Medes their exceptional interest. There are many books on the subject, and for this reason we may be excused from entering into a description of this habitat that would go beyond the scope of this book. The vegetation of the Medes Islands is very similar to that found on the cliffs of the Montgrí massif, of which they form part geologically. Halophilous plants that can endure high salinity, and xerophilous ones, such as Sea-side Carrot *Critnum maritimun* and Sea Fennel, that resist long periods of drought, are predominant on the islands. Another determining factor for the vegetation is the huge colony of Herring Gulls (8,000 pairs). Plant species abounding are those adapted to soils rich in nitrogen, such as common mallow, thistle, saltwort and the introduced species, cammock. As for trees, only olive trees and the odd carob tree are to be found on the Medes Islands.

On the flood plain of the lower Ter, at the Ter Vell marshes, on the lagoons at the mouth of the river and at the Basses d'en Coll, at Pals, the vegetation is similar to that described at the Roses Bay Aiguamolls (marshes) in chapter 2. Once again, dunes, saltmarsh, freshwater lagoons fringed with reed and bulrush beds, paddy fields and riverside woodland are encountered.

On the road between Pals and Blanes that crosses the Begur, Gavarres and Cadiretes massifs, you will pass through areas of scrub made up of heather and rockrose, as well as Aleppo and stone pine woods, and, above all, thick cork oak woods. It is not surprising, then, that this part of the Costa Brava has been one of the first and foremost places in the Iberian Peninsula for the cork industry.

How to visit the area

Itineraries in the southern part of the Costa Brava begin at L'Escala and finish at Blanes. It is very easy to reach L'Escala if beforehand you have been visiting the Aiguamolls de l'Empordà Nature Park, since the last itinerary for the Aiguamolls area finishes up at Sant Martí d'Empúries-L'Escala. If you are arriving at L'Escala straight from Barcelona or from the French frontier, you must take the L'Escala turning off the motorway. You can also reach L'Escala by bus from Figueres.

You will need at least two days to visit this area. Itinerary 3A requires half a day, though if you can follow it at a slower pace, it is better to spend a

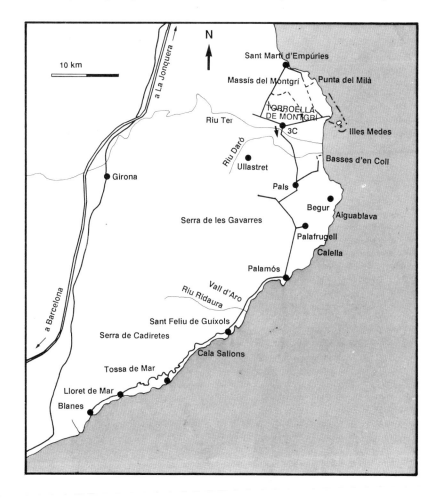

whole day. Itinerary 3B, a boat ride to the Medes islands and along the coast, lasts between 2 and 4 hours, and may be combined with itinerary 3A. It is better to cover it in the morning or in the evening if you want a calmer sea, since the midday period is when the sea breeze normally blows. In any case, the early morning is better for the visit because the sea often calms down late and there may not be enough time to carry out the full trip.

L'Estartit is the point at which both itineraries 3A and 3B finish up, so it may be the best place to make your base. Hotels of all kinds (cf. board and lodging) and a camping site called "Castell Montgrí" may all be found. This camping site has an ornithological trail in a very interesting part of the Montgrí massif.

A whole day will be necessary to cover itinerary 3C in an unhurried fashion, allowing time for the recommended stops, although, at a push, you can cover it in less time. You must bear in mind that the distance from Torroella de Montgrí to Blanes is almost 100 kms.

The climate in this area is very mild, and so any month of the year will be suitable for the visit. The breeding colonies on the Medes Islands, and the fact that the area's most attractive species -amongst them Red-rumped Swallow, Spectacled Warbler and Orphean Warbler- are summer visitors, make Spring (when fewer tourists are around) and Summer the most interesting times of the year from the ornithological point of view.

Bird-watching

3A. Itinerary in the Montgrí massif

Starting point: l'Escala **End of the itinerary**: Torroella de Montgrí **Time needed**: half a day
Means of transport: by car and on foot **Observations**: best in spring

The itinerary begins at L'Escala. You must head in the direction of Montgó along Riells Avenue (Avinguda de Riells). The starting point of the itinerary (**km 0**) is the entrance to the L'Escala marina. On your left you pass a military area that may be recognized by its barbed wire fences which have ensured that (at least) one section of coast has remained free of development. After one kilometre you come to a junction where you must take the right-hand road descending to Punta Montgó, which is sign-posted. At **km 1.3**, you must turn right towards the "Neus" camping site, which you will come to 300 m farther on at a point where the tarmac road ends giving way to a perfectly passable track. After this point, the track passes through an Aleppo and Stone pine wood. The undergrowth and open areas are composed of thick, almost impenetrable scrub. Warblers and woodland birds, especially finches such as Serin, Goldfinch and Greenfinch, will begin to make their appearance.

At **kilometre 4.**2 of the itinerary, you must take a turning to the left, followed shortly by another turning to the left; this is the path that will lead you to the Punta del Milà (Kite Point). After a further 200 metres on this path (**Km 4.4**), you will see a quarry on your right which is now an excellent watering place. Limestone areas, it must be remembered, can often be very dry because rain water tends to permeate rapidly through the rock. Regular visits to watering places are thus obligatory for many species of birds, especially in summer, and so it is well worth waiting at this spot to see what turns up. In summer, the local warblers - Sardinian, Spectacled and Subalpine -as well as several finches, Black-eared Wheatear, and more rarely Black Wheatear and Rock Sparrow, may all be seen here. Larger birds such as Hoopoe and Wood Pigeon also come to the watering place.

Continuing on your way to Punta del Milà, you will go through another pine plantation, which is pretty sparse due to the poor quality of the soil. One need only compare these trees with those growing on the continental dune on sandy soil, as you will see shortly.

At **km 5.6**, you will reach Punta del Milà cliff. Be careful, especially if there are children in your party, because the cliff edge is very close at hand and is very sheer. From the point, walk along towards the left, in a northerly direction, until you reach a concrete platform that was built as a cannon emplacement. In the breeding season there is a small Herring Gull colony just below you, on a small island. Crag Martin and three species of swifts can also be seen skirting the rock faces with their shrill cries. This is a good spot for observing the difference between Common Swift and Pallid Swift, since the latter species is numerous and both species can be seen from close up. Blue Rock Thrush and Black Wheatear can be seen singing from nearby rocks, and with a little bit of luck, a Peregrine might fly over the area. In winter, Peregrine, Blue Rock Thrush and Black Wheatear are all still around, and may be joined by the odd interesting species, such as the rare Wallcreeper. During migration, the possibilities are thrown wide open, although there is no shortage of better spots for observing passerines.

After this stop, you must drive back to the turning marked at **kilometre 4.2**, which you will come to when your kilometre-gague marks **km 7**. Here you must now turn left along the same track you were on before, and drive towards L'Estartit. After 500 m, you will see a small disused military base. On **km 8**, you will come to a ruined farm house, beside which there are a few fields where cereals are grown. It is worth keeping an eye out for Red-legged Partridge, and after the harvest, a good number of seed-eating birds should be around.

At **km 8.7**, a track leads off to the right across the plateau towards Bellcaire, and on the left there is a very stony track. You will later keep on straight, but first, it is not a bad idea to stop at this point, and walk along this left-hand track. It crosses an area of scrub which is rich in warblers. Sardinian, Subalpine and Dartford Warbler are all to be seen as well as the rarer Spectacled Warbler, for which this spot is one of the most regular observation sites in the whole country. Black-eared Wheatears are also common here.

Once back at the car, drive on along the main track, and at **km 10**, you will have a good view of the plateau, with the mountain on which the castle is built in the background (the castle, however, cannot be seen from here). In the troughs between you and the mountain there are continental dunes, covered in pines. You will be visiting the area later. For the moment, scan the area from this vantage point to see if there are any raptors around. The locally-breeding pair of Bonelli's Eagle might well be seen, and if it is winter time, you might see Hen Harrier.

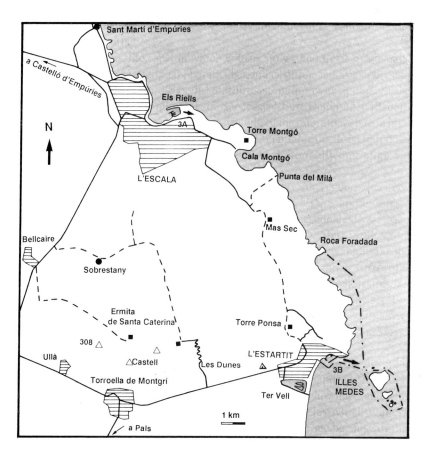

At **km 10.6**, the main track twists round to the left and L'Estartit is signposted. Keep on straight, though, along a track that passes a large *mas* (farmhouse) with a massive tower known as Torre Ponsa. In this area, the watering places available and the conservationist attitude of the owners ensure the presence of many species of passerines. Care must be taken, however, not to damage crops or fences in the area. During migration, the abundance of migrants in this small though lush valley is often surprising. Icterine Warbler and Wood Warbler have been seen here on several occasions. Orphean Warbler and Nightjar also breed here. An ornithological trail starts at the "Castell Montgrí" camping site (cf. board and lodging), and skirts part of the area.

At **km 11.8**, and after bordering the fields at the bottom of the small valley, you will once again come to the main track which you had left at km 10.6. Drive along it as far as L'Estartit and at **kilometre 12.5** you will come to an obligatory diversion to the right which leads to the L'Estartit-Torroella road. At **kilometre 13.2** you must turn left, and of the three possible routes to be taken, take the one furthest to the right. Driving along this road to the end, you will come to a row of tamarisk trees. Turn left and you will come to the beach. Among several blocks of flats you will come across a small treasure -the Ter Vell (the old mouth of the river Ter)- that has been converted into a Nature Reserve by the Torroella de Montgí Municipality.

Reed-dwelling and freshwater marsh birds can be seen at the Ter Vell, where a nature trail and several hides are to be made. In the breeding season you can see Great Reed, Reed, Moustached, Fan-tailed and Cetti's Warbler as well as the odd Little Bittern, Coot and Mallard. During migration and in winter, almost all species of birds associated with this kind of habitat are to be seen, and occasionally, good numbers of waterfowl. In winter it is especially worth looking out to sea. Apart from the excellent view you will get of the Medes Islands, you may well spot divers or Razorbill near the beach.

From the Vell Ter, you make your way back to the L'Estartit-Torroella road. You can now continue to Torroella or else interrupt the itinerary on land to visit the Medes Islands (itinerary 3B), the starting point of which is at L'Estartit. Since those of you who have opted for itinerary 3B will by now have lost count of the distance in kilometres of itinerary 3A, it is best to reset **km 0** at the exit of L'Estartit beside a playground on the left-hand side of the road.

After **2.3 km** you come to a *mas* (farmhouse) with a defence tower (this kind of farmhouse was built as a defence against the attacks of corsairs, who often used the Medes Islands as a base for pillaging raids against inland villages) and after a further 200 m, at **km 2.5**, if you wish to visit the pine wood on the continental dune, take a right-hand turning to "Urbanització Les

Dunes". Drive straight along this track and soon you will come to the pine wood. The undergrowth is generally poor partly because of the sandy soil. At **km 4.9** you will come across a junction where the left-hand track should be taken. At **km 5.4**, you pass by a forestry hut, and the track now deteriorates, becoming very stony. You must at all times follow the main track, but do stop at clearings and areas where birds are more in evidence. Here woodland species such as Great Tit, Blue Tit, Long-tailed Tit and Crested Tit are to be spotted, along with Jay, Spotted Flycatcher, Bonelli's Warbler, Short-toed Treecreeper and, sometimes, Crossbill. Buzzard may be seen from time to time, as well as the odd Goshawk on the wing or dashing off rapidly among the trees.

At **km 8.4**, the track turns sharply to the right, and at **km 9.5**, when you reach the crossroads, you must keep straight on until you reach another fortified *mas*, and from there, drive on to the village of Sobrestany. From here you will enjoy a good view of the higher summits of the Montgrí massif.

When you get to Bellcaire, you may care to drive on to Torroella de Montgrí to start itinerary 3C, or you may prefer to extend your itinerary and take in Santa Caterina hermitage (Ermita de Santa Caterina). The track is well signposted and in good condition, starting at Bellcaire itself. You first cross an area of pines and pass beneath some cliffs where the odd pair of Raven breed. Then the track crosses an area of scrub which extends as far as the hermitage. This extension of the itinerary, apart from adding to the bird-watching, will also give you a better idea of the inner structure of the massif.

3B. Itinerary to the Medes Islands

Starting point and end of the itinerary: l'Estartit **Time needed**: 3 hours **Means of transport**: by boat **Observations**: best in spring and summer

This itinerary has to be covered by boat, and starts at L'Estartit, though it may also be started at L'Escala.

At L'Estartit port there are several large boats that run trips for tourists, and there are also several smaller boats that have fixed itineraries to the Medes Islands and to the Montgrí cliffs, normally as far as the Roca Foradada (Pierced Rock). At L'Escala there are also boats for the Medes Islands, but only in summer. Obviously, there is no problem if you have a boat of your own! Just remember to keep outside the established boundaries of the protected area around the Medes (75 m from the perimeter): it is forbidden to fish and to extract materials of any kind from the sea; boats may not drop anchor; 3 knots is the speed limit in the area; and boats may only visit the area between sunrise and sunset.

If you disembark on the Meda Gran (the largest of the Medes Islands and the only one that may be visited), you must respect the signs and keep to the trails. It is forbidden to take samples of animals or plants, to light fires, to take dogs, and to camp or spend the night on the island.

The boats from L'Estartit only operate as from the end of spring and in the summer during the breeding season, when it is well worth a visit. You may also care to do the trip in winter, especially if you are keen on seeing wintering seabirds such as Cormorant, a species with a sizable roost on the islands, Red-necked and Black-throated Divers, quite abundant in the area around the Medes and off Pals beach, as well as other marine species such as Gannet and Razorbill.

During the breeding season the Medes Islands stand out for their large Herring Gull colony. There are about 8,000 pairs, covering almost all the Meda Gran and Meda Petita islands. This colony is becoming larger, to the detriment, probably, of other seabirds, the growth being due to the Herring Gull's great capacity for making use of all kinds of resources, including those of which they have an unlimited source, viz. rubbish tips.

In the breeding season, Herring Gull are very territorially-conscious aggressive, and you must therefore be very careful if disembarking on the island since visitors tend to be attacked. It is advisable not to disembark, but to see the islands from the boat. You will see the same amount of birdlife, and maybe even get better views than from on land. The elaborate behaviour of the Herring Gull may be observed. It is based on an intricate language of cries and gestures with which threats and warnings are expressed, and courtship and social relations are acted out and established. The first clutches -normally of three eggs- are laid in mid-March, and the chicks begin to hatch in mid-April, one month later. Their first flight -at least five weeks later- normally takes place in June.

Several pairs of Storm Petrel have also been found nesting on the Medes Islands, though they are very difficult to see because of their tiny size and their almost imperceptible and nocturnal habits.

A few years ago, a Cormorant's nest was found on a solitary island. It is the only breeding site to have been recorded so far for this species in the whole Iberian Peninsula. The Shag is also beginning to breed there again after a few years' absence. Incidentally, summer numbers have been growing (up to 40 individuals now), almost certainly due to the better protection of the islands. This makes one hope that the small breeding population may soon grow into a a regular colony, albeit small.

On a cliff facing east, that is to say towards L'Estartit, in a clump of olive trees, a small heronry has established itself in the last few years. In fact, it harbours most of the birds that used to breed in the Ter riverside woods, and which were forced to move because of increased pollution in the river and direct persecution. This small yet curiously-situated heronry, situated on a sea cliff, is used by Night Heron, Little Egret and Cattle Egret. Both the difficulty of the terrain and the need to leave colonies of this kind (very sensitive to human disturbance) well alone, call for visitors to keep their distance.

Blue Rock Thrush, Common Swift, Pallid Swift, Alpine Swift and Common Kestrel also breed on the islands' cliffs. Lesser Kestrel also used to breed here, but unfortunately no longer do so.

If the boat trip continues as far as Roca Foradada, you will be able to have a good look at the impressive Montgrí sea cliffs, where, with a bit of luck, you may be able to see Peregrine Falcon, and, maybe, Eleanora's Falcon, sightings of which have recently become more frequent.

To get an idea of the interest this coast offers, it must be remembered that in 1974 a pair of Ospreys was still breeding here; it is also one of the last sites on the Costa Brava where the rare Mediterranean Monk Seal was seen. This species is getting rarer and rarer (there are thought to be about 500 individuals, most of which would be on the North African and eastern Mediterranean coasts).

Once you are back in L'Estartit, if you have been on the boat trip in the afternoon and it is now dusk, you may be lucky enough to see an Eagle Owl flying over the rocks or perched on a boulder, outlined against the ruddy sky - you would not be the first visitors to see one!

3C. Coastal itinerary in the Begur, Gavarres and Cadiretes ranges

Starting point: Torroella de Montgrí **End of the itinerary**: Blanes **Time needed**: one day (it can be covered in less time) **Means of transport**: by car and on foot
Observations: very windy road

The starting point for the itinerary is Torroella de Montgrí, which you will leave on the Pals road. You will cross a plain where you may sometimes spot the odd Hobby in spring or summer, although care has to be taken in identifying falcons in June and early July when there is a regular passage of Eleanora's Falcons, which are especially active at sunset catching flying beetles (especially *Melanontha melanontha*, locally known as Saint John's Beetle, because it is common at the end of June, coinciding with the Saint John's festival).

Before reaching Pals, you must turn left towards Masos de Pals, a hamlet you will leave behind you on your way to Pals beach, where you take the turning to the golf course. Shortly after the golf course, at a point where the road turns sharply to the right, you must leave the car and follow a path on the left. It is called the "islands' path" (camí de les illes), and takes us through paddy fields to the Coll lagoons (**Basses d'en Coll**), a small yet interesting area of marsh that is unfortunately in danger of being developed with the inexplicable consent of the Pals town council. In winter, excessive hunting eliminates practically all the birdlife. However, over the course of the two periods of migration in spring and summer, the marsh area, especially the paddy fields, are a good shelter for many waders and different species of passerines. Purple Heron, Bittern and Marsh Harrier are three species that are reluctant to leave the area, which in the breeding season is frequently visited by the herons breeding on the Medes Islands. Penduline Tit may also be seen and heard in the riverside woodland. The presence of all these species should be more than ample reason for the Government to protect this area and ensure that what is laid down in the law is observed.

After Pals you must go through a built-up area in the direction of Palafrugell, Palamós and Sant Feliu de Guíxols. It is at this latter point that the most beautiful and characteristic section of the itinerary along this part of the Costa Brava starts. The **Sant Feliu de Guíxols-Tossa de Mar road** is infamous for its bends, but famous for its beauty. It was on this stretch of road, in 1936, that some English bird-watchers saw a flight of Red-rumped Swallows. It was practically the first recording of this species in Catalonia, and the first nest was found here in 1959. If you wish to see this species, take a good look at the tunnels and bridges along the way, and you may well come across one of their typical and unmistakable nests.

Red-rumped Swallow

The road skirts the coast, and there are occasional stopping places with marvellous views of the cliffs. Observation of the cliffs and of the cork oak woods makes the itinerary most rewarding. You can stop wherever your ornithological instinct or the view call for it, although a few tips are given: just beside the signpost that indicates you are entering the county called "La Selva", there is a steep and humid gully that could provide interesting observations. The abundance of Nightingale in the breeding season is also truly remarkable.

After Salions cove (Cala Salions), and after passing through a tunnel, you will cross over a bridge, after which there is a turning to the right that winds down and passes under the bridge. If you follow this track and stand beneath the bridge, you will be able to see several Red-rumped Swallow nests. Further nests of the same species may also be seen beneath the bridge that crosses over above the Pola camping site, a few kilometres further on.

Once you are in Tossa, which is possibly the most typical of the towns in the southern part of the Costa Brava, you must drive on towards Lloret. Now the road goes through an area which is less wild, where the stone pine is predominant. After Lloret you will come to Blanes, where the **"Mar i Murtra" botanical gardens** are well worth a visit. Apart from the botanical interest of the rare plants to be found there, a visit to the garden may well result in good bird-watching, especially during passage. The abundance and variety of the flora means that there are almost always plants in flower or bearing seed, attracting different species of birds to the garden. Numerous Nightingale, Sardinian Warbler, Blackcap, Great Tit, Crested Tit, as well as Serin, Goldfinch and Greenfinch, all breed in the garden.

Itinerary 3C finishes at Blanes, the last town on the Costa Brava.

Board and Lodging

The importance tourism has in the area means there is a wide range of hotels and restaurants of different categories and prices.

If you have chosen L'Estartit as your base for the itineraries, the Hotel Coral or the Torre Gran are good places to sleep, and the food there is very good. The Aiguablava "Parador Nacional" (State Tourist Hotel) near Begur is another possibility; it has marvellous views of the sea. The Hotel Terramar at Llafranc, the Hotel Rosamar at Sant Antoni de Calonge and the Panorama-Park or the Montecarlo at Sant Feliu de Guíxols are all further alternatives. Needless to say, for the summer months, you must book well in advance since all this part of the coast is overrun by tourists in July and August.

For those who prefer camping, the presence of an ornithological nature trail at the "Castell Montgrí" camping site makes it the most recommendable one in the area.

In so far as restaurants are concerned, you will find a whole series of restaurants serving typical Catalan food at a fair price a few kilometres inland and in towns that have not yet been spoilt by tourism. Can Bech at Fontanilles, Mas Pou at Palau-Sator, El Burinot, La Riera or Can Bonay at Peretallada, Can Oliveres at Vall-Llobrega and La Sala Gran at Llofriu, to mention but a few.

Others places of interest

- Ullastret Iberian Village. The remains of an ancient Iberian settlement on a small hill, with a wonderful view of the Empordà plain. The village has a wall around it and pre-Roman remains dating from the time of the Indiketes, an Iberian tribe that lived in this area. It is about 1 km. from the modern village of Ullastret. The village and the museum are open from 10.30 am to 1 pm, and from 4 pm to 8 pm from June to August, and from 10 am to 2 pm and 4 pm to 6 pm during the rest of the year.

- Pals. A small medieval town that has recently been beautifully restored, an operation for which it won an award. It is delightful to wander through the streets of Pals, even at night, for the town is well lit up. It is 7 km south of Torroella de Montgrí (cf. itinerary 3C).

- Sant Sebastià Lighthouse (Far de Sant Sebastià). One of Catalonia's most beautiful lighthouses. It was built in 1857. Although the lighthouse itself is out of bounds, the view of the Mediterranean from the area around it is truly spectacular. There are roads up to the lighthouse from Llafranc and Palafrugell.

- The Cap Roig Botanical Gardens. They are to be found on one of the Costa Brava's most beautiful estates. Both the gardens and the nearby house used to belong to a retired Russian colonel who had them built in 1923. They are to be found at the southern tip of Calella de Palafrugell, and can be visited every day of the week from 9 am to 5 pm.

4

THE MONTSENY MASSIF NATURAL PARK

This park is situated at the point where the Selva, Osona and Vallès Oriental *comarques* (counties) meet. The area forms a well-defined sub-county known as "Conca del Tordera" or "Baix Montseny". It is the highest massif in the Catalan *Prelitoral* Range (which runs inland, parallel to the coast). The highest peaks are Turó de l'Home (1,712 m) and Les Agudes (1,706 m).

Park foundation date: The Patronat de la Muntanya del Montseny (Montseny Mountain Conservation Board) was founded in 1928, and in 1977 the Montseny Natural Park Special Protection Plan was put into effect. In 1978, the Park was declared to be a Biosphere Reserve by UNESCO.

Surface area: 30,000 ha.

Office address: Servei de Parcs Naturals de la Diputació de Barcelona
 Sant Honorat, 1
 08002-Barcelona

Habitats: ilex woods, cork oak woods, oak woods, fir woods, beech woods, pine woods, chestnut groves, heath, subalpine meadows, rocky areas, rivers and mountain streams, cultivated areas.

Interesting species:
-*Present all the year round*: Goshawk, Red-legged Partridge, Woodcock, Crag Martin, Dipper, Dartford Warbler, Sardinian Warbler, Crested Tit, Nuthatch, Rock Bunting.
-*Summer visitors*: Short-toed Eagle, Alpine Swift, Rock Thrush, Bonelli's Warbler, Golden Oriole, Red-backed Shrike, Woodchat Shrike.
-*Winter visitors*: Alpine Accentor.

Description and habitat

From the ornithological point of view, the Montseny Natural Park is not especially outstanding. However, the more inaccessible parts and the thickest forest areas on the massif are an important refuge for several birds such as Goshawk, Peregrine Falcon and Eagle Owl, species which were formerly widespread throughout Catalonia but which have been severely reduced in numbers or cut back in their distribution range in large areas of the country because of the enormous population boom there has been over the last thirty years and the environmental changes that have come in its wake. Apart from the area's importance as a refuge, another outstanding feature about the birdlife of the Montseny is that several north European species -Woodcock, Red-backed Shrike, Goldcrest, Bullfinch or Marsh Tit- have their southernmost breeding area here.

Environmental variety is without doubt the Montseny massif's most important feature. It comes as a consequence of the great variation in altitude and the climatic changes that this implies from one area to another. Annual rainfall, for example, ranges between the meagre 700 litres/m^2 of the lower areas and the more than 1,300 litres/m^2 in Santa Fe valley. It can therefore be stated that the Montseny harbours features -in different proportions- of the main biogeographical regions that make up Western Europe. In the lower areas, up to approximately 900 m, typically Mediterranean habitats are to be found; from 900 to 1,600 m, especially on north-facing slopes, Euro-Siberian biotopes are predominant; on the peaks, over 1600 m, there are patches that stand out for their Boreal-Alpine characteristics.

The Euro-Siberian and especially the Boreal-Alpine biotopes are highly isolated, and have probably been so since the last Ice Age. This factor explains the presence of three endemic species of plants in the Montseny, the most characteristic of which is the small saxifrague known as "Sant Segimon" (*Saxifraga vayredana*), and about fifteen Arthropodae species. Also worthy of mention are the local populations of land vertebrates with specific forms, especially the Agile Frog and the Pyrenean Newt.

Of the Boreal-Alpine or Atlantic biotopes, the most predominant ones on the massif are **Subalpine meadows** and **heath**, which have a very variable range of animal populations according to the season: limited during the harsh winters and very numerous in spring and summer, when these habitats become very rich and productive because of the dense and diverse plant and animal biomass in the area.

The **rupicolous habitat** is represented by areas of schist and the very resistent granite blocks at the summits, these being an important breeding area for some of the shyer species, especially the birds of prey, which also take advantage of the rising thermal currents produced by the effect of the sun on the stone faces.

The **fir woods**, due to their small size, contain the same species as the neighbouring **beech** and **oak woods**. In these latter woods there are also marked seasonal differences because of the great changes in light and foliage cover from winter to summer.

The areas associated with Mediterranean habitat, the most abundant of the massif's habitats, the forested areas -**ilex, cork oak, stone pine and Aleppo pine woods**- all have seasonal stability as a factor in common. The evergreen nature of the foliage bears a direct relation to the fact that the majority of the bird species living in the woods are sedentary.

The rest of the species, except for those living near the water, may be divided into those associated with man, and a few ubiquitous ones, that live in open areas such as waste and arable lands.

How to visit the area

Whether you are coming from Barcelona or from the Costa Brava, the best way of approaching the Montseny area by car is the A-7 motorway, which goes from La Jonquera to Barcelona. Come off the motorway at exit 11, marked "Sant Celoni-Montseny", if you wish to visit the itineraries that are described here. However, if first you wish to visit the Arbúcies valley, you must leave the motorway at exit 10, at Hostalric. Two main roads pass through the centre of the massif by means of two mountain passes. They are BV-5301, from Santa Maria de Palautordera to Seva, and BV-5114, from Sant Celoni to Viladrau, which are taken to follow itineraries 4A and 4B respectively.

The Montseny area is also well served by public transport systems. Two railway lines cross two valleys that lie at the foot of the massif: the one which passes along the Congost valley, on the Barcelona-Puigcerdà line, and the Barcelona-Girona-Port Bou line, which passes along the Tordera valley, with about one train an hour at peak hours. There are also three bus lines, two of which leave from Barcelona: one run by the Hispano Hilarense company, in Plaça Palau, with stops at Sant Celoni, Breda and Arbúcies, and another run by the Sagalés company, which leaves from Fabra i Puig in Barcelona, and stops at all the villages on the Congost valley run. There is also a bus line run by the Barba company which runs from Granollers to Sant Celoni, Santa Maria de Palautordera, Sant Esteve de Palautordera and the village of Montseny. Furthermore, on summer Sundays, a bus of the same company covers the run to the Santa Fe valley, leaving Sant Celoni station at 9 am (coinciding with the arrival of a train from Barcelona).

Both of the itineraries described here each call for a full day's excursion, and even then, there will not be a lot of time to be lost! If you have more days available for the area, it is best to split up the itineraries and to cover them in different shorter and more relaxed outings.

As almost everywhere, spring is the most pleasant time of year for mountain walks, and also the time of the year birds may most easily be observed. The Montseny may be visited at any season of the year, howvever, because the climate is relatively mild on the massif in comparison with Pyrenean high mountain areas, and the fact that most of the principal Montseny bird species, those of a Central European origin, are present on the mountain at all times of the year.

Bird-watching

4A. Itinerary to the Formic pass, Matagalls and Pla de la Calma

Starting point: Santa Maria de Palautordera **End of the itinerary**: Seva **Time needed**: one day **Means of transport**: by car and on foot

Take road BV-5301, which goes from Santa Maria de Palautordera to Seva, stopping off at various points of interest on the itinerary. The first stop will be at the Can Pagà spring at **km 2**. In this area, which is principally made up of quaternary sedimentary materials, dry farming is predominant. In summer, there will be several breeding colonies of Common Starling on the farm roofs, there may also be the odd pair of Spotless Starling, a species which is rapidly spreading northwards and eastwards in the country. You will almost certainly spot the odd Tree Sparrow mixed in among the House Sparrows. Near the farms, where there are dunghills, Magpie and the odd Hoopoe are to be seen. Dunnock may also be seen and heard in the hedgerows, and Yellowhammer might well be perched in the branches of the sloe trees nearby. Keep an eye on the solitary fruit trees which are sought out by finches such as Serin and Greenfinch. It is also worth scanning telephone poles and wires and other similar perches where, apart from Swallow, it would not be too uncommon to see the odd Corn Bunting or Red-backed Shrike. Nor would it be rare to hear a male Quail calling from the fields.

Drive on along the same road and after passing Sant Esteve de Palautordera, stop once again before reaching **km 8**. At this point, you can follow the path that leads to Fluvià castle. In the fields of crops and stubble, you should hear the cooing of Wood Pigeon and Turtle Dove and you might well see a Little Owl asleep on the telephone poles. On the edges of the fields, and near the forest, Chaffinch, Blackbird and Blackcap are normally abundant. Make your way back to the car along the same path or by way of Can Panxasec (another farm).

The second stopping off point will be Can Coca (Coca Farm) at a place where the road crosses over the Tordera river, after approximately **11 kilometres** of the itinerary. You must now follow the path that starts off at the side of the bridge, following one section of river upstream in a parallel fashion. Nightingale will be heard all the time, and Crag Martin will be seen on the wing. Dipper breed on this part of the river, but they are difficult to see because excessive hunting has made them very wary. Grey Wagtail can be seen perched on the large boulders in the river, as can the much more common White Wagtail. The Chiffchaff fidgets about in the vegetation at the side of the river and the bushes further away are visited by Melodious Warbler. Look out for animal droppings on the boulders in the river bed; unfortunately they are not the droppings of Otter but of American Mink, the modern usufructuary of the river.

Once again back at the car, drive on up the road, along which Blackbird and Jay will doubtless come into view, stopping at the Coll Formic (Formic mountain pass), at km 26. This pass, where you may leave the car, will be the starting point of two further walks, each of which will take two hours to

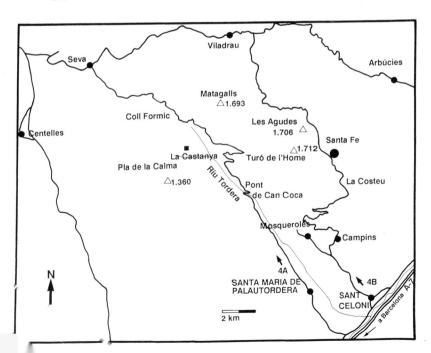

complete. If you take the path upwards on the left, you will be headed for one of the most beautiful sites on the mountain, the Pla de la Calma (Calma Plateau), which is covered in broom-brush, heather, ling, fern and pastures. Red-legged Partridge, Red-backed Shrike, Common Wheatear and Stonechat are common here. You will also hear the non-stop song of the Skylark and Rock Bunting. On the stonier ground, there is the odd pair of Rock Thrush, though their behaviour is rather shy. Mistle Thrush make their nests in the branches of wild apple trees and hawthorn, while Linnet breed in the smaller bushes. Tree Pipit, Water Pipit, and less frequently, Dartford Warbler, may also be seen. Do keep an eye on the sky, where Short-toed Eagle, Bonelli's Eagle, Kestrel or Hobby can come into view at any moment.

From Coll Formic itself, you may also choose to take the path up to the right (where you left the car). It passes in front of the highest inhabited *mas* (farm) on the mountain, Sant Andreu de la Castanya, at 1,300 m, and climbs up to Matagalls peak (1,693 m). One of the most beautiful views in all Catalonia is to be had from this point. However, the birdlife is very much the same as on the Pla de la Calma, with the sole -though significant- addition of the Ortolan Bunting.

Once back at Coll Formic, you may drive on in the direction of Seva. After you have reached this town, it is possible to see the odd pair of Stock Dove, and if you arrive in the evening, it should not be too difficult to hear the Scop's Owl, which must not be confused with the Midwife Toad an amphibian with an equally repetitive call.

Once you get to Seva, you can return to the starting point by turning to the left towards Tona, and driving to Santa Maria de Palautordera via Granollers. On the other hand, if you turn to the right, towards Viladrau, you can return by way of Sant Marçal or further still, by way of the Coll de Ravell (Ravell Pass) and Arbúcies. Whichever route you choose, you are likely to be returning in the dark, making it worth keeping a look out for Tawny Owl in wilder areas, and Barn Owl near farms and villages. It will take a little bit more luck to see a large mammal such as a hare, marten, genet, badger or fox crossing or following the road along.

4R. Itinerary in the Santa Fe valley and to the Turó de l'Home peak

Starting point: Sant Celoni **End of the itinerary**: Viladrau **Time needed**: one day **Means of transport**: by car and on foot

At Sant Celoni you must take road BV-5114 towards Viladrau. The first stop is at **kilometre 2**, at a place known as Can Reberté (Reberté Farm) where there is a large oak tree. This is a good spot for observing all species associated

Red-backed Shrike

Zitting Cisticola

with woodland edges, thickets, fences, and fields of crops and stubble. Crested Lark and Fan-tailed Warbler should be immediately visible. If you carry on along the path, you will soon come to Partegàs stream. Green Woodpecker breed in the tree trunks of streamside poplars. Golden Oriole do so in the tips of the highest branches. On the way, you are sure to have heard Nightingale and Ceti's Warbler, and maybe even Great Reed Warbler. This is the breeding area (among the pines and higher ilex trees) and the hunting ground (among the fields of crops and stubble) of Sparrow-hawk and Common Buzzard.

Drive on in the car as far as the Mosqueroles and Campins crossroads, where you should once again leave it. Walk along the Mosqueroles road for a hundred metres until you come to a mature stone pine wood on your right. This is typically Mediterranean woodland scenery with rockrose, furze and gorse with heather, where Great Tit, Blue Tit, Coal Tit and Serin abound. Cuckoo can easily be heard here too.

On the way back to the crossroads, and once again in the car, take the other road that leads to Campins. Shortly after passing through this village, at **km 10.5**, on a bend known as the "Revolt de la Cadena", you must take a path that leads off to the left to Can Riera de Ciuret Farm. Leave the car here and walk on through a landscape of mixed woodland, with stone pine, Aleppo pine, ilex, cork oak and oak (*Quercus pubescens*). Chaffinch and Robin are abundant here, and the Common Nightjar breeds in the area.

Once you have had a good look around this particular wood, make your way back to the car once more. Drive on up the main road you left before until you come to **km 14**, where another stop can be made. You are now 800 m high, on the very boundary of the Natural Park, which you will now enter. A beautiful view is to be seen: in front of you, to the east, is the Coastal Range (Serralada Litoral) with the wild Montnegre massif that rises to 760 m; then, to the south, are the Corredor and Montalt massifs, separated from the Montseny by the Vallès depression, with Barcelona in the background. From this point, you make walk on into the forest until you come to Can Rubí Farm. The landscape, here, is mainly composed of mountain ilex woods, where species such as Short-toed Treecreeper, Sardinian Warbler and Rock Bunting are common. The pair of locally-breeding Short-toed Eagle may sometimes be seen hunting in the area.

Take the car again and climb on up the road, noting how the ilex woods gradually give way to chestnut and oak woods. At **km 17**, the road suddenly changes direction, and the first beech trees begin to appear. You are now in the Costeu area, in the Gualba valley, where spectacular outcrops of granite and schist cliffs are common. You must stop at a small parking area after **km 18**, about fifty metres before you come to a tunnel known as La Foradada. This is a good area for looking out for botanical species, especially the plant known as Sant Segimon, an endemic Montseny saxifrague, round patches of which abound throughout the rocky area. At the end of autumn and at the beginning of spring, you may see the rare Wallcreeper if you climb up the rocks. Alpine Accentor, Crag Martin and Raven are also abundant, the latter species breeding just above the Foradada Rock. Long-eared Owl also breed in this area.

Drive on and you will soon come to an area of typically Central European scenery. It is the Santa Fe valley. The botanical characteristics of the valley (it is like an island of Central European environment surrounded by a sea of Continental Mediterranean environment) are the result of the 1,300 litres of rain that fall per square metre every year, thus making it the wettest part of the whole massif. At **km 21** you will come to the hamlet of Santa Fe, with the hermitage up against the hotel wall. You may leave the car at the Park's Information Centre car park at Can Casades, right beside the road. Notice the exotic four-footed sequoia tree which is over 40 metres high. To take a good walk in the Santa Fe valley, you are advised to take the circuit around the small lakes, leaving from the Can Lleonart Nature School, which is 300 m from where you left the car. It is a circular path that first skirts the old and abandoned reservoir. When the river narrows again, the path continues alongside the stream leading us to the larger lake, a site where Osprey and Black-necked Grebe have been seen on migration, along with Black-winged Stilt and Snipe on the banks. On the various stages of the circuit where there are beech trees, you may see any one of the breeding species for which the Santa Fe valley is the southernmost limit of their breeding range in the western palearctic region. These species are Woodcock, Goldcrest, Bullfinch and Marsh Tit, although other interesting species, such as Goshawk, Nuthatch, Short-toed Treecreeper, Firecrest, Chiffchaff and Bonelli's Warbler and other tits such as Crested Tit and Long-tailed Tit, are also to be seen. Woodlark and Red-backed Shrike are also present on the woodland fringes and in more open areas, while Dipper and Grey Wagtail breed on the stream. On the banks of the stream there are plenty of Wren nesting, and you could hear this species' rich song at any point.

Another splendid -though more tiring- excursion, is the climb up to the massif's highest peak, the Turó de l'Home (1,712 m). You must once again take the road as far as L'Espinal, a clearing with a building, the Friars' Convent, where you may leave the car. Right in front of this clearing, though on the other side of the road, there is a wide path that after three quarters of an hour's walk will lead us to the Briançó spring, which is litle more than a small patch of dampness. Two small paths lead off from this point; the one on the right takes you to Les Agudes peak (1,706 m), and the one on the left, which is the one that is recommended, to the Turó de l'Home. You should be able to reach the top in half an hour. At the top you can take a look at the meteorological observatory and have a cool drink at the shop there. This peak is a magnificent observation point, and on a clear day a large portion of the Catalan lands can be seen.

Above the beech and fir forests there are subalpine meadows where Rock Pipit, Common Wheatear, Black Redstart, Rock Thrush, Yellowhammer, and in winter, Snow Finch, may all be seen. Other fairly common vertebrates are the Asp Viper and the agile Green Lizard.

It is better to make your way down by way of the short-cut through the fir woods. You will not get lost because it is a very clearly marked path. Both Goshawk and Goldcrest breed in this forest. If you keep an eye out for them, you should see animal droppings on prominent points along the way. These are the territorial markers of the Marten, a very abundant carnivore in this biotope. The few pairs of hares that remain in this mountain area have their breeding grounds in clearings where young fir trees grow. Continuing downwards along this mule path, you will be able to admire the beauty of the fir wood undergrowth, with soft carpets of a species of fescue (*Festuca gautieri*). If you carry on walking along the same path, you will pass by the Pou del Comte (the Count's Well), a large stone ice pit which is a reminder of a time when snow was stored and sold in the form of ice. This activity was an important source of income until the turn of the century. Nearby is the now dry and abandoned Font del Llop (Wolf Spring), a name that evokes the presence of that great predator in the massif until the turn of the century - like the activity associated with the ice pit. If you have not lingered along the way, you should have completed the climb down in an hour and a half.

Once again on the L'Espinal Plateau, and if you still have the time, you may care to take a walk in the Font de Maçaners broad-leaved oak wood, one of the most beautiful of the Montseny's forest landscapes. You should now take the path to the Garolera estate that you will find behind the convent. After about one kilometre you will come to a very sharp right-hand bend, where there is a forestry track that leads to a plantation of exotic ornamental trees (Douglas Firs) which in the last few years has become the breeding ground of the Woodcock. Continue walking for a further couple of kilometres until you reach the oak wood. Some trees are fully thirty metres high. The birdlaife is rich, with Goldcrest, Short-toed Treecreeper, Nuthatch and Marsh Tit.

After this nice walk, you can either turn round and drive back to the starting point, or else continue along the road in the same direction as before, and, after crossing the beautiful Sant Marçal area, arrive in Viladrau, a popular summer resort where this itinerary comes to an end.

Board and lodging

The Montseny area has a wide range of board and lodging. There are over 80 establishments in the massif where you can stay, and a number of categories is also available. As all these establishments cannot be all mentioned, only those that are within the limits of the Natural Park, and those that are to be found at Santa Maria de Palautordera and Sant Celoni (being the points where the itineraries start) will be listed. On the road from Sant Celoni to Viladrau, on km 21 of itinerary 4B, you will come to Hostal Santa Fe, in the valley of the same name. On the same road, 7 kms from Santa Fe in the direction of Viladrau, you will come to the hotel-cum-hermitage of Sant Marçal. At km 20.5 of the Coll Formic road, along which itinerary 4A passes, you will find on your right the track that after one kilometre comes to the Hotel Sant Bernat. Those who prefer to stay at places nearer to the starting point of the itineraries may choose between the Hostal Turó de l'Home at Santa Maria de Palautordera, or Sant Celoni, where you will find the Hostal els Avets, Hostal Corbaire and Hostal-Restaurant Suizo in the main street (Carrer Major).

For those wishing to camp, there is a camping site within the Park itself. It is called "Càmping Fontmartina" and is 16 km from Sant Celoni, just after the Costa del Montseny parish church on the Mosqueroles road.

Insofar as cuisine is concerned, the range of possibilities is equally varied and rich. Apart from those establishments that have already been listed as suitable places to spend the night, at Santa Fe you will find the Restaurant Avet Blau and "El Racó de Can Faves" at Sant Celoni; the latter is recommended by the famous Michelin gourmet guide.

Other places of interest

-Josep Aragay Monographic Museum. An important collection of pottery, tiles, painting, drawing and prints by the *noucentista* (fin de siècle) artist Josep Aragay is to be found in the Santa Maria de Breda Romanesque church, 11 kms north of Sant Celoni.

- "La Gabella" Montseny Ethnological Museum. A display on the history and human activities of the northern Montseny area. It is to be found in the Plaça de la Vila (Town Square) in Arbúcies, where the historic, century-old Plane Tree is to be found. It was planted as a symbol of freedom in 1873 to commemorate the first Republic. Arbúcies is 24 kms north of Sant Celoni.

- Masjuan Arboretum. A living display of century-old Coniferae, at Espinelves, 6 km north of Viladrau.

- "La Tela" Museum. An exhibition of the natural biotopes of the Vallès Oriental *comarca* (county). At Granollers, 20 kms south-west of Sant Celoni.

- Montseny Fauna Museum and Bush and Tree Botanical Gardens. As yet uncompleted, this is to be found at Santa Maria de Palautordera, the starting point for itinerary 4A.

5

BARCELONA
AND ITS SURROUNDING AREA

Barcelona is the capital of Catalonia. It is on the coast, and is enclosed by the rivers Besòs and Llobregat, which run into the sea to the north and south respectively. In the delta of the latter river, there are still some important areas of marshland, most of which form part of two Nature Reserves that were set up in 1987. The city is also surrounded by hills; the Corredor, Sant Llorenç del Munt, Collserola ranges as well as the Montserrat and Garraf massif all run in a north-south direction, and have all been made into Natural Parks, with the exception of the Collserola range, which is a Metropolitan or city area park.

Habitats: Urban environment, parks and gardens, coastline, ilex woods, pinewoods, scrub, rocky areas and cliffs, crops.

Interesting species:
- *Present all the year round*: Bonelli's Eagle, Peregrine Falcon, Red-legged Partridge, Monk Parakeet, Rose-ringed Parakeet, Eagle Owl, Thekla Lark, Crag Martin, Black Wheatear, Blue Rock Thrush, Dartford Warbler, Sardinian Warbler, Dartford Warbler, Crested Tit, Rock Bunting.
- *Summer visitors*: Great Spotted Cuckoo, Nightjar, Pallid Swift, Alpine Swift, Bee-eater, Wryneck, Black-eared Wheatear, Rock Thrush, Cetti's Warbler, Spectacled Warbler, Subalpine Warbler, Orphean Warbler, Bonelli's Warbler, Golden Oriole, Woodchat Shrike, Ortolan Bunting.
- *Winter visitors*: Gannet, Mediterranean Gull, Little Gull, Razorbill, Wallcreeper, Alpine Accentor.
- *Migratory species*: herons, wildfowl, raptors, gulls, terns, waders and passerines.

Description and habitat

This chapter aims to deal with a very heterogeneous area. The only real main common factor throughout the area is its proximity to the city of Barcelona. The area may however be divided into three main areas: firstly, the city area itself, with its gardens and city parks. Next, the coastal area that includes marine habitat and marshland (in the Llobregat delta, south of the city). The third area comprises the mountainous zones surrounding the metropolitan area. Despite the adjacency and apparent similarity of these areas, they are quite different in terms of orography, vegetation and fauna.

From the ornithological point of view, the area within the city is of interest both for its typically city birds and for its garden and parkland birds. Some of these parks support birdlife which would normally be associated with natural Mediterranean habitats. This is possible because of their peripheral situation and the presence of spontaneous natural vegetation in these parks - a form of vegetation that is in keeping with areas outside the city limits. Likewise, the city itself is in contact with the port area, and thus with the coast, and it is here that interesting marine life is to be seen, especially in winter.

As regards seabirds and wetland species in general, the Llobregat delta calls for special attention. Despite its nearness to the city and the high degree of human disturbance affecting the area, the delta is the third most important wetland area of Catalonia, and is noteworthy for the great variety of species (over 300 have been recorded there) and for being a stepping stone for migratory species. Some of the delta's most interesting parts have recently been made into a Nature Reserve. Unfortunately, it is not possible to visit the reserve as yet. Hopefully, necessary arrangements permitting nature trails to be followed in these interesting marshes will soon be made.

The mountainous areas near the city form part of a range that runs along the whole of the Catalan coast. These hills have a mild climate and the vegetation is mainly made up of ilex woods, Aleppo pine woods and large areas of scrub. On some of the hills there are also rocky areas. The Corredor range, the Sant Llorenç del Munt massif, the Collserola range, Montserrat mountain and the Garraf massif may be listed as the major mountainous zones around Barcelona.

The Corredor range (Serra del Corredor), which is now a Natural Park, is to the south-east of the Montseny massif (cf. itineraries 4A and 4B), and is fairly well forested. The Sant Llorenç del Munt massif has also been a Natural Park since 1974, and is to the north-west of the city. Its landscape and fauna are similar to those of Montserrat. The Collserola range borders the city on the west and is a Metropolitan Park. Although it is near to the city, it still conserves a considerable botanical and zoological interest. The mountain of Montserrat and the Garraf massif are described in more detail below, since they are areas with recommended itineraries.

The mountain of Montserrat, with a surface area of about 3,700 hectares, is to the north-west of Barcelona. A Natural Park, it is without any doubt the most famous mountain in Catalonia because of its very special morphology and the importance of its abbey (Abadia de Montserrat). The rocky massif rises straight up from the plain, and the effect of the erosion of the elements on the conglomerate stone has given rise to a unique landscape, the whole mountain being in the form of high, slender, rounded needles of rock. This feature gives the mountain its name of "Montserrat" or "sawn mountain".

Despite the predominance of rocky areas, the mountain's vegetation is not sparse. It used to be quite lush and was made up of thick ilex woods, with Aleppo pine on the lower slopes. We say "used to be" because a disastrous forest fire burned most of the mountain in the summer of 1986. At present, most of the non-rocky areas are only covered in scrub. However, in areas that remained unaffected by the fire, splashes of green ilex wood can be seen climbing up between the rocky peaks in magnificent combination. Nowadays, vineyards, olive and almond groves can only be found on the lower slopes.

It must also be added that Montserrat Abbey is the most important religious centre in Catalonia. The *Mare de Déu de Montserrat* (Our Lady of Montserrat) is adored as one of Catalonia's Patron Saints (along with Sant Jordi). The Monastery receives an extraordinary number of visitors over the course of the year, and the mountain itself is also a mecca for mountain-climbers due to its exceptional characteristics.

The **Garraf massif** is situated to the south-west of Barcelona on the south side of the river Llobregat. It covers an area of about 10,000 hectares and was made into a Natural Park in 1986.

The principal feature of the Garraf massif is its karstic nature: most of the area is made up of calcareous rock, which has undergone severe decomposition that has given rise to karrens and dolines, as well as countless gullies and a few caves. Surface water is almost non-existent since rain water seeps into the rock. The hills are not high and have smooth weathered forms, although there are sudden deep gullies as well as cliffs on the coastal side of the massif.

The Garraf massif vegetation is low and typically Mediterranean. Although this poor and stony area may never have been too fertile, it is now recovering from the forest fire that in 1984 destroyed almost all the massif's vegetation. In some spots there are small pinewoods that survived the fire, though the area is principally covered in low scrub, with lentiscus and kermes oak as predominant species. Two very interesting species are palmetto scrub

(*Chamaerops humilis*), the only autoctonous species of palm in Europe, and the reed *Ampelodesma mauritanicum*, a large species of Gramineae with a basically African distribution.

Away from the developed coastal areas, the massif is an almost deserted area, with an arid look about it. Agriculture and the rearing of livestock have been almost totally abandoned here.

Unfortunately, conservation, in the form of the Natural Park status it now enjoys, arrived too late to prevent gypsum-quarrying and the establishment of a huge rubbish tip in one of the most beautiful valleys in the massif. Nonetheless, the park can still boast of large wild and deserted areas with noteworthy flora and fauna.

How to visit the area

Even though your stay in Catalonia may be limited to the city of Barcelona, you will still have the opportunity to get in some good bird-watching. Furthermore, several nearby sites will enable you to get to grips with a handful of intriguing species, adding interest to your visit and to giving you an idea of what some of the country's most widespread habitats are like.

Within the city of Barcelona and in its surrounding area, birds may be seen at many sites. As regards city parks, itinerary 5A describes a few of those that hold most species, as well as the Ciutadella Park itself, which is the largest and most important park within the city precincts. Also within the city area, the trip to the port quays, described in the same itinerary, may to light interesting species, especially in winter. As regards the districts surrounding the city, two excursions have been chosen out of the wealth of possibilities there are. Itinerary 5B gives advice on the trip to Montserrat mountain, which many visitors to Barcelona will be visiting anyway, so that it may also be interesting from an ornithological point of view. Itinerary 5C, in the Garraf massif, has been chosen as it is the region nearest to Barcelona where interesting species such as Bonelli's Eagle may be seen. The other ranges in the Barcelona area also have very similar birdlife. Hopefully, further editions of this book will include an itinerary to the Llobregat delta, thus greatly increasing the total number of species to be seen in the metropolitan area. There are various projects to open the area to visits, but for the moment, these wetland areas are closed to the public.

You will have no problem getting to the city parks and the port area (itinerary 5A) with the aid of the city transport facilities (underground and bus). It is advisable to consult the city transport guides first.

Insofar as itineraries to the mountains of Montserrat and the Garraf massif are concerned (itineraries 5B and 5C respectively), you will only have to travel short distances from Barcelona.

To go to Montserrat, you must take the A-7 motorway in the direction of Tarragona, leaving it at exit 25 (at Martorell). You would have to carry out the same exercise if you were coming from Tarragona or Girona on this same motorway. After this, you have to continue along the N-2 road (in the direction of Lleida and Madrid), and, before Esparraguera, you must take a turning to the right along the C-1411 road leading to Manresa. When you come to Monistrol, take the road signposted to Montserrat Monastery (Monestir de Montserrat), where you will leave the car. You can also get to Montserrat by way of the Generalitat train service (from Plaça Espanya in Barcelona), getting off at the "Aeri Montserrat" station and taking the funicular up to the monastery. You

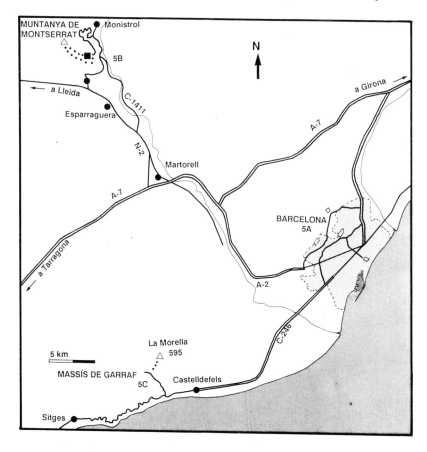

may also care to go by bus (Julià bus company, on the corner of Plaça Universitat and Ronda Universitat in Barcelona). The itinerary will take you about 5 hours at a bird-watcher's gait. You should wear sports footwear or light mountain boots. As you will not be coming across any springs or rivers, it is advisable to bring water with you. Since the path you are to follow is initially quite steep, it may be better for senior ornithologists to follow the itinerary in the opposite direction, which will make the slopes easier to climb; however, this change does have one disadvantage: it may be diificult to find your way down from the "pla dels ocells" (Bird Plateau). You are also advised not to leave the itinerary path at any point since this mountain is quite dangerous.

It must be remembered that the abbey and mountain of Montserrat are visited by many people, especially at weekends, on holidays and in summer months (July and August). If you do not want to come across too many people on the itinerary, it is advisable to avoid these periods, or to start off early in the morning.

The Garraf massif is even easier to get to. Take the Castelldefels dual carriageway out of Barcelona (this is the C-246 road to Barcelona airport which will soon be extended to Sitges). You arrive at the massif just after going through the large coastal development of Castelldefels (see Itinerary 5C). You may also reach Garraf by train from Barcelona (Sants Station) getting off at "Castelldefels-platja" (Castelldefels beach). From this point, you will have to walk 2.5 km (in the opposite direction to Barcelona) until you come to the massif area. You can also reach Castelldefels by bus (from Plaça Universitat in Barcelona).

The itinerary will take you about three hours on foot, with additional time for those extra options that are listed, as well as the car ride. The latter involves a 4 km drive between the point where you turn off the C-246 and the begining of the itinerary on foot. The ground is very stony and you are advised to wear light boots or thick-soled sports footwear. For this very reason, it is not advisable to wander off the recommended itinerary. Thorny plants are common so it is not a good idea to wear shorts. Furthermore, the lack of springs and water courses makes it necessary for you to bring water on the walk.

The best time of year to observe birds in the Barcelona area is spring, although any other season may proove interesting. The mild winter climate means that the itineraries can be followed in pleasant conditions, thus enabling you to see large quantities of wintering passerines. Summer, however, is very hot, and a good way of getting round this inconvenience is to start off on the itineraries early in the morning.

Bird-watching

5A. Itinerary in the Barcelona city parks and on the pier

Starting point and end of the itinerary: Barcelona **Time needed**: one day (it can be covered in less time) **Means of transport**: city transport

Barcelona has numerous good bird-watching sites. It is not possible to give a full and detailed list here, so only a few of the more representative sites, where all the city's most interesting species are to be seen, have been chosen.

Several of these species cannot be pinned down to any one particular site, such as the Jackdaw, for example, or the yellow-legged Herring Gull, which breeds on rooftops in the city centre and can be seen throughout the city area. In districts in the higher areas of the city, it is not at all rare to see flights of Alpine Swift, mixed in with plentiful Swift, from March through to mid-October. On winter evenings, it is spectacular to watch Jackdaw and huge flights of Starling swirling in the sky on their way to their Plaça Catalunya tree roosts.

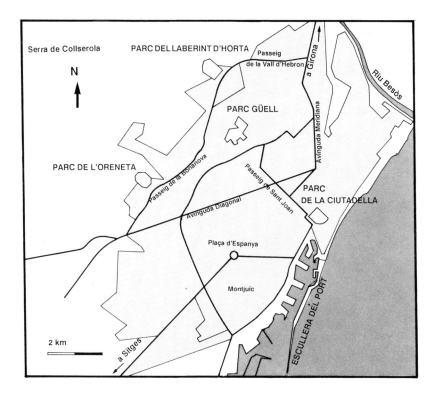

The best area for birds, though, are the parks and gardens, as well as for sea birds, the coastal area. The network of paths in the city parks makes bird-watching both thorough and easy.

From an ornithological point of view, the parks in the higher part of the city are the most interesting, since their vegetation and close contact with the Collserola range provide them with a few of the more typical woodland species.

The **Parc de l'Oreneta** (Swallow Park) is largely made up of spontaneous Mediterraean vegetation such as ilex, stone and Aleppo pine, and a thick undergrowth of scrub. Carob and almond trees are to be found in some parts, as reminders of former agricultural activities. Paths in these areas have an anarchical layout, and cross areas of differing levels of woodland growth.

The presence of Mediterranean vegetation and the relatively small index of human disturbance makes it possible for several Mediterranean species to abound in this park. Sardinian Warbler is present all the year round and Subalpine Warbler in migration and to a lesser extent in summer. Of th tree species, the tits are particularly numerous. Long-tailed Tit, Great Tit, Blue Tit, Coal Tit and Crested Tit are to be found there all the year round, along with the equally common Firecrest and Short-toed Treecreeper. Blackbird and Black-cap are also common throughout the year. Of the summer visitors, Golden Oriole, Nightingale, Melodious Warbler and Bonelli's Warbler stand out.

In areas with less woodland coverage, several species of finch are to be found breeding, such as Goldfinch, Greenfinch and Serin. Linnet, Siskin and Crossbill are rarer, and usually visit the parks in winter only. In these more open regions, Hoopoe and Redstart are to be seen in spring and summer, and the odd pair of Woodchat Shrike breed in some years. Common Starling and Black Redstart are to be seen in clearings and on buildings in winter, and, more rarely, Dartford Warbler in areas of scrub.

Robin and Wren breed in the cooler spots, and are joined by Dunnock in winter.

The **Parc del Laberint d'Horta** (Horta Maze Park) is similar to the Oreneta Park, with which it has many features in common. It has some more humid areas, but also suffers from more human disturbance. Some parts of the Parc del Laberint d'Horta can be described as having a "romantic" air about them, with walks, buildings, lakes and a maze that gives the park its name.

The wooded area is much thicker and has a greater proportion of deciduous trees than the Parc de l'Oreneta. This factor accounts for the presence of Turtle Dove, Wryneck and Green Woodpecker, species that are rare in the Parc de l'Oreneta.

The ponds in the park also provide a habitat for White and Grey Wagtails. This latter species breeds in the park.

The remaining species are practically the same as those in the Parc de l'Oreneta, with a significant presence of tits, Short-toed Treecreeper and Firecrest. Hoopoe, Nightingale, Melodious Warbler, Sardinian Warbler and Bonelli's Warbler are other species of interest to birdwatchers that can be found here.

Other interesting species may well turn up in the fringe areas of the park, alongside the Collserola range. Two such species are Great Spotted Cuckoo (as a result of the large amount of Magpies in the area around Barcelona), and Bee-eater, especially towards the end of summer. This phenomenon also occurs in the Parc de l'Oreneta and other peripheral parks in Barcelona.

The **Parc de la Ciutadella** (Citadel Park), as against the other parks mentioned previously, is in the centre of the city. A large part of the park is taken up by Barcelona Zoo. This causes several feral species, mainly "escapes" from the zoo, to be found in the vicinity. Among these species, Monk Parakeet and Rose-ringed Parakeet are particularly noteworthy. The former species is very common and has colonized most of the parks and tree-lined avenues in the rest of the city area, making its huge nests in palm trees.

From the point of view of the landscape, the Parc de la Ciutadella combines two kinds of garden styles: areas with flower-beds and few trees,

Great Spotted Cuckoo

situated in rows, contrasting with those with much denser clumps of trees. Blackbird is very common throughout the year, with Robin, Song Thrush and Chiffchaff also common in winter. Although not abundantly present, the following species are also regular: Great Tit, Blackcap and Spotted Flycatcher, this latter species in spring and summer. Sardinian Warbler may also be found in winter. As regards the finches, Serin, Greenfinch and Goldfinch stand out, with Chaffinch joining them in winter.

Black Redstart can be seen on buildings and constructions within the park in winter, while Jackdaw and yellow-legged Herring Gull are seen there all year.

An interesting factor about the Parc de la Ciutadella is that there are two relatively large ponds, which are responsible for the presence of such water-loving species in the park as Mallard, Red-crested Pochard and Grey Heron. These birds, although born within the zoo (especially the Grey Heron), may now be seen about the city. In winter, Black-headed Gull is very common, much more so than Lesser Black-backed Gull and Mediterranean Gull, species that are to be seen alongside the yellow-legged Herring Gull on the roofs of buildings, especially on the Catalan Parliament building.

The ponds also encourage the presence and breeding of White and Grey Wagtail. They also bring in odd ducks, Moorhen or Coot, attracted by the "decoy" ducks on the pond. Reed Warbler and Cetti's Warbler are also to be seen (and the latter's powerful song is sometimes heard too) along with rather rarer Kingfisher.

Finally, the **Parc Güell** (cf. Other places of interest) also deserves mention. This park has the same sort of spontaneous vegetation, with carob and olive trees, as the Parc de l'Oreneta, and although it is not in direct contact with the Collserola range, it has most of the same species as the other park, albeit in lesser numbers.

To observe seabirds, it is worth going to the **port mole**, which you can reach by car or on foot from the colourful Barceloneta district, or by taking one of the typical "*golondrines*", pleasure boats that leave from the wharf opposite the Columbus monument.

The large surface area covered by Barcelona port means that the mole is very long. It juts several kilometres into the sea. This factor enables bird-watchers to see seabirds especially during migration. Yellow-legged Herring Gull, Black-headed Gull and Sandwich Tern are the three main species that can be observed all the year round.

The mole becomes really interesting outside the breeding season, when other species of gulls can also be seen. Mediterranean Gull is one interesting species, and is very common from the end of August up until April. In winter there may be flocks of several thousand Mediterranean Gulls in the sea off the jetty, where they spend the night. In winter, Lesser Black-backed Gull is also common, more so than Little Gull, which is mainly seen towards the end of winter. Skuas are also occasionally seen, especially the Long-tailed Skua.

Apart from the gulls and terns, other water birds are also to be seen: Great Crested Grebe, Cormorant and to a lesser extent Shag, Razorbill and Gannet. Divers and ducks are somewhat rarer, although many of the species turning up along the western Mediterranean coast have in fact been recorded here. During migratory periods, the range of species to be seen swells considerably. Some of the more regular species are Common Tern, Black Tern and Whiskered Tern, as well as Cory's and Manx Shearwater. Nor is it rare to see flights of waders and herons.

5B. Itinerary to Montserrat mountain

Starting point and end of the itinerary: Montserrat monastery **Time needed**: 5 hours **Means of transport**: by car and on foot **Observations**: wear sports footwear or light mountain boots

The itinerary begins at the Font del Portal (Gateway Fountain) in the most western part of the monastery, behind a square with fir trees and street stalls with fruit, honey, etc. Go up the stairs to the left of the fountain, and cross over a little bridge. Keep on climbing up, generally up steps, leaving the gully behind to your left. The ilex wood is thick, but you should be able to see birds such as Blue Tit and Great Tit, Blackcap, Nightingale, Robin, Serin and Blackbird. Further up, the steps pass between two rocks ("pas dels Francesos"), and soon you will come to a small clearing. Of the three paths leading off it, take the middle one. You will see some extraordinary needle-like peaks on the left-hand side of the valley: the one on the left is called "Gorra Frígia" (Phrygian cap) because of its shape. Once you reach the Pla dels Ocells (Birds' Plateau), where there is a small stone monolith, you will once again be confronted by paths to your left and right. Follow the path that gently makes its way up the valley, a few metres to the left of the dry river bed of the Santa Maria "torrent" (in Catalan "torrent" means a dry, seasonal water course). In the very thick woods you may well see Firecrest, Bonelli's Warbler, tits, Garden Warbler, Wren and Robin. You will soon come to a path leading off to the left. Although wider than the path you have been following up till now, it is a dead-end, so keep on along the original path. After a few metres you will pass beneath a monolith called "Cap de mort" (Dead man's head), since it is shaped like a skull. Next, a path joins you from the right, and after a short climb, the path leads into another larger one which you should follow up the valley.

Once you reach the Sant Jeroni (Saint Jerome) chapel, take the path to the left, which leads to an abandoned building and to a beautiful view from the left-hand side of the path. Keep on climbing up the steps and you will reach the top of the peak called **Sant Jeroni** (1,236 m). It is the mountain's highest point. Beneath you are great rocky cliff faces, and a fine view of Catalonia (to the north are the Pyrenees, to the north-east the Montseny massif and the Sant Llorenç del Munt massif nearer at hand, etc.). In this area you may see rupicoline species such as Crag Martin, Black Redstart, Raven, and Peregrine Falcon, as well as Alpine Swift in summer and Wallcreeper in winter.

The return trip to the monastery can be made along the wide path you found at the end of the climb, before the Sant Jeroni chapel. The path down does not have too many steep sections and offers a better view than on the way up.

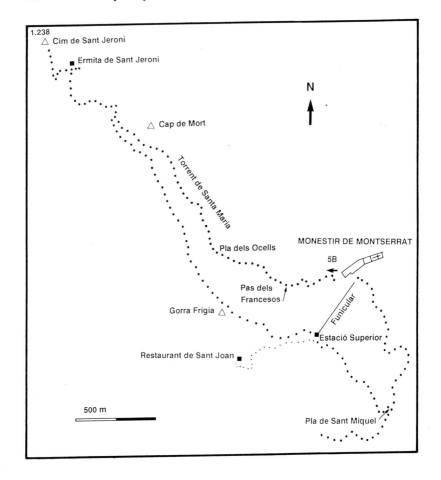

It will therefore be easier to spot birds such as Jay, Wood Pigeon, Raven and possibly Sparrowhawk. It is a good idea to stop off at the lookout points to enjoy the view. The odd lizard (*Podarcis hispanica*) may dash across the path before you. The path passes right beneath the "Phrygian cap", and at this moment the monastery will once again be beneath you. Soon you will come to the top funicular station from where the funicular descends to the monastery. On your right a path leads off to the Restaurant Sant Joan, a quarter of an hour's walk away. However, to continue the itinerary, take the path on the left leading down the Sant Miquel plateau, where you will come across larger paths. The one on the left (northwards) leads straight down to the monastery. The one of the right skirts the mountain round to the west. Before returning to the monastery, you may care to follow this path round to the right until it begins to slope in a more pronounced fashion (about 2.5 km further on, at the point, the village of Collbató is beneath you). As against most of the itinerary, this area was very much affected by the 1986 fire. The vegetation is very low and suitable for birds such as Sardinian Warbler. You may also be lucky enough to see Bonelli's Eagle. After this, you should go back along the same path as far as the Sant Miquel plateau, and make your way down to the monastery.

Once you have finished the itinerary, and if you wish to get a fuller picture of Montserrat, instead of returning to Barcelona along the route you came, you may care to complete the full loop around the mountain, without in this way greatly increasing the mileage. Rather than driving down to Monistrol, take the road to the left to Can Massana, 1 km beneath the monastery. Once you get to Can Massana take the road to the left which leads to the N-2 road and Barcelona.

Near the village of Collbató there are the **Coves del Salnitre** (Saltpetre Caves - cf. Other places of interest), near which you may care to do some further bird-watching. You can reach Collbató from Monistrol along the road turning off the C-1411 right in front of the funicular station. Otherwise, if coming from Can Massana along the N-II, you can take the turning off at Collbató. Once in the village, follow the road as far as the caves (less than 2 km from the village). From this point, you must drive for a while along a track signposted "camí de Les Feixades" in an easterly direction. It is rocky terrain with scrub, very much affected by the recent forest fire. But it is a good habitat for observing Sardinian Warbler, Subalpine Warbler, Blackcap, and more rarely, Dartford Warbler. Rupicoline species are also common: Crag Martin, Blue Rock Thrush, Black Redstart, raptors such as Peregrine Falcon and Bonelli's Eagle, and Wallcreeper in winter. Other birds that may be seen in the area are Green Woodpecker, Great Tit, Swallow, House Martin, and finches such as Serin and Goldfinch.

5C. Itinerary in the Garraf massif

Starting point and end of the itinerary: Cornudella **Time needed**: half a day (the itinerary on foot takes about 3 hours) **Means of transport**: by car and on foot **Observations**: wear light mountain boots

e 31

If you come from Barcelona along the C-246 road, you will find an endless area of development in the Castelldefels zone. Bearing this in mind and the fact that the present route of the main road is to be changed, the best directive that you can be given to find your way up to the massif is to look for a turning to the right signposted "Platja Port Ginetsa" and "Palau Novella". You will come to this a few kilometres after the turning to the Castelldefels town centre, and once you come alongside the Garraf range foothills. After taking this turning, you will come to another junction after a few metres. The main road follows on to the right (to "Platja Port Ginesta"), but you should keep straight on towards Palau Novella, crossing through the Rat Penat housing development.

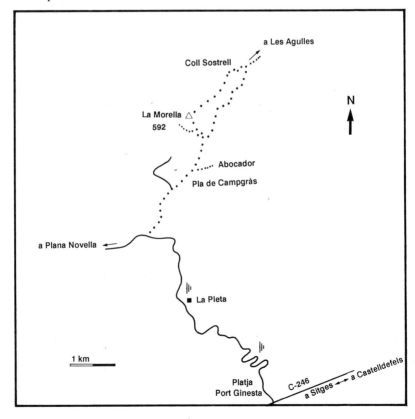

The road soon starts to climb, and you leave the development area. Shortly after beginning the climb, you might stop on the second large bend to the left. Although still quite a way off, in the distance you will see the white cliffs of Vallbona, where cliff-dwelling birds such as Kestrel, Stock Dove, Alpine Swift, Crag Martin and Blue Rock Thrush all live. The road continues to climb steeply until it comes to a flatter area, with a small Aleppo pine wood and a house in ruins (**La Pleta**), together with its old abandoned fields. Here a brief walk should reveal Great Grey Shrike, Hoopoe, Great Tit and Crested Tit, Green Woodpecker, as well as Sardinian Warbler, Blackcap and Dartford Warbler. If you stop off here in the evening, you may be lucky enough to spot a Nightjar or hear Eagle Owl. At night, you will probably see Moorish Gecko on the road itself in the right season.

Following on along the road, at about 1.5 kms from La Pleta, you should take a turning to the right (if you went straight you would come to Plana Novella). Leave the car right on this junction and continue on foot, following the right-hand turning. The relief is quite flat here, and as the vegetation is low, there is a very good field of vision, enabling you to get good sightings of birds such as Black-eared Wheatear, Great Grey Shrike, Sardinian Warbler, Dartford Warbler, Rock Thrush, Kestrel, etc.

Further on, you should take a right-hand turning off the main road, which is closed to the public and leads to a telecommunications centre situated on a local hilltop. You are now on the **Campgràs plateau**, a small plain that is cultivated some years. Thekla Lark can be seen around along with Red-legged Partridge, Ortolan Bunting, Tawny Pipit, Stonechat and Wren. In winter, finches are common (Goldfinch, Linnet, Serin, Chaffinch, Greenfinch, etc.).

About 300 metres after the last junction, take a track to your left, ignoring the chain that bars the way to cars. On your left you will see a small hill with a broadcasting station on its summit. On the right, there are some rocks that are a very good spot for Blue Rock Thrush. About 700 metres further up you will come to a path leading off to the right (on a bend), with black, blue and yellow painted signs. Take this path and climb up the hill facing you, which is known as "La Morella". It is 592 m high, and it is the highest point in the park. There is a very good view of the massif from here, and on a clear day, you should be able to see the mountains of Montserrat and even the Pyrenees (to the north), and Montseny (to the north-west). Keep a special look out for the warblers, because here you may spot Whitethroat and, very locally, Spectacled Warbler.

From La Morella make your way down to a rocky hillock at a lower level, which is quite close at hand to the north-east. It has some ilex bushes on its summit. The path is none too clear at this point, and you must head off

Sardinian Warbler

slightly to the left to look for a small, very narrow path with blue and yellow markings. This path leads to the right around the hillock. Its is impossible to get lost, but the rocky nature of the ground makes it very uncomfortable if you leave the path. Another reference for finding the path is that it passes a little to the left of a very visible clump of ilex trees that conceals a pothole. These trees are situated about half way between La Morella and the hillock.

Beyond this point, the birds will not change substantially, but you are recommended to follow the full itinerary to get a fuller picture of the local birdlife, and maybe even see rarer birds such as Bonelli's Eagle. Follow the path that now descends sharply towards a wide pass where there are some electric power cables. Just before arriving there, you will find a wider path to the right, which runs at an oblique angle into the one you are on. Take this path, although you can also descend as far as the pass if you wish (Coll Sostrell). A few paths lead off from this point; the one furthest to the right leads to a smaller pass which has an electric cable running along it with an electric pylon. Following this path you will soon come to some brown cliffs (**Les Agulles**), a very good spot for rupicoline species such as Blue Rock Thrush, Rock Thrush and Kestrel, among others. It is also a good area for Subalpine Warbler. After this minor deviation from the regular itinerary, make your way back to the Coll Sostrell and follow the normal itinerary.

Climb in the opposite direction to the path you were following before the optional deviation, looking out for black markings. You will see La Morella once again and soon you have to take a narrow path leading off to the left (the black markings continue). In the background, to the south-east, you will see the rubbish tip mentioned in the area description. You then leave La Morella on your right and come to the track you climbed to the summit on. Take this same track as far as Pla de Campgràs (Campgràs plateau) and continue along the same path you came on.

Once back at the car, you may care to drive to **Plana Novella** (about 78 kms away). The road passes over several valleys, all of which are rocky and lacking in vegetation. Blue Rock Thrush, Black-eared Wheatear, Red-legged Partridge, Raven and, if you are lucky, Bonelli's Eagle, are all species you may see. On the right you will find a track leading to the Park Information Centre (Open from 10 am to 3 pm). Keep going as far as Plana Novella, where there is an old palace (now restored). The palace gardens contain species such as Golden Oriole, Woodchat Shrike, Spotted Flycatcher, Turtle Dove, Hoopoe, and the Scops Owl may be heard.

Board and Lodging

In Barcelona and its surrounding area, there is an extraordinary abundance and diversity of hotels and restaurants. There is also a wide range of camping sites, mainly to be found on the coast to the south of Barcelona (Gavà-Castelldefels area). They are therefore near the Garraf massif, where itinerary 5C is set.

At the Abbey of Montserrat there is a hotel and a camping site, as well as restaurants, a self-service restaurant, bars and several shops. Furthermore, half-way through itinerary 5B, you will come to the Sant Joan restaurant.

As regards the Garraf massif, there are many restaurants in the Castelldefels area, although the nature of itinerary 5C makes it advisable to go to the restaurant which is at Plana Novella (see Itinerary 5C).

Other places of interest

The immense cultural and historical interest of the city of Barcelona calls for the expert advice of a specialized guidebook. However, a few of the most interesting sites are listed below:

- The Sagrada Família Temple. An impressive and unfinished cathedral, the work of the genius Antoni Gaudí, a late 19th century Art Nouveau architect.

- The Art Nouveau style took on great importance in the city, and some of the most significant other examples are: La Pedrera and Casa Batlló (buildings on the Passeig de Gràcia), the Güell Park (an urban park, with many architectural and artistic features, in the Gràcia district), the Torre Güell doorway (situated behind the Pedralbes royal palace), the Palau de la Música (Carrer Sant Pere més Alt, near Plaça Urquinaona).

- The old city (Ciutat Vella). The historic city centre: the Barri Gòtic (cathedral, Plaça del Rei, remains of the Roman and medieval city walls, etc.), the Gothic church of Santa Maria del Mar, the stately palaces of Montcada street, etc.

- The Gothic monastery of Pedralbes, with its magnificent cloister and Religious Art museum. In the district of Pedralbes.

- Picasso Museum. Important collection of the painter's work. Housed in two palaces in the Carrer Montcada.

- Museu d'Art de Catalunya (Catalan Art Museum). The largest and most important collection of Romanesque art in the world (also contains Gothic and other forms of art). On the mountain of Montjuïc.

- Fundació Miró. A collection of the works of the painter Joan Miró, with frequent short-term exhibitions of a miscellaneous nature. On the mountain of Montjuïc, in a building designed by the architect Josep Lluís Sert.

- The Zoo (Parc Zoològic). The home of the only known albino gorilla. The zoo is in the Ciutadella park.

In the Montserrat area, the following are of interest:

- The Abbey of Montserrat. An historic building in the most beautiful setting. There is a museum with an outstanding collection on biblical archaeology, Catalan, Italian and Spanish painting, liturgical objects etc.

- Cova del Salnitre (Saltpetre Caves). A 530 metre long subterranean cave. Near Collbató.

6

MONTSANT MOUNTAIN RANGE AND THE SIURANA MOUNTAINS

These mountains are to the north-east of the cities of Tarragona and Reus, and to the south of the Catalan coastal mountain range, of which they are an important part.

At present the project to convert the Serra del Montsant (Montsant Mountain Range) into a nature park is under consideration.

Area: approximately 15,000 hectares.

Habitats: pine and ilex woodland and scrub, cliffs and extensive rocky areas, sparsely-vegetated mountain tops, cultivated land (vineyards, hazelnut plantations, almond and olive groves) and Mediterranean mountain streams (the Montsant and the Siurana).

Interesting species:
- *Present all the year round*: Golden Eagle, Bonelli's Eagle, Peregrine Falcon, Red-legged Partridge, Eagle Owl, Thekla Lark, Crag Martin, Sardinian Warbler, Dartford Warbler, Blue Rock Thrush, Black Wheatear, Rock Bunting, Rock Sparrow, Spotless Starling.
- *Summer visitors*: Short-toed Eagle, Alpine Swift, Bee-eater, Hoopoe, Red-rumped Swallow, Tawny Pipit, Woodchat Shrike, Melodious Warbler, Orphean Warbler, Subalpine Warbler, Bonelli's Warbler, Rock Thrush, Black-eared Wheatear.
- *Winter visitors*: Alpine Accentor, Wallcreeper.
- *Migratory species*: Honey Buzzard, Black Kite and other raptors.

104

Description and habitat

The Montsant and Siurana mountains are typically Mediterranean mountain ranges and form part of the Catalan coastal range. This mountain system runs parallel to most of the Catalan coast and is made up of a number of smaller ranges, all of which have their own particular features. The Montseny (highest of the coastal range mountains), Montserrat and the Garraf mountains also form part of this mountain system.

From the point of view of the birdlife and the fauna in general, the Montsant and Siurana mountains are a place where the ranges of Mediterranean and Central European species overlap. Central European species find suitable habitats in these mountains and are thus to be found in typically Mediterranean surroundings. The most interesting group, both in number and in variety, are the rock-dwelling (rupecoline) birds which are very much attracted by the craggy nature of the area.

The biological wealth of the Montsant makes it one of the most interesting Mediterranean massifs in the country, and for this reason a nature park is planned here in the near future. The protection of the area, however, is not fully guaranteed yet because there is a project to dam the river Montsant. This project has provoked a forthright defence campaign led by Catalan ecological groups.

The Monstant is a long mountain range and stands out from the surrounding landscape with its magnificent sheer cliff (the "Cingle Major") which is almost 12 kms long on its southern face. The conglomerate nature of the rocks causes erosion to give them rounded shapes of a kind not associated with the Siurana mountains. The crest of the Montsant range is very smooth, having small vales and a series of spurs leading to a major ridge called the "Serra Major", which runs like a backbone from one end of the Montsant to the other. The highest point is the Roca Corbatera which is 1,166 metres high. To the north of the Serra Major there are many gullies heading down towards the Fra Guerau canyon, where the Montsant river flows. It is another spot of great beauty and ecological interest where one of Catalonia's last remaining otter colonies can still be seen.

The imposing cliff known as the "Cingle Major" is on the southern slope. The landscape is very rocky with low vegetation (thickets and scrub) including rosemary, kermes oak and ling. Former woodland had been destroyed not long ago by devastating forest fires. There are still small patches of ilex and pine in odd ravines and sheltered spots. The higher parts of the massif were over-grazed and vegetation is now very stunted. The northern side of the massif, however, has a fine mantle of trees, principally pine and ilex, as well as well-conserved riverside woodland along the course of the river Montsant.

From the south you can only reach the higher areas of the Montsant along small paths leading up the Cingle Major (cliff) by way of clefts and ledges in the cliff face itself. What from below may seem to be an impregnable rock face can in fact be climbed without too much difficulty. The points at which these paths reach the top of the cliff are known as "graus". Some *graus* are very difficult to reach but are quite breath-taking. Some were frequently used by flocks on their way over the ridge, and others were sometimes used as short cuts.

Siurana is to the south-east of the Montsant range and very close at hand. It is an attractive village (cf. Other places of interest) perched on an impregnable cliff, which permitted the Arabs to make it their last stronghold in Catalonia (it was not conquered by the Catalans until 1153). The cliff, on the southern side, towers above the Siurana river which flows through the canyon beneath the village. In this area the mountains are a little lower and more highly vegetated than the Montsant, with pine (especially drought-resistant Aleppo pine) and patches of ilex.

Years ago most of the mountains and hills of this *comarca* were covered in vineyards, a crop that was of great importance. Nowadays vineyards cover a very much smaller area, although wines of great (and ever-improving) quality are still produced locally. At present, the principal crops are hazelnut, almond and olives which are mainly cultivated in flatter areas and on small hillocks near the villages. Large areas of abandoned fields (especially vine-yards) are being progressively overgrown, a process which is only halted by the bush fires which cause so much damage in summer.

How to visit the area

To get to the Montsant or Siurana mountain areas you must first reach the village of Cornudella. Whether coming from Barcelona or from the south, once you get to Tarragona you must drive to Reus. From Reus you must continue along the N-420 road towards Falset, turning right after a few kilometres on to the C-242 road to Les Borges del Camp, Alforja and Cornudella (22 kms farther on). After Alforja you drive through a small mountain area which forms part of the Siurana massif and reach the Alforja pass. From this point there is a splendid view of the Montsant range in the distance. Drive along the main road as far as Cornudella, which is the starting point (km 0) for all the itineraries.

It is also possible to go to Cornudella by coach from Barcelona (the coach company is called "Hispania", and leaves from 52, Passeig de Sant Joan) or from Tarragona (coach leaving Plaça Tarraco). There is a train line from Barcelona to Tarragona.

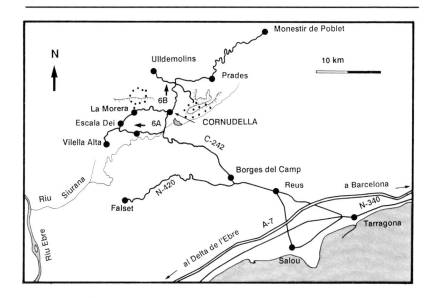

The itineraries described here are nature trails. Trail 6A takes between 5 and 6 hours (at a birdwatcher's gait) and has an additional section which can be covered by car; the best time of day to start off is the early morning. Trail 6B is less demanding and may take up to 4 hours. It can be left for the afternoon although this will depend on how much time you spent on the first trail, and the amount of day-time available at different times of year. If you lack time in the afternoon or are tired, you can drive to Siurana village and have a look around the surrounding area (cf. itinerary 6B for more details). But if you intend to leave trail 6B for the morrow, there is another possibility (cf. end of itinerary 6A). You can motor over to the Carthusian monastery of Scala Dei where interesting species are to be seen in the vicinity.

Itinerary 6A, which climbs and then descends considerably (passing through passes or *graus* on the Cingle Major cliff), calls for a little physical exertion, although any normal person will certainly be up to it! Those who suffer from severe vertigo will only have problems at the Grau dels Barrots despite the handrails which provide extra safety for hikers at key places. The use of mountain boots or other thick-soled, sturdy shoes is almost obligatory on this rocky trail. It is also advisable for you to take drink because there is no drinking water along the way. If you take a canteen, you can fill it up at the public fountain in Cornudella or La Morera, in the Plaça del Priorat (Priorat square). You may also care to take a little food with you on this long trail. However, if it is foggy, you are strongly advised not to go on this walk because you might get lost on the higher ground.

Itinerary 6A winds its way up the Grau dels Barrots cleft and descends by way of the Grau de la Grallera. There is another easier (though less spectacular) way up: the Grau de l'Agnet, from where you can descend by way of the Grau de la Grallera; if you take this route, part of the instructions given for itinerary 6A will apply. The Grau dels Barrots path may well supply you with unexpected surprises such as the view of a falcon flashing past. You are therefore recommended to take this route unless you really are very "squeamish"!

Itinerary 6B is not too difficult at all, although you are strongly advised to wear good walking shoes for added comfort. In summer it may be pleasant to make your way to the Siurana river and have a plunge in one of its very inviting pools.

As regards the season you choose (or have available) for your visit, spring is by far the best (April-June). Summer months are very sticky, as can be expected in a Mediterranean area, and not so good for birdwatching. Autumn and winter are good for migration and the arrival of wintering species which are generally attracted to the lower cultivated zones of the massif, except in a few cases such as Wallcreeper and Alpine Accentor. Resident species are not as conspicuous in winter as they are in the breeding season. Nevertheless, it is not usually very cold here, and pleasant and profitable birding is to be had by all!

Birdwatching

6A. Itinerary on the Cingle Major cliff in the Montsant range

Starting point and end of the itinerary: Cornudella **Time needed**: 5-6 hours **Means of transport**: by car and on foot **Observations**: sections with some difficulty. Do not do itinerary in fog. Best in the morning

The starting point for the itineraries is **Cornudella**. This village was one of the first in the Iberian Peninsula to have resident populations of both Spotless and Common Starling (both species are spreading their range). They can be observed together throughout the year, especially in the breeding season. They breed side by side on the church bell tower.

From Cornudella you drive along a road leading to La Morera (8 kms away). The road at first crosses an area of vineyards, hazelnut and almond groves, with odd patches of woodland (Aleppo pine, oak and ilex). On the right-hand side of the road you will see the cliff face of the "Cingle Major". It has rocky areas at its base with great conglomerate boulders (which have broken away from the cliff) scattered here and there. Blue Rock Thrush is often seen here. If you are passing through this area at dusk, stop for a while before reaching La Morera and listen for the calls of Eagle, Tawny, Little and Scops Owls.

Once you have reached **La Morera,** leave your car at the entrance to the village or in the square by the Town Hall (Plaça del Priorat). The itinerary starts at this square. Walk up Ciutadella street and when you reach the end, turn right for a few metres until you come to a path that leads to the cliff. As soon as you are out of the village, you will find the first junction in the path. Take the left-hand path which is marked with red and white parallel markings (it is a "Grand Route" path). You will immediately come to a signpost. Grau de Sanfores is straight on, Grau de Grallera (50 mins.) is on the downhill path to the right and Grau dels Barrots (1 hour 15 mins.) is the path you want. Those of you wishing to follow the easier path to Grau de l'Agnet (rather than the Grau dels Barrots route (cf. How to visit the area)) should follow the Grau de la Grallera path as far as a sign indicating the way to Grau de l'Agnet to the right.

On this first stretch of the itinerary, species such as Stonechat, Black-eared Wheatear and Black Redstart should be spotted without too much difficulty along with birds which generally nest below the village, such as Bee-eater and Golden Oriole. You will then pass through an area with great blocks of stone where you have good chances of seeing Black Wheatear.

Further along the path you will come face to face with a great vertical rock face called the **Roca Falconera** (Falcon Rock). You may indeed see a Peregrine Falcon (or a Raven) fly past as you climb. Be sure to keep your eyes open. Raptors such as Short-toed Eagle and Kestrel can also be seen alongside other species such as Crag Martin and Alpine Swift. In tree-clad areas, Robin, Wren, several species of tit, Bonelli's Warbler, Jay and even Green and Great Spotted Woodpecker are present. Sardinian and Dartford Warbler, Linnet and Tawny Pipit are to be seen in the more sparsely vegetated areas. You may encounter the odd Wood Pigeon, and there may be Stock Dove on the cliff face.

Further on you will come across a new metal sign which indicates that the Grau Carrasclet is straight on and the Grau dels Barrots to the left. Take the left-hand path which has double red and black markings painted regularly along the way. At the foot of the cliff there is another metal sign which indicates the way to the Grau de l'Agnet (along a fairly treacherous path), La Morera (the place you have left behind you) and Grau dels Barrots, to the right of the Roca Falconera. You must take this last path.

From your present location it may well appear madness to try and climb up the cliff. The truth is that there is a way up a cleft, providing a splendid route up the cliff face. At the bottom of the cleft there is a short metal ladder which can be scaled without any difficulty at all. A little further up you will find a large boulder "barring" the way up. But you will be able to get round it by using the hand supports. The way up will now take you along a ledge on the cliff face which you follow to the east. The view will now open up before your eyes. Keep a look out for raptors, and for birds such as Wallcreeper and Alpine Accentor in winter. You will soon come to a vantage point called the "Balcó del Priorat" (Priorat Balcony) which is situated on an overhang. You can get there with the aid of a handrail, and the view is breath-taking. To the south-east is the village, the Siurana mountains and the reservoir. On a clear day you will be able to see the sea; to the south-west, far beyond Morera, a whole series of mountain ridges rise up, the furthest of which are the Ports de Tortosa-Beseit (Itineraries 8A and 8B).

The path then leads past a few clumps of ilex, sycamore and savin trees (*Juniperus phoenicea*) -the few ones to have survived the fires. Soon you will come to another metal sign. It indicates the way to Serra Major/Corbatera to the left, and straight on (bearing left), the way to Serra Major/Barranc Falles. You want this second path. To begin with the path is not very clearly marked. You must keep to the left and pass through an intriguing hole in the rock. After

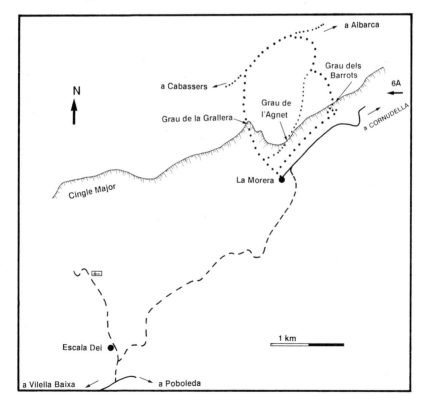

that point, the path is once again marked out with red and black markings. You are now on the cliff top. This area is not even but rugged and very craggy, with plenty of small gullies and sparse vegetation: ilex, sycamore, savin and the odd yew tree. Rock Bunting, Dartford Warbler and Robin can be seen here, as well as Red-legged Partridge, a species which can in fact be seen at almost any point on the itinerary.

You climb through stony ground following the red and black marks. The path is not too clear but you will soon come to another metal sign which indicates the way to the various *graus* (Agnet, Barrots, Espinós, Carrasclet). Those of you who have come via the Grau de l'Agnet will also arrive at this point and will have to follow the directions from this point to the Serra Major and to a metal sign which you will be able to see in the distance. It can be reached along a path marked with white and red markings. This new sign indicates the way to the Serra Major, to the right to Albarca and to the left to Cabassers, which is the route you must take. You are now on the crest of the range. The path links up the highest peaks of the Montsant. You must head for Cabasset. This area continues to be very rocky, with odd patches of savin trees *Juniperus phoenicea* and dogwood, a bush with beautiful spring blossom. To the north there are abrupt ravines with more trees. They lead to the splendid Fra Guerau canyon where the Montsant river flows.

From this point you can see a fine view of the snow-capped Pyrenees on clear winter days. Wood Lark, Raven, Great Grey Shrike and sometimes Golden Eagle can be seen, along with Alpine Accentor in winter. Stay on the path with the red and white markings until you come to another sign which indicates you are on the Serra Major, and the direction to be taken if you want to go to the Cova de l'Os (Bear's Cave) and Cabassers. You must take the path to Cabassers until you come to a third sign indicating you are on the Serra Major, and the way to Albarca (where you have just come from), Grallera-La Morera, Cabassers, Comellar-Cova de l'Os and Comellar del Riu Bidobar. Descend in the direction of Grallera-La Morera, and the path will lead towards the Grau de la Grallera, a much easier way down than the Grau dels Barrots. Keep walking until you reach La Morera, the place where you left the car. On your way down the Grau de la Grallera, you may well see Rock Sparrow, Wallcreeper, and, in the vicinity of the village, in rocky areas, Black Wheatear. The birdwatching on the way down should in fact be very similar to the birdwatching you had on the way up, but in the reverse order! Near the village, Cirl Bunting, Corn Bunting, Goldfinch, Serin and Linnet can all be seen.

Once you have reached La Morera, if you do not wish to go straight on to itinerary 6B (it is better to leave it for the next day), you can round off the day's birdwatching by going on an additional section of the itinerary in the car. The route is as follows.

Take the La Morera to Scala Dei road (it lacks tarmac for much of the way, but does not present serious problems). You will get marvellous views of the Montsant. When you reach **Conreria d'Scala Dei**, you can drive or walk for a further kilometre as far as the Carthusian monastery (Cartoixa - cf. Other places of interest). All around you there are abandoned vineyards. Before you is the Cingle Major cliff. Peregrine Falcon, Kestrel, Blue Rock Thrusk and warblers can be seen here. You must then drive on the tarmac road to Vilella Baixa (11 kms from La Morera). On the way back, you can drive along the road which goes through Poboleda and links up with the C-242 road again (the crossroads is just before Scala Dei).

The birdwatching is good all the way along this drive: raptors such as Bonelli's and Short-toed Eagle or Kestrel as well as Bee-eater, Black-eared Wheatear, Woodchat Shrike or Red-legged Partridge can all be seen.

6B. Itinerary in the Siurana mountains

Starting point and end of the itinerary: Cornudella **Time needed**: 4 hours **Means of transport**: by car and on foot **Observations**: best in the afternoon

Drive towards Ulldemolins from Cornudella. Very soon you will pass a tarmac road on your right. Do not take the turning. Continue along the main road and you will come to another turning to the right in the next kilometre. A sign indicates the way to Siurana along an uneven earth track. Although it has a very variable gradient, you should not have any problems driving along it.

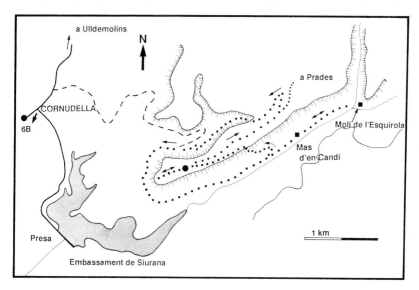

You will come closer to the reddish cliff face as you pass through Aleppo pine woods with scattered ilex trees. After about 3 kms, you will come to a turning to the right (on a bend). It is normally chained off. Park the car at this point, leaving the track to Siurana on your left (you will later make your way back to the car along that track). Take the right-hand path which is almost completely flat.

You cross an area of hazelnut and almond groves, with odd thickets and clumps of trees here and there. Above you is the cliff the village of Siurana is perched on. Raptors such as Peregrine Falcon, Kestrel and Short-toed Eagle can be seen alongside Raven and beautiful Golden Oriole and Bee-eater. Flights of partridge and smaller birds such as Stonechat, Melodious Warbler, Rock Bunting, Sardinian Warbler, Dartford Warbler and several species of finch can also be seen.

The path turns to the left and enters the valley of the river Siurana and soon after forks into three paths. The middle path heads towards the river, and the path on the left (which is closed off to vehicles) is the one you are to follow. The river will always be on your right, giving you good views of Grey Wagtail dashing across the water.

Aleppo pine is the predominant tree in the valley, but there are also patches of Scotch pine and pinaster. There are white and orange limestone cliffs at the top of the canyon. Further down the cliff is a deeper red once again, having plenty of little cavities which are ideal for Stock Dove and owls (Eagle, Tawny, Barn and Little Owl). Five species ot tit (Great, Blue, Coal, Long-tailed and Crested) can also be seen here.

The path goes past a ruined *mas* (farm house) and then past one that is still in working order (Mas d'en Candi). Soon after you come to an area of abandoned fields where the odd almond tree and the remains of old stone walls can still be made out among the trees of the wood, which is becoming more and more overgrown. Here you can see Great Grey Shrike, Blackcap, Wood Pigeon, Jay and Green Woodpecker. At this point you must also keep an eye out for Bonelli's Eagle flying overhead. The valley is very much boxed in, and though you may well see the eagle, the view will probably not last long! Sightings of Golden Eagle are also possible here, though a good deal rarer.

You will soon come to a place called **Molí de l'Esquirola** (Squirrel's Mill) where there is a broken down mill. The path ends here at a point where two valleys converge. Go back along the path and approximately half a kilometre after the Mas d'en Candi you will find a small path to the right. This path initially leads you up quite steep slopes (and gentler ones later) to the top of the cliff where Siurana is situated. You will continue seeing small birds such as Short-toed Treecreeper, warblers, Firecrest (and Goldcrest in winter). Once you have climbed up a reasonable distance, the path heads west and you will see limestone cliffs above and below you. It is a good spot for Blue Rock Thrush and Alpine Accentor, as well as the somewhat rarer Wallcreeper in winter.

The path finally leads out of the canyon and comes to a small clearing which the **Siurana** villagers use as a car park. In front of you are the ruins of an old Arab castle, where Rock Thrush and Rock Bunting are often to be seen. There are four hirundines to be seen here: House Martin, Crag Martin, Swallow and Red-rumped Swallow. This last species is the rarest of the four, but if you have a close look at the swallows swirling around the village outskirts, you are sure to see it. You will also probably see Alpine Swift flashing past.

Bonelli's eagle

You must then cross the village. Look out for Black Redstart and Rock Sparrow in the vicinity of the church. Follow a small path westwards as far as a vantage point on some rocks. There is a beautiful view of Siurana's gardens and the reservoir. You can also see the Montsant mountains. You may well see Blue Rock Thrush as well as many small birds such as tits, warblers, Goldfinch and Rock Bunting in the small gardens at the foot of the cliff.

You must now cross the village again (in the opposite direction) and take the only track leading out of it. After 1.5 kms you will come to a turning to the left which takes you back to Cornudella (the right-hand path heads towards Prades). Follow it down a wooded ravine (Aleppo pine) skirted by rocky cliffs. You will reach your car two and a half kilometres beyond the turning. If you are on this path at dusk, you might well see a Red-necked Nightjar.

Board and lodging

There are many places to dine and sleep at Tarragona and Reus. At coastal towns such as Salou and Cambrils, there are many hotels of various categories but in summer you may find it difficult to find a room. In the inland area around the Montsant and Siurana mountains, villages are smaller and hotel rooms are harder to come by, though you are unlikely to be left out in the cold! Lodging is to be found at two guest houses in Cornudella (Fonda del Racó and Fonda Montsant), as well as at Poboleda (Hostal Antic Priorat), Ulldemolins (Fonda Toldrà), La Bisbal de Falset (Cal Ramonet) or Les Borges del Camp (guest house).

Restaurants are also to be found at Siurana, La Vilella Baixa (Restaurant Racó del Priorat) and La Venta del Pubill (C-242 and Poboleda road crossroads).

There are mountain huts for hikers at Siurana and Albarca.

Other places of interest

- Siurana, small medieval village on a clifftop, with ruins of an old Arab castle and a Romanesque church.

- Scala Dei Carthusian monastery. Founded in the XIIth century, it was the first to be built in the whole Iberian Peninsula. The practice of vineyard cultivation began at this point. The monastery was abandoned in 1835 and is now in ruins, although restoration is now under way.

- La Vilella Alta. One of the most typical villages in the Priorat, with a beautiful little high street.

- La Vilella Baixa. A very picturesque village built on a steep slope causing houses to be many floors high, with the main door on the fourth or fifth floor.

- Poblet monastery. An important architectural ensemble founded in the XIIth century. It has a mixture of monastic (cloister), civil (Palace of King Martí) and military elements (walls, gates). It is an excellent combination of successive architectural styles. There is a museum of architectural and artistic interest. Weekdays and holidays from 10 am to 1 pm, and from 3 pm to 6 pm.

- Tarragona. Important Roman remains (aqueduct, amphitheatre, walls) at different sites around the city and on the outskirts. The cathedral reflects the transition between the Romanesque and Gothic periods. There are several museums of archaeological and artistic interest.

7

EBRE DELTA NATURAL PARK

The Delta of the river Ebre (in Catalan Ebre, in Spanish Ebro) is at the southern tip of Catalonia, in the Baix Ebre and Montsià *comarques* or counties. It is the foremost wetland in Catalonia, and one of the major ones in Europe. It is considered to be a wetland of international importance in the Ramsar Convention list.

Inaugural date: the left-hand part of the delta was given park status in 1983; the whole of the delta was finally made into a park in October 1986.

Surface area: 7,736 hectares (of which 2,505 form a Partial Nature Reserve)

Park offices address:
Parc Natural del Delta de l'Ebre (information centre).
Carrer Ulldecona s/n
43580-Deltebre

Habitats: marine bays, beaches and coastal dunes, salt pans and saltmarsh, coastal lagoons, riverside woodland, paddy fields, crops and orchards.

Interesting species:
-*Present all the year round*: Black-necked Grebe, Little Egret, Cattle Egret, Bittern, Flamingo, Red-crested Pochard, Shelduck, Marsh Harrier, Avocet, Kentish Plover, Slender-billed Gull, Sandwich Tern, Whiskered Tern, Hoopoe, Lesser Short-toed Lark, Moustached Warbler, Cetti's Warbler, Fan-tailed Warbler, Sardinian Warbler, Bearded Tit, Penduline Tit, Reed Bunting (*whitherby* subspecies), Spotless Starling.
- *Summer visitors*: Purple Heron, Night Heron, Squacco Heron, Little Bittern, Water Rail, Black-winged Stilt, Pratincole, Audouin's Gull, Gull-billed Tern, Lesser Crested Tern, Little Tern, Black Tern, Bee-eater, Short-toed Lark, Melodious Warbler, Savi's Warbler.
- *Winter visitors*: Great White Egret, wildfowl, Hen Harrier, Peregrine Falcon, Merlin, waders, Mediterranean Gull, Short-eared Owl, Bluethroat.
- *Migratory species*: Manx Shearwater, Black Stork, Glossy Ibis, Spoonbill, Osprey, Little Crake, Temminck's Stint, Marsh Sandpiper, Red-necked Phalarope, Caspian Tern, Subalpine Warbler, Spectacled Warbler, Black-eared Wheatear.

Description and habitat

The Ebre Delta is situated in the north east of the Iberian Peninsula. It is a large delta-shaped alluvial flood plain covering 32,000 hectares, with two coastal limbs enclosing two bays, one in the north and the other in the southern part of the delta.

It is an area with a high level of human activity, and at present, a large proportion of the delta's surface area is used for agriculture (15,000 hectares of paddy fields, 9,500 hectares of orchards and market gardens). Despite the intense agricultural activity, there are still large areas of natural marine and marsh habitat, especially in coastal zones. Almost all these areas form part of the natural park's 7,736 hectares. In the delta there are five different environmental categories: coastal zones; salt pans and saltmarsh; coastal lagoons; paddy fields; orchards and market gardens.

The **coastal zones** are made up of sandy beaches, dunes and bays. The delta's coastal fringe is one of the most important habitats in the park. This is primarily due to the fact that this zone (along with the Coto Doñana) is one of the Spanish State's last large stretches of unspoilt beach. Furthermore, it is in this coastal habitat that the large breeding colonies of gulls and terns are to be found. This factor makes this habitat the most characteristic and outstanding feature in the delta.

The wide Fangar and Alfacs bays are other characteristic elements of the delta's make-up. They are very shallow, and the variation in the depth of the water is caused mainly by the influence of the winds, since in this area the tides are very weak. Huge sand and mud bars appear, providing endless feeding grounds for waders and gulls.

Behind the beaches and coastal dunes, there are stretches of **salt pans** and **saltmarsh**. Here the high salinity of the ground is the predominant factor. This phenomenon is caused by the evaporation of salt water brought in by coastal flooding. The vegetation of these areas is largely composed of salicornia and, to a lesser extent, rushes. At times, when the paddy fields are dry or covered in rice plants, these areas are of great importance as feeding and resting areas for a wealth of species, especially waders, though gulls and terns are also common. They are also important in the breeding season, and the small islands in the salt pans are the main site for the colonies of waders, terns and gulls breeding in the delta.

The Delta's **coastal lagoons** are shallow -normally between 1 and 1.5 metres deep- and their water is quite salty (less so in the spring). The lagoons are surrounded by large reedbeds and bulrush beds, and in some zones, by rushes and salicornia, as well as by large subaquatic meadows which at their peak period cover very extensive areas. The various lagoons in the delta are of relatively different characteristics. At present, there are seven principal lagoons (L'Encanyissada, Els Calaixos de Buda (the Buda Lagoons), El Canal Vell, La Tancada, La Platjola, L'Alfacada, and Les Olles) as well as several other small lagoons that have almost totally dried up. They are of all sizes, the largest being L'Encanyissada (1,200 hectares), and one of the smallest being El Lluent de la Nòria, which only covers 8 hectares. The physical properties of the lagoons, such as, for example, salinity, also vary greatly.

The **paddy fields** are the most widespread habitat in the Delta, and rice-planting is the basic factor for the control of the freshwater cycle in the Delta. Rice-planting begins at the end of April when the irrigation canals are opened, and the whole rice-growing area is flooded; planting continues in May, and the harvest is in September and October. The irrigation network is closed off at the end of October and in November until the following year, when the cycle begins again.

This activity brings about a strong seasonal variation in the appearance of the paddy fields: in Spring they are flooded and the rice plants are just peeping out of the water, making the area look like a true marsh; in summer the rice has grown up and covers the whole surface area of the paddy fields; in autumn it is reaped and all the agricultural activities associated with the harvest take place. So there is a good deal of variation from field to field, some having stubble, others having already been ploughed, some still deep in water, others almost dry...; in winter, the paddy fields gradually dry out, giving the Delta an arid and sad appearance after the month of February.

Zones with deeper soil and less salinity along the banks of the rivers and furthest away from the sea have almost entirely been taken over for agricultural purposes. There are only a few remaining areas of the original **riverside woodland** (Illa de Mar, Illa de Gràcia, Illa de Sapinya). These woods are the only truly original Delta woods left, and are made up of poplars, willows, alders and a great wealth of bushes and creepers. Most of the surface of this habitat is at present covered in large tracts of **orchards and fields**. The principal crops are maize, barley, lettuce, artichokes and oranges.

How to visit the area.

To visit the Natural Park, the best idea is to make your way to one or other of the two information centres. One is at Deltebre (Delta Ecological Museum) and the other on L'Encanyissada lagoon (the "Casa de Fusta" (Wooden House) refuge-cum-museum). From the national road N-340, you should take any one of the turnings off to Deltebre. If you wish to go the "La

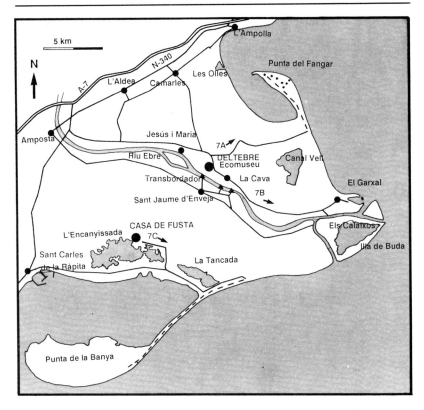

Casa de Fusta", leave the road at Amposta, head for Sant Jaume d'Enveja and follow the signposts to "Refugi-Museu de la Casa de Fusta". You may also leave the national road at Sant Carles de la Ràpita, take the road to Poble Nou, and then look out for the same signposts (to the "Casa de Fusta"). If you are coming along the A-7 motorway, you must come off it at the L'Aldea or Amposta-Sant Carles de la Ràpita exits, and follow the afore-mentioned roads. If coming by train along the Barcelona-València line, you must get off at L'Ampolla, Camarles or L'Aldea-Amposta. There is also a bus service between Barcelona and València and between the various Delta villages and towns.

You will be able to get maps and general information brochures in different languages at the Park information centres. All kinds of information is also supplied for tourists at these centres. It must be stressed that the road network in the Delta is very complicated, and that there are few signposts, so it is vital to have a good map! The Deltebre information centre is open throughout the year from 10 am to 2 pm, and from 3 pm to 6 pm (on week days) and from 10 am to 2 pm, and from 3.30 pm to 6pm (on holidays).

There is a very complete road network in the Delta, and roads cross or skirt most of the principal areas of interest. All the itineraries are therefore by car. This offers the added advantage that birds will not be so wary and you will be able to get closer to them than if you were on foot. It is also possible, however, to carry out the itineraries by bicycle. There are several rent-a-bike enterprises in the Delta (information on this or any other subject related to the itineraries can be obtained from the Deltebre information centre).

Itinerary 7C is without doubt the most complete, and a whole day will be needed if all the areas are to be covered in detail. The other itineraries are shorter and can be carried out in half a day or one whole day, according to your whim, and the birdlife! Although in regions such as the Ebre Delta there are always things to see, mid-May to mid-July is the most interesting time of the year since the breeding activity is at its peak; the period from mid-October to December, between the harvest and the drying out of the paddy fields, is also excellent, offering peak numbers of wintering wetland species.

Bird-watching.

7A. Itinerary in the northern part of the Delta: Fangar point

Starting point and end of the itinerary: Deltebre **Time needed**: half a day **Means of transport**: by car

Both the itineraries in the northern part of the Delta begin at the Natural Park information centre and Delta Ecological Museum (Eco-museu del Delta) at Deltebre (cf. other places of interest). The itinerary is 15 kms long and starts off from the information centre. Take the track that leads to the local Deltebre-L'Aldea road, where you should turn left to drive out of the village. Then, take the first tarmac road on your right just after the cemetery, and follow it until you come to a crossroads where you should turn left. Keep on this road for about 1.5 kms until you come to a junction, where you should take the turning to the right before coming to another crossroads 2 kms further on. Turn left there and drive on for 100 metres until you come to another crossroads, where you are to turn right towards the east, keeping on until the road ends at La Marquesa beach. The paddy fields will have begun as soon as you left the village, and is a habitat that will have accompanied you as far as the beach. Once you are in this area, drive along the track that leads off to the left behind a house (Bar "Los Vascos").

This track first passes through paddy fields on the left, with the Marquesa beach and its dunes on the right. Afterwards, you have to cross an area of dunes and you will then start to drive along the Fangar point, where the sandy track skirting the bay should be followed. Despite its precarious appearance, this track is quite reliable and firm. Do not, however, leave the track because there is a real danger of getting bogged down! In winter, it is also worth pointing out that some gales flood the Fangar point making the use of a four-wheel drive vehicle very much more necessary.

Autumn - winter: From October to March, Cattle Egret, Little Egret, Grey heron, Lapwing, Black-headed Gull, White Wagtail, Meadow Pipit and Water Pipit are common here, and can be seen along the whole itinerary. The abundance of herons and gulls in the period after the harvest (October-November) is remarkable. Keep an eye out in areas where tractors are ploughing in the stubble, for there are sure to be flocks of birds after the insects and worms the tractor is unearthing. When most of the paddy fields are already dry (February - April), the section of the itinerary that passes beside the Fangar bay or along the Canal Vell lagoon may be interesting, especially those paddy fields that are not yet dry where there may well be flocks of waders generally made up of Common Snipe, Black-tailed Godwit, Redshank, Spotted Redshank, Little Stint, Dunlin and Ruff. It may also be possible to see flights of (lagoon - or) bay-dwelling birds flying from one area of the Delta to another: Cormorant, wildfowl or Flamingo for example.

Once you are on the Fangar point, it is a good idea to stop off at the beginning of the bay, since in this area of very shallow waters, shore-loving waders are to be found in good numbers: Grey Plover, Sanderling, Dunlin, Curlew and Redshank. If from this point you scan the southern shore of the bay, flocks of Flamingo and Coot are often to be seen, along with the odd Shelduck. It is worth stopping at regular intervals along the point in order to scan the bay. With a bit of patience you should see isolated individuals or small flocks of Great Crested Grebe, Black-necked Grebe, Cormorant, Red-breasted Merganser and, occasionally, other species of ducks too; divers, Common Scoter and Velvet Scoter are also to be seen, and even Eider Ducks, though these are somewhat rarer. Huge flights of Black-headed Gull and Herring Gull join together in the evening to roost out in the bay. You must also look out for wader roosts in the areas near the tip of the Fangar point. This same zone is also very good for spotting sea ducks and waders such as Oystercatcher; furthermore, this area - and that of the Fangar lighthouse (reached along a turning to the right off the main track 3 kms after the Marquesa beach) are very favourable for seeing sea-birds. In winter, yellow-footed Herring Gull, Lesser Black-backed Gull, Black-headed Gull and Sandwich Tern are all very common. In the evenings, it is especially interesting to watch thousands of Mediterranean Gull, along with other species, flying to the north west to their L'Ametlla de Mar roosts.

For sea-bird enthusiasts it is well worth going to L'Ametlla de Mar harbour to see the arrival of the gulls in the wake of the fishing boats (cf. other places of interest). A close scan of the sea might well reveal Gannet, Manx Shearwater, Kittiwake, Great Skua, Razorbill as well as gulls. Puffins are a good deal rarer, as they normally stay further out to sea. In migration time Long-tailed Skua are also common, though they are rare in winter.

Spring - summer: After they are flooded the fields and planted the rice, the paddy fields (that in winter are dry and with little sign of life) awake to their full splendour. From the month of May onwards, the fields begin to fill with herons such as Cattle Egret, Little Egret, and more rarely, Purple Heron (this itinerary is far from the breeding grounds of this species, which will not be plentiful here until late summer). It is also the migratory period for many species of waders, although the paddy fields tend to be too deep, and only a few areas are suitable for feeding. Look out for one of these areas along the way (the exact situation will vary from year to year). When you find it, you will be sure to find many species such as Black-winged Stilt, small waders (plovers, Dunlin etc.), godwits, Ruff, Redshank, Green, Wood and Common Sandpiper. Have a close look at these flocks of waders since Temminck Stint is a regular migrant, as is Marsh Sandpiper, especially in the month of April. Common,

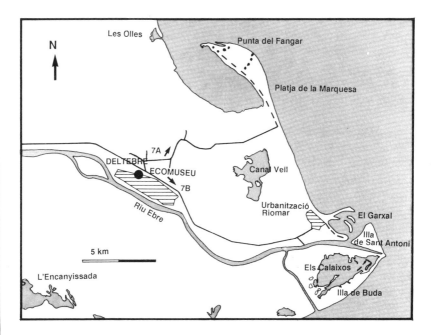

Little and Whiskered Tern also arrive in spring, being very common and present in all zones, hunting in the paddy fields.

At the beginning of the itinerary, in the vicinity of the cemetery, be sure to look out for the Gull-billed Tern that daily come to feed in these paddy fields. As you drive along, you should also watch out for both species of starling breeding on isolated farms. Hoopoe are also very common. You will often see it in the neighbouhood of these farms or flying across the road.

In the Marquesa beach and dunes area, Crested Lark are very common, and on the extensive stretches of sand at the tip of the Fangar point, there is a large colony of Common and Little Tern. At this time of year, extra precautions must be taken. Please do not get out of your vehicles and under no circumstances wander into the signposted breeding area. From your car window you will be able to see tern and Kentish Plover nests a short distance away. Oystercatcher also breed in this area, but it is quite rare. The best place to see this species is along the shoreline at the tip of the point. This same area of the point is good for gulls (yellow-legged Herring Gull and Black-headed Gull), and among them it is relatively easy to see the odd Audouin's Gull or Slender-billed Gull, especially young birds. At this time of year, sea-watching from the tip of the point, or better still from the lighthouse, is almost sure to raise Cory's Shearwater, a very common species in the Delta's off-shore waters. With a little bit of luck, you may also see Storm Petrel. Both of these birds have their breeding colonies on the Columbretes and Balearic Islands.

7B. Itinerary in the northern part of the Delta: el Garxal

Starting point and end of the itinerary: Deltebre **Time needed:** half a day **Means of transport:** by car

Leave the Natural Park information centre in the same direction as for the previous itinerary. You will come to the local Amposta-Deltebre road, and you turn to the right. Drive through Deltebre in the direction of the Riomar housing estate (Urbanització Riomar), and 9 kms further on you will come to a crossroads. The right-hand turning leads to the Buda island landing stage (Buda island is one of the most interesting points on the itinerary). The left-hand turning leads to the Riomar housing estate, from where the Garxal area may be visited. In all, the itinerary is 15 kms long.

The paddy fields between the crossroads and the Buda island landing stage, and extending as far as the Riomar Development are especially interesting since they hold water until late on in the season, and remain semi-flooded in February and March, being one of the best areas for waders at the end of the winter period. For example, it is common to see flocks of hundreds and even over a thousand Black-tailed Godwit and other waders, as well as herons, all feeding in the fields. In spring and summer, the proximity of this area to the Buda island breeding zones causes there to be plenty of Cattle Egret, Little Egret, Purple Heron, Black-winged Stilt, Black-headed Gull, Common Tern, Little Tern, Whiskered Tern and also the odd Little Bittern and Squacco Heron. Both at dawn and dusk, the Buda island landing stage is a good spot for watching the movements of birds to and from their roosting sites on the island. Especially in autumn and winter, it is a fine sight to see the arrival of Cormorants, Cattle Egret, Little Egret, Black-headed Gull, Black-tailed Godwit and starlings, in flights made up of dozens or hundreds of birds. You should be able to see plenty of Grey Heron and Marsh Harrier, and if you are lucky, you may see the rarer Bittern, which leaves the island at dusk to go and feed on the nearby Canal Vell lagoon. Glossy Ibis, Spoonbill and even Great White Heron are also to be seen at times. The movement of wildfowl leaving the island after dusk is very spectacular, and you may hear the whistling of wings and the calls of the different species. From the landing stage itself, you will also be able to see several species of raptor such as Hen Harrier, Buzzard, Merlin, Kestrel or Peregrine Falcon, all of which are attracted by the wealth of prey in the area. During migration, Osprey may also be seen flying up the river.

You can reach the Garxal area (where a lagoon is being formed) by taking a track to the right from the housing estate in the direction of the

Audouin's Gull

lighthouse. You then follow another track that skirts the lagoon in a north west direction until you come to the sea. Be sure to leave the signposted out of bounds area to your right.

This Garxal area combines some features of a marine bay and some of a coastal lagoon. It is an interesting zone all the year round, though especially so from March to May when most of the Delta is dry, so that this area becomes one of the principal centres for wildfowl, waders, gulls and terns. During this period, Little Egret are particularly common in this area, along with Red-crested Pochard, a species that gathers here in hundreds just before the breeding season. Mallard, Gadwall, Garganey, Coot, Moorhen and thousands of waders (almost all the species that can be seen on the Delta) are also to be found at this spot. All the Delta's species of gulls and terns (except for Gull-billed Tern and Lesser Crested Tern) also gather here in their thousands before the breeding season. Audouin's Gull and Slender-billed Gull, for example, are relatively easy to see. The Garxal area is also very good for Caspian Tern, the presence of which can almost be guaranteed during the months of March-April and August-September.

Later on in the year, in spring and summer, larks are particularly numerous on the saltmarsh and in the dunes: Crested Lark, the locally rare Short-toed Lark and the more common Lesser Short-toed Lark all being present. Also common are Kentish Plover; and lastly, the very interesting presence of a colony of Pratincole, a species that is very easy to see in the divide between the housing estate and the beach.

During the autumn migration, from July to September, the area becomes vey interesting once again as a shelter zone for migrants that cannot take refuge in the paddy fields, which are now covered in rice plants. Large numbers of wildfowl, waders, gulls and terns are again to be seen.

The area is much less interesting, however, in autumn and winter, and is invaded by large quantities of gulls. The odd Audouin's Gull or Slender-billed Gull can indeed be spotted, as well as flocks of waders of the same species as mentioned for the Fangar bay (cf. itinerary 7A). The Garxal area is also interesting for seabirds, and the same species as described in itinerary 7A can be seen here.

7C. Itinerary in the southern part of the Delta: l'Encanyissada, la Tancada and the Banya point

Starting point: Casa de Fusta **End of the itinerary**: the Banya point observatory **Time needed**: one day **Means of transport**: by car

This is by far and away the most complete of the Delta's itineraries and the one that gives you the fullest picture of the Delta's diversity. The southern part of the Delta is also the better conserved, and is better for bird-watching than the northern part.

The itinerary is 25 kms long, and starts at the "Casa de Fusta", a centre where there is a Natural Park information office and a museum with a collection of stuffed birds (cf. other places of interest).

There is an observation tower in front of the house and beside the landing stage on the lagoon. From here you will be able to get a good view of much of the Encanyissada lagoon, the largest lagoon in the Delta. Once you have come down from the observatory, drive east along the tarmac road. In a little over one kilometre you will cross a small bridge over a canal, and soon after you will come to a junction. The road to the right leads to Poble Nou, crossing over the lagoon by means of a small bridge, which is a good place to get a look at the eastern and western reaches of the lagoon. If you keep straight on, you will soon come to Poble Nou village, although it is normally better to drive back from the bridge, and take the road to the right (before, it was the road to the left) when you get back to the junction. Drive on along the left-hand side of the lagoon, skirting the small Roseldo lagoons, until you come to a crossroads where you should turn right. At this point, you will see an area of reeds called El Lluent de la Nòria to your left. It is what remains of the old Embut lagoon. Keep on along the same road and in a little over one kilometre you will come to another crossroads. If you turn right, you would be heading for Poble Nou again; you must therefore turn left to the east, and drive on until you come to the Sant Antoni salt pans and the beach. Almost at the very end

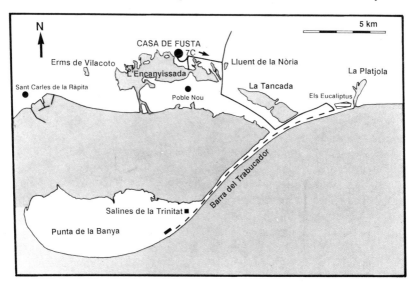

of the tarmac road, another road leads off to the left and skirts the Tancada lagoon (it is a road called "Carretera dels Baladres"). It is worth taking this road to see this region of saltings, rushes and the shores of the lagoon, stopping at regular intervals to scan the area for birds. Once you have had a good look around, drive on to the end of the road in the direction of the "Els Eucaliptus" housing estate. Once you have reached the beach, turn right once again (towards the south) and take the track along the beach that leads along a spit called "Barra del Trabucador" as far as the Banya point (be careful not to turn right into the Trinitat salt pan works, which are closed to the public). After several kilometres you will come to the Banya point observatory, which is the end of the itinerary (you will have covered 11 kms after the housing estate).

Autumn - winter: the itinerary begins at the "Casa de Fusta" centre where it is worth taking a look at the starlings on the roof and in the surrounding trees. Both species should be visible and it is one of the best places for observing Spotless Starling. From the Casa de Fusta observation tower, as well as from the bridge on the Poble Nou road or on the Roseldo lagoons, you should be able to see all the typical lagoon species such as Great Crested Grebe (although at this time of year it is more common out in the bays), Little Grebe, Cormorant (often perched on the posts and markers in the lagoon), surface ducks of several species, but especially Mallard, diving ducks such as Red-crested Pochard or Common Pochard. Also raptors such as Hen Harrier, and the much more abundant Marsh Harrier, as well as Moorhen, Water Rail, and Coot (although this species is quite rare on L'Encanyissada lagoon), Snipe, Black-headed Gull, which roost in their thousands on the lagoon, and Flamingo which come to drink water in winter. Many species of heron are also to be seen, especially in the evening when they come to roost in the lagoon reedbeds. The best places from which to see these species (Cattle Egret, Little Egret, Grey Heron) are: the bridge that crosses the lagoon (because in the western branch of the lagoon, to the right of the bridge, there is a small reed-covered island which is often used as an autumn roost) and El Lluent de la Nòria.

At this time of year you may see, or better still hear, the rather rare Bittern in the area around the bridge. The best way of pinpointing this species is to to be on the alert at dusk, and to listen for the raucous call it makes as it takes off and flies towards its feeding sites. Look out for Cetti's Warbler, Fan-tailed Warbler, Reed Bunting (very common), and the rather rarer Penduline Tit, Bearded Tit, Moustached Warbler and Bluethroat.

From the moment you leave the observation tower of the "Casa de Fusta" until you reach the Sant Antoni salt pans, you will be skirting or crossing through large expanses of paddy fields. The birds you may see in these fields are the same as those described in the paddy fields in itinerary 7A. The best areas are those on the edge of L'Encanyissada lagoon and those near to the salt pans. Once again, in winter be sure to look out for the last flooded fields, for it is here that the birds will be concentrated.

Once you have left the paddy fields behind you, and after crossing a fish hatchery area, you will enter a region of saltings and small lagoons which are the abandoned Sant Antoni salt pans. A great variety of waders can be seen in this area, especially at the end of the winter period, when the lack of water forces the birds to gather in the few flooded areas that remain. The species you may see here are Avocet, plovers, Dunlin, Redshank and godwits; gulls, Sandwich Tern, Little Egret and Grey Heron are also abundant. The Grey Heron is especially common, as it tends to gather in the saltings on the left-hand side of the road during the day.

If, as you are advised to do, you take the road to the left ("Carretera dels Baladres"), you will be seeing the same species more or less, as well as

Moustached Warbler

Flamingo, Cormorant, Great-crested Grebe, Black-necked Grebe, Marsh Harrier and Hen Harrier as well as several species of wildfowl and a large quantity of Coot on La Tancada lagoon. This road, which skirts the estern edge of the lagoon, is one of the best areas in the Delta from which to get a close and comfortable look at the wildfowl and other lagoon species. The area of vegetation-free saltings to the right of the road is also one of the best in the Delta for Lesser Short-toed Lark. If you keep on along the same road, the saltings and rushes on either side might well hold waders and herons.

   Once you have seen this area, follow the instructions given for this itinerary and make your way to the Trabucador spit ("Barra del Trabucador"). It is worth looking out to sea at this point to see if there are any sea ducks. The area in front of the "Els Eucaliptus" housing estate is the best in the Delta for seeing Common Scoter, and Velvet Scoter can also be seen there occasionally.

   The Alfacs bay has very similar birdlife to the Fangar bay described in itinerary 7A, though it is much better for divers, which are regular, if not numerous, and also for grebes, which are very common here. It is a good idea to stop at regular intervals and look out for birds, although the best places to stop are the beginning of the spit, beside the salt pans, where, apart from the typical bay birds, Flamingo, Coot and several species of waders may be seen. It is also a good idea to stop at the point where the spit ends and the Banya point begins to widen out. On the way, keep an eye open on the bay side for small flocks of waders such as Grey Plover, Kentish Plover, Bar-tailed Godwit, Sanderling, Turnstone, and sometimes even Oystercatcher. You should also look out for rarer gulls, for among the commoner species it is relatively easy to see flocks of Slender-billed Gull fishing in the shallow waters of the bay, and the rarer Audouin's Gull.

   At the end of the Trabucador spit, you will come to the Banya point, perhaps one of the most spectacular ornithological sites in Europe. The track passes along the left-hand edge of saltings and the Trinitat salt crystallization pans until you come to the Banya point observatories. Here you should be able to find all kinds of shoreline waders to be seen in the Delta. Avocet is especially abundant at the salt works' deposits, where groups of gulls are also to be seen. Audouin's Gull is common in autumn, although this species's autumn migration is very rapid and after the October-November period, only small flocks are to be seen because only a few of these gulls winter in the Delta.

   In autumn and winter, if you look out over the vast expanse of salt pans to the west and south-west of the observatories, you should see the same species as described earlier, but in greatly superior numbers. It is common, for example, to see flocks of over a thousand Flamingo, thousands of Dunlin, hundreds of Cormorant, and, above all, enormous concentrations of tens of thousands of wildfowl. The most common species of duck is without doubt

Mallard, which is almost the only species of duck that comes close to the observatories. Further afield you should be able to see Wigeon, Teal, Shoveler, Gadwall, Pintail and also Shelduck. Diving ducks are somewhat rarer, but you might well see the odd Red-crested Pochard or Pochard. If you are lucky, this site might also attract flights of Grey Lag Geese which often visit the Delta from their more customary wintering areas. Marsh Harrier frequently fly over the flocks on the pans in search of wounded or weak birds. Peregrine Falcon sometimes visit the area, attracted as well by the abundance of available prey. If you are lucky, you may see the rare Great White Egret or Spoonbill mixed in among the flocks of Grey Heron and Little Egret.

From the observation tower it is also worth looking out to sea for seabirds. The same information as supplied for itinerary 7A at the Fangar point will apply for this area, though the movements of gulls here are normally in a south-westerly direction, in the wake of fishing vessels making their way to Sant Carles de la Ràpita or Alcanar.

Spring - summer: from the same observation tower at the "Casa de Fusta", or from the bridge, you should be able to see many duck, especially Mallard and Red-crested Pochard, as well as Marsh Harrier, Great-crested Grebe, Moorhen and the odd Coot. Water Rail and Little Grebe will be more often heard than seen, unlike Stilts, which will be plentiful, and Avocet that will be present in small numbers. Other common birds will be Purple Heron, which will often be seen flying from their breeding colonies to the feeding grounds in the paddy fields, as well as Little Bittern, which are very common along the edges of the reedbeds. This species is especially easy to hear and see in the months of May and June, when its characteristic squawks can be heard and the male bird carries out his display flights.

Savi's Warbler, Reed Warbler, Reed Bunting, Fan-tailed Warbler, and, with a little bit of luck, Bearded Tit, can all be seen from the observation tower, though maybe the bridge across the lagoon or La Nòria might be better sites from which to see these species. To see Great Reed Warbler, you must watch the denser areas of reedbed from the bridge or at La Nòria. This latter spot is also the best for spotting Moustached Warbler. In all these areas, Cuckoo are very common, and can be seen scouting around for nests of these species to lay their eggs in.

In spring, special mention must be made of the area around La Nòria since this small lagoon has an extraordinary wealth of species, and is very easy to observe from the car. It is without doubt the best area for spotting herons, since a mixed colony with hundreds of pairs (Purple Heron, Squacco Heron, Little Egret, Night Heron, Cattle Egret, Little Egret) is to be found here every spring. All these species can be observed as they leave or arrive at the nest, or while feeding in the surrounding fields. In the last few years, Glossy Ibis has become a regular species at this spot. This area is also good for observing grebes, several species of duck (Mallard, Red-crested Pochard, Gadwall, Shoveler, Garganey, Pochard), Coot, and most of the typical lagoon species. In the nearby irrigated fields to the north, Gull-billed Tern and Pratincole are also a common sight; in summer, when the paddy fields are covered in rice plants, this area of flooded fields is very attractive for many birds (Stilt, Avocet, Kentish Plover, gulls and terns).

In the canals in this area alongside L'Encanyissada lagoon, it is very common to see families of Mallard and Red-crested Pochard (Gadwall are rarer), and it is specially rewarding to see the female birds followed by the ducklings swimming up and down the canals (try not to disturb or frighten the mother birds!). Here too, you will see the typical paddy field species described in itinerary 7A. It must be added that the paddy fields between the last section of L'Encanyissada lagoon and La Nòria are usually full of Black-winged Stilt, herons, terns and the odd Avocet. All these birds come to feed in this area from their nearby breeding grounds.

The Sant Antoni salt pans are a very interesting vantage point for observing waders, gulls and terns during both the migrations. It is a good site, for instance, for Caspian Tern in spring and autumn; Slender-billed Gull are also common here, and in the months of September and October, it is not impossible to see the odd Red-necked Phalarope. The saltings and rushes between the road ("Carretera dels baladres") leading to the housing estate and the sea is also very interesting. It is without doubt, the best area in the Delta for larks: Short-toed Lark are very common in the salicornia, and Lesser Short-toed Lark are common on the sparsely-vegetated saltings, where Crested Lark, Skylark and Blue-headed Wagtail are also to be found. Waders such as Kentish Plover are also numerous, and Pratincole have their major breeding site in Catalonia here. One frequently sees this species flying over the area and even sitting on the road. During migration, you should watch out for migratory passerines in the meadows and in the few trees there are in the zone.

On the nearby La Tancada lagoon you will be able to see a similar variety of birds as on L'Encanyissada. Of special note are the large quantities of Mallard and Red-crested Pochard on the beaches at the north-eastern tip of the lagoon in summer. Osprey may be seen on this lagoon, as they can on L'Encanyissada, especially in the months of March, April and September/October.

In spring and summer the Trabucador spit is disappointing for birdlife and too full of tourists, so you will have to drive on as far as the Banya point, where you will once again find birdlife in abundance. The Banya point is unquestionably the best area on the Delta for gulls and terns. You should be able to see all the Delta's species from the observatories. Audouin's Gull, for example, will often be found on the salt pans and even more frequently flying along the beach; Slender-billed Gull is very commonly found feeding on the salt pans. If you are lucky, you may see Mediterranean Gull, Caspian Tern, and maybe even the rare Lesser Crested Tern, on their way to and from the nearby tern colonies on the islands in front of the observatory. Shelduck should also be around, for although not very numerous, they do breed in this area; there should also be large numbers of Flamingo, Avocet, and, during migration, a wealth of waders. You should also note that, as on the Sant Antoni salt pans, Red-necked Phalarope are regularly seen on passage at this spot as well.

Board and lodging

On the itineraries in the northern part of the Delta, there are plenty of restaurants at L'Ampolla, Deltebre, Riomar housing estate (Urbanització Riomar) and its surrounding area. On the itinerary in the southern part of the Delta, restaurants are to be found at Sant Carles de la Ràpita, Sant Jaume D'Enveja and El Poble Nou. Typical Delta food can be ordered at all these establishments. Hotels are also available at L'Aldea, Amposta, Deltebre, Sant Jaume d'Enveja, and above all, at Sant Carles de la Ràpita.

For those wishing to camp on the Delta, there are two camping sites at Riomar housing estate (L'Aube and Riomar), and there is also one at Els Eucaliptus development (Mediterrani Blau); there are further camping sites at L'Ampolla and at Les Cases d'Alcanar.

Other places of interest

- Tortosa. An important town in the area, it is interesting here to visit the Jewish medieval district, the XIVth century Gothic cathedral (finished in the XVIIth century), and Zuda castle, a pre-Roman settlement and Roman acropolis that was used by the Moors. Tortosa is 17 kms inland from Amposta.

- L'Aldea hermitage. An old XIIth century Islamic farmstead. On the 340 national road, halfway between Amposta and L'Ampolla.

- Montsià Museum, Amposta. A collection based on the archaeology, human traditions and natural history of the area. Open on weekdays from 11 am to 2 pm, and from 3 pm to 8 pm. Closed on Sunday afternoons and Mondays.

- Delta Ecological Museum (Ecomuseu del Delta). A display of the different habitats and traditional human activities in the Delta. There is an aquarium and a terrarium with a collection of the majority of fish and reptile species in the area. There is also an artificial lagoon with different species of birds. Deltebre. Weekdays from 10 am to 2 pm, and from 3 pm to 6 pm. Saturdays from 10 am to 1 pm, and from 3.30 pm to 6 pm. Sundays from 10 am to 1 pm.

- "Casa de Fusta" (Wooden House) Refuge and Museum (L'Encanyissada lagoon). An interesting collection of stuffed local animals, especially birds. Beside L'Encanyissada lagoon (cf. itinerary 7C). In summer from 9 am to 1 pm, and from 3 pm to 8 pm. In winter, from 9 am to 1 pm, and from 3 pm to 6 pm. Closed on Mondays.

- Fish markets. The fish auction can be seen every weekday from 5pm onwards at Sant Carles de la Ràpita and at L'Ametlla de Mar.

8

THE TORTOSA AND BESEIT MOUNTAINS (PORTS DE TORTOSA I BESEIT)

Situated at the extreme southern tip of Catalonia, just to the west of the Ebre Delta, this is a very mountainous and rocky massif, and is the home of the Spanish Ibex. A large part of the area is a National Game Reserve, and there is a project to make the area into a Natural Park.

Surface area: 60,000 hectares.

Habitats: Cliffs and rugged mountain areas, gullies, pine woods, ilex woods, scrub, Mediterranean mountain streams, dry farming.

Interesting species:
- *Present all the year round*: Griffon Vulture, Golden Eagle, Bonelli's Eagle, Peregrine Falcon, Red-legged Partridge, Eagle Owl, Thekla Lark, Crag Martin, Spotless Starling, Chough, Sardinian Warbler, Dartford Warbler, Black Wheatear, Blue Rock Thrush, Rock Sparrow, Rock Bunting.
- *Summer visitors*: Short-toed Eagle, Red-necked Nightjar, Alpine Swift, Bee-eater, Hoopoe, Tawny Pipit, Woodchat Shrike, Melodious Warbler, Orphean Warbler, Subalpine Warbler, Spectacled Warbler, Bonelli's Warbler, Black-eared Wheatear.
- *Winter visitors*: Alpine Accentor, Wallcreeper, Citril Finch.
- *Migratory species*: Honey Buzzard, Black Kite and other raptors.

Description and habitat

The Tortosa and Beseit Mountains (Ports de Tortosa i Beseit) are a very mountainous massif at the extreme southern tip of Catalonia. They form the easternmost part of a system of mountains stretching southwards and westwards into Valencia and Aragon respectively. They are mountains with a Mediterranean climate and a very rugged relief, with a whole series of valleys, gullies, cliffs and rocky pinnacles. The combined effect is breath-taking.

The highest peak is Mont Caro (1,447 metres), but there are many others of about the same height. Many zones of the massif are over the 1,000 metre mark. From Mont Caro, and from other high points on the eastern side of the massif, there is a magnificent view of the mouth of the river Ebre and the lands it has claimed from the sea by the formation of its distinctive delta.

The most characteristic element about the "Ports" massif is the combination of rocky areas with others of lush vegetation. The vegetation is extremely rich. About 1,300 different botanical species have so far been recorded in the area, as well as a good number of endemic ones. The landscape is made up of large tracts of pinaster, Scotch pine and Aleppo pine on the lower slopes. There are also ilex woods in many parts. On the summits of the mountains, the typical low mountain bushes of the Iberian ranges are to be found. On the drier coastal side, the forest has been very much damaged by forest fires, and there are large areas of bushes (scrub, brushwood etc).

The physical and climatological characteristics peculiar to the Ports de Tortosa i Beseit cause there to be botanical species normally associated with more northern latitudes, such as Beech trees, and breeding birds not normally associated with Mediterranean climate coastal zones, such as Wheatear, Nuthatch, Dunnock and Nightjar.

The rugged nature of the Ports also made it possible for the Spanish Ibex to survive in these mountains, although the species did in fact come close to extinction at one stage. The creation of a National Game Reserve in 1966 enabled Ibex numbers to recover, and it is today a common species to be counted in thousands (around the 6,000 mark within the Reserve). The most spectacular gullies are in the innermost precincts of the massif (in the west and north-west). Here, the waters of the rivers are clean, and Dipper and the odd Otter are to be counted among the local fauna. One of the most beautiful valleys is El Parrissal above the village of Beseit; the river Matarranya flows down this valley. Other mammals that are to be found here are rabbit, hare, red squirrel, fox, badger, marten, genet, wild cat, wild boar and Mouflon. This latter species was introduced into the area a few years ago, but it has not extended its range and population. Only a few of these animals are to be found at the head of La Galera gully and its surrounding area.

There used to be *masies* (farmsteads) with single-family arable and livestock farming in the Ports area. Nowadays, what farms there are in the massif area are all derelict, and crops are only grown on the lower slopes, and around the villages. The dryness of the climate means that olive and almond groves predominate, and fruit orchards and market gardens are limited to the area nearest the river Ebre and its Delta. The vast olive groves on the plain between the Ports area and the coast are particularly impressive, being a wintering area for large quantities of birds such as Song Thrush, warblers, larks and finches.

The predominant birds in the Ports are the rupicoline species, especially the raptors. Golden Eagle and Peregrine Falcon are very common, and Griffon Vulture and Bonelli's Eable also nest here. Egyptian Vulture became extinct in the area but it is possible that it will soon come back to breed again. Blue Rock Thrush, Chough, and, in winter, Wallcreeper and Alpine Accentor are other inhabitants of the massif's cliffs.

How to visit the area

To reach the Ports area, you must first pass through Tortosa. If coming from Barcelona along the A-7 motorway or along the 340 national road, you should turn off on the Tortosa road when you reach L'Aldea. You may also reach Tortosa by train (from Sants Station in Barcelona) and by bus (Hife Company, c/ Numància, 162, Barcelona).

Once you get to Tortosa, do not cross the town. Cross the bridge you will find before entering the town. This bridge will lead you to the 230 local road (carretera comarcal 230) towards Gandesa and Móra d'Ebre. To follow itinerary 8A, you should turn left to Roquetes soon after taking the Gandesa road. Roquetes is a village right next to Tortosa. In the centre of Roquetes, take a road off to the left of the main road, which is signposted to La Sènia and Mas de Barberans (16 kms away). Mas de Barberans is a small village where the itinerary starts. To follow itinerary 8B, follow the 230 local road (carretera comarcal 230) to Xerta, a small village where you should look for the road that leads to Paüls.

You may reach both Paüls and Mas de Barberans by bus from Tortosa (Hife Company, adjoining the railway station).

Itinerary 8A consists of following 17.5 kms of forest track, and is to be carried out by car, stopping off at areas that provide interesting birdwatching. The time taken at each stop will be the factor that decides how long the itinerary is to take, although it should be about 4 hours, without taking the return journey into consideration. Itinerary 8B may be undertaken on foot and, at a bird-watcher's gait, should take about 5 or 6 hours. If you do not have much time, but wish to get a general idea of the massif's characteristics and to see as wide a range of birds as possible, you are advised to follow itinerary 8A and part of 8B. Begin this latter itinerary from the point 8A comes to an end (according to these instructions), covering as much ground as possible in the time you have available.

The track you are to follow on itinerary 8A is no motorway, but you will be able to drive along it without any problem at least as far as observation point number 4 (cf. itinerary 8A). After this point you may choose to proceed on foot for the remaining 4.5 kms according to the kind of vehicle you are in and the prevailing weather conditions.

Itinerary 8B is mainly on tracks and so comfortable walking shoes should suffice, although the rocky nature of the ground and the climb up to the Coll d'en Roger (Roger's Pass) along a small steep and stony path call for thick,

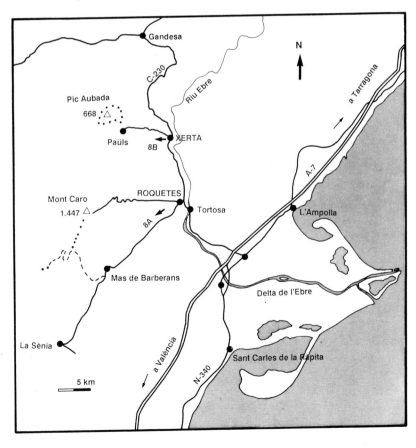

non-slip soles. The length of the itinerary makes it advisable to take a lttle food and drink, since there are no fountains along the way. The first sector, as far as the Coll d'en Roger, is the only steep part of the itinerary and the climb may prove tiring. From this point onwards, however, the itinerary proceeds along a track that descends gently to the end without any difficulties.

Apart from the two itineraries decribed here, it is also worth driving up Mont Caro if you have the time. It is the highest point in the massif. Take the tarmac road that leads up to the television repeater station from Roquetes. On clear days the view is truly magnificent and interesting birds are also to be seen!

The Ports massif may be visited at all times of year, for the birdwatching is always interesting, with raptors and a wealth of small wintering birds, as well as the rich Mediterranean area birdlife present there in the breeding season. The weather is mild throughout the year, although there may be windy days in autumn, making birdwatching a litle difficult. If your visit is in spring, and even more so in summer, you are advised to start off early in the morning when birds are most active. The midday heat greatly reduces the activity of the birds. Early morning and evening hours are also the best for watching Spanish Ibex.

Birdwatching

8A. Itinerary in the Galera gully

Starting point and end of the itinerary: Roquetes **Time needed**: 4-5 hours **Means of transport**: by car and on foot

If you are coming from Roquetes, you will arrive at the small village of Mas de Barberans at the foot of the massif. It commands a view over a large plain covered in olive groves that are also excellent for birdwatching. In Mas de Barberans, as in all the villages in the region, Swallow, House Martin, Swift, House Sparrow, Hoopoe and Spotless Starling (on rooftops) are all very common. Drive through the village towards La Sènia, and after 2.5 kilometres, between Km 13 and 14 of the road, you will find a track leading off to the right. There is a sign of "dangerous bends for 1 km" right beside this turning which should help you to find it.

Once you are on the track, and before driving up into the massif area, you may choose to stop and stroll among the olive groves (this stop, and all other stops on this itinerary, is clearly marked on the map). In fact, any path leading through the crops on this plain will reveal birds, which use the olive groves to breed in as if they were areas of sparse woodland: Hoopoe, Turtle Dove, Wheatear, Crested Lark, Woodchat Shrike, Short-toed Treecreeper, Sardinian Warbler, Orphean Warbler, Serin and Cirl Bunting. Bee-eater may also be seen and Wryneck heard. In autumn and winter, the number of passerines increases sharply, as is often the case in Mediterranean countries. Warblers, Song Thrush, larks and finches are very common, feeding on the nutritious olives. Recent agricultural techniques, however, have almost totally eliminated the presence of grasses in the olive groves, thus making this habitat less attractive for birds feeding on insects and small seeds. The plain that lies between the Ports massif and the sea is also a very good area for observing large migratory birds, such as raptors (Honey Buzzard, Black Kite, Marsh Harrier etc.), both species of stork and Crane.

Once you set out along the track that leads to La Galera gully, and after crossing a short stretch of olive groves, you will notice that the crops are progressively becoming restricted to the valley bottom. The higher slopes hold abandoned terraces, and are covered in bushes and odd Aleppo pines. It is in these zones of sparse scrub and recently burnt areas that Tawny Pipit breed. About 1 kilometre along the track, you will find a junction. Follow the left-hand track, and after a further kilometre, the track crosses over the river and divides into two smaller tracks. Take the right-hand one which goes into the **Galera gully** (Barranc de la Galera) itself, following along the water course on its left-hand bank. Soon the gully will become very narrow, and two kilometres after the last turning, in an area where the gully's cliff-face is quite close (especially on the right), you may choose to stop again (there is a place to leave the car). Griffon Vulture, Peregrine Falcon, Kestrel, Rock Dove and Chough can all be seen here, as well as Sardinian Warbler and Dartford Warbler in the scrub on either side of the gully. Blue Rock Thrush and Black Redstart are also common on the rocky parts of the gully, and in winter it is also possible to see Wallcreeper, quite a common species on the massif at that time of year, although quite difficult to spot.

The track continues on up the gorge, with cliffs on either side. The vegetation is made up of thick Kermes oak, ling, lentisk and box scrub, with odd ilex trees, and, further up the slopes, Scotch pines. Over the course of the whole itinerary, you should keep scanning the slopes with your binoculars, as you may well spot Spanish Ibex among the vegetation or on the rocky crags. Crag Martin are very common on the cliffs, and Alpine Swift can also be seen there. After about 5 kms, the track crosses over the river and continues on up the gully on its right-hand bank. The valley sides now have more trees, with clumps of Scotch pine here and there, and more extensive tracts of Aleppo pine. Several tracks and paths will break off to the left, but you should follow the main track at all times. Keep an eye out in areas where visibility permits, because it is possible to catch a glimpse of Golden Eagle flying above. You may also put up flights of Red-legged Partridge at any point on the itinerary.

After passing a track leading to the right that normally has a chain barring the way, you will once again cross the river over a small bridge, and

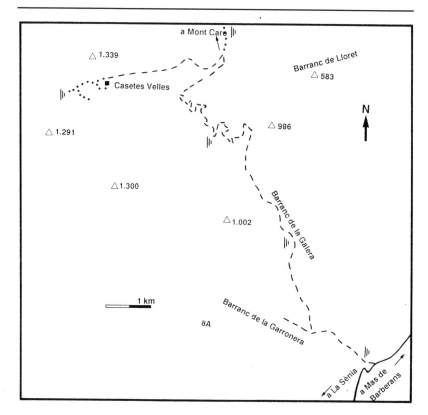

then the track will wind its way up through a mixed ilex and pine wood. It is worth stopping on one of the bends with good visibility; maybe the one marked on the map is the most suitable. It may be recognized by the fact that there is a place to leave your car and a track leading off to the left just after it. From this point you will get a marvellous view of the valley and the mountain ranges about you. The chances are you will spot birds of prey such as Griffon Vulture, Golden Eagle, Short-toed Eagle, Peregrine Falcon and Kestrel. You will be able to see that a large portion of the valley is covered in low vegetation, and is recovering from a forest fire that burnt most of the eastern slopes of the massif in 1983.

Four kilometres further on along the track you will come to a bend, where another track in very bad condition leads off to the right. This point may also be recognized by the fact that there is a white and red sign painted on a rock. Leave the car here and follow the track adjoins a meadow, skirts a wood and leads to the head of a gully 300 metres further on. This gully is called **Barranc de Lloret** (Lloret Gully). If you scan the large rocky areas before you, it is often possible to spot Mountain Goats from this observation point. The Mont Caro, highest point in the massif, can be seen in the distance to the north-west. It is easy to recognize because of the TV aerials on its summit. On a clear day, you will also get a good view of the Ebre river and a large part of its delta. Among other birds, you may see Wood Pigeon, Jay, Raven and Chough in this region.

If you wish to carry on walking, you may choose to take the small path leading off to the left at the point where the first track comes to an end. The path crosses woods and passes above the spectacular gullies in the eastern part of the massif. Eventually you will come to Mont Caro.

On your return to the car, drive on along the track, although its condition worsens somewhat and some stretches become quite bad. If need be, you may continue on foot, although there are still 4.5 kms before you come to the end of the itinerary. After 3 kms you will come to an area known as **Casetes Velles**. It is a flat piece of land that was formerly cultivated and now consists of meadows with trees here and there. There are also a few chalets. On the right of the track there are rocky areas with scattered box and juniper bushes, where Alpine Accentor are to be seen in winter. This area is one of the best in the whole massif for spotting Mouflon. There are also forested areas with Scotch and stone pine. Soon after passing the last house, after a bend, the track is usually impassable because there is a very muddy sector. You should therefore leave your car and continue on foot for the last kilometre or so, until you come to the end of the track, from where you will get a view of the interior part of the massif. If you take a walk through this final zone, you should come across Green Woodpecker, Nuthatch, Short-toed Treecreeper, Firecrest (in winter Goldcrest are also to be found here), Crested Tit, Coal Tit, Mistle Thrush, Crossbill etc.. Dartford Warbler will be found in bushy areas; and in the meadows, Dunnock, Stonechat, Black Redstart, Melodious Warbler, Garden Warbler, Rock Bunting, Cirl Bunting as well as Meadow Pipit and sometimes Siskin in winter. Raptors such as Griffon Vulture, Golden Eagle, Goshawk, Sparrowhawk, Peregrine Falcon and Kestrel can also be seen. In autumn, there is a heavy passage of thrushes, among which the presence of migratory Ring Ouzel is particularly interesting.

The return journey is along the same track you came on. You have a 17.5 km drive back to the itinerary starting off point. If you are making your way back in the evening, Tawny Owl and Eagle Owl may be heard, and you might see or hear Little Owl, Barn Owl and Red-necked Nightjar in the lower parts of the valley or in the olive groves.

Griffon Vulture

8B. Itinerary in the Bages valley gully

Starting point and end of the itinerary: Xerta **Time needed**: 5-6 hours **Means of transport**: by car and on foot **Observations**: wear thick-soled sports shoes. Take drink

Shortly after leaving the village of Xerta, on km 30 of the local 230 road (carretera comarcal 230), you must take a road on your left leading to **Paüls**, ten kilometres from the turning. You will start driving through market gardens and orange orchards, but soon dry farming areas with carob trees and olive groves will become predominant. The road soon enters a valley called **Barranc de les Fonts**, and first proceeds along the left-hand bank of the river, and later on the right-hand side. It climbs through sparse Aleppo pine woods, Rosemary and palmetto scrub, as well as old abandoned farmlands. Farming is only kept up on the valley floor, near the river, where you may come across the beautiful Golden Oriole in spring. As you climb up, you will become aware of some mountains to your left, where it is possible to see Golden Eagle.

About 2 kms before you come to Paüls, right beside the road on the right-hand side, there is a small cliff. This is a good spot for observing Blue Rock Thrush and Rock Sparrow, as well as Crag Martin and Alpine Swift.

Shortly after, you will cross a small bridge and Paüls will come into view. Then, just before crossing another bridge, about 1.5 kms from the village, you will come across a crossroads with a tarmac road and a track leading off from the same point to the left. Here you should leave the car and continue on foot. Now you take the track, though you will later be coming back along the road. Remember that if you do not have a great deal of time to do the itinerary, it is advisable to start off along the tarmac road first, since this will eliminate the climb up to the Roger pass (Coll d'en Roger), and will enable you to have an easier birdwatching walk through farmland and, if you get far enough, through scrub and pinewoods too.

If you wish to follow the full itinerary, though, take the track through an area of agricultural lands composed basically of olive groves and carob trees. These cultivated zones are interesting all the year round, for in summer Woodchat Shrike, Turtle Dove, Red-legged Partridge, Bee-eater, Wryneck, Short-toed Treecreeper, Sardinian Warbler, Mistle Thrush, Crested Lark, Wood Lark, Black-eared Wheatear, Spotted Flycatcher, Serin, Greenfinch and Goldfinch are all common, and in autumn and summer Blackcap, thrushes, Skylark and flocks of finches (Chaffinch, Linnet etc.) also abound.

Keep straight on along the path, which after about 1 km (soon after passing a farmhouse) will turn to the right and enter the gully you are to climb up, thus leaving to one side the main gully, which continues straight on and is crowned by high and rugged mountains. Soon you will come to a wide path

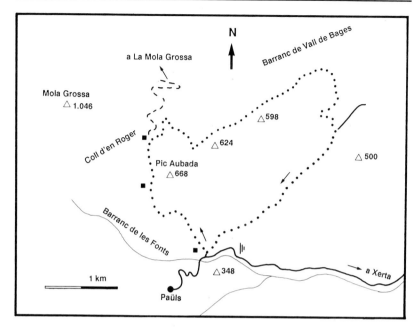

turning off to the right, at an acute angle, but do not take it. Afterwards, you will come across several tractor lanes that alternately split off to the left and to the right, but keep on walking up the main path, which is more worn and follows along the right-hand side of the gully. There will be several scattered farms to your left set among olive groves. Here you may observe Blue Tit, Cirl Bunting and Rock Bunting all the year round. If you keep an eye on the higher ground, you may well see the odd raptor such as Kestrel or Short-toed Eagle.

In front of you will be the gully with the rocky and pointed Aubada peak to the right and a range of crags to the left. In the background, the forested range slopes down to the Roger pass, the point you are headed for. The track will have been becoming narrower and narrower as you climb, until disappearing at the last farm you come to. Behind this *mas* (farmhouse) there is a threshing floor and a huge unmistakable Ilex tree. Besides the last cultivated area, at the very point where the path dies out, you must look for a small path, that may only be followed on foot. It breaks off to the right and climbs up amongst scrub, clumps of trees and abandoned fields. This rocky path ascends the left-hand side of the gully, and, towards the end, crosses over to the right by means of some old terraces (be careful here for the path is not very clearly marked), leading finally to the Roger pass, where you will arrive approximately two hours after having left the car.

Once you are on the pass, you should climb to the left until you come to a track. You will see almond trees all around, and a farm nearby. Take this track, which in not is very good condition as it is not much used, in a north-easterly direction, that is to say, away from the *mas*, and cross over the pass, entering the zone of ilex and pine woods. From the pass itself, it should not be difficult to see flights of dozens, maybe even a hundred Chough, as well as Raven and Golden Eagle. Smaller birds such as Rock Bunting, and in winter, Meadow Pipit, should also be visible.

Once you enter the wood, this narrow track soon runs into another much wider track (on a bend). Turn right and descend along this wider track. You are now in the Bages Valley, which is very closed in, having rocky cliffs on the higher parts and the odd *mas* and cultivated land along the valley bottom. On the south-facing slopes, the vegetation is not very dense, with odd clumps of Scotch pine. On the north-facing slopes, there is a young Aleppo pine wood, with plenty of clearings and quite a rich undergrowth, allowing you to observe birds such as tits (Crested, Long-tailed, Great and Coal), Firecrest, Short-toed Treecreeper, Subalpine Warbler, as well as Wood Pigeon, Green Woodpecker, Crossbill, and, in the breeding season, the common Bonelli's Warbler.

Follow on along this track, which descends along the right-hand side of the valley. You will come across several paths to the right and even more to the left, but do not leave the main track. Remember to keep looking at the mountain tops where Raven and raptors such as Kestrel, Peregrine Falcon, Sparrow-hawk, Short-toed Eagle, and, especially on the lower reaches of the valley, Bonelli's Eagle, are all to be seen. Shortly before leaving the Bages Valley, you will come to another turning that is more important-looking than the others, but keep on to the right, where you will soon come to the tarmac road. The pines now give way to scrub and the odd cultivated field. Subalpine Warbler will be found here in summer, Sardinian Warbler and Dartford Warbler all the year round, and in winter, Dunnock and finches such as Serin, Goldinch, Green-finch and Chaffinch are all very common.

A little farther on, you will come to another tarmac road to your left, but you should follow the tarmac road to the right. It will pass through agricultural land, mainly olive groves, Carob and almond trees, with the odd fruit orchard, leading you back to the place where you left the car. On this last section of road, you will once again come into contact with the birds associated with agricultural land that were described at the beginning of this itinerary.

If yu have not come across Orphean Warbler at any stage of the itinerary, you may try to spot it in the orchards and olive groves in the vicinity of Xerta, since this species, along with Melodious Warbler, prefers the lower areas to the central part of the massif.

Board and Lodging

Tortosa is a town near the itinerary route, and is big enough to guarantee a wide range of hotels and restaurants, among which the following may be recommended for meals: "El Recó de Mig Camí", the "Parador Nacional de la Zuda" and the Berenguer IV hotel. The latter two establishments are also recommended for lodging. In the villages, the following are recommended: "Hostal dels Alls" at L'Aldea, Hotel Montsià, Hotel Bajo Ebro in Amposta, and , a little further afield, in Sant Carles de la Ràpita, there are plenty of places to eat and sleep, although you must remember that coastal towns receive a flood of tourists in summer.

There are many camping sites, but all are situated in coastal towns: L'Ampolla, Sant Carles de la Ràpita and Alcanar.

As regards the small villages near the itineraries themselves, you may dine at Paüls and Mas de Barberans (Mario Restaurant), but there are no places to sleep there.

Other places of interest

- Tortosa (cf. page 133).

- Ulldecona. A medieval village with a beautiful square, surrounded by arches, and a Gothic church. It is 30 km south of Tarragona, almost on the border with the País Valencià (Valencia).

- Cave paintings in the vicinity of the Pietat hermitage and the Iberian settlement of Ferradura. These are two of the outstanding sites in this area of great archaeological interest. You should ask the way in the village of Ulldecona.

- Santa Maria de Benifassar monastery. Romanesque style (XIIIth century), it is at present the only enclosed Carthusian monastery in the whole of the Spanish State. It is near La Pobla de Benifassar, 52 kms south of Tortosa, in the province of Castelló, and can be reached by driving along the Mas de Barberans and La Sènia road.

- Vall-de-roures. Ancient village with a beautiful Gothic church and an XIth century Castle-cum-mansion of Moorish origin. It is in the province of Terol. You can reach it on the road that skirts the inland part of the Ports massif and which starts 12 kms north of Xerta.

- Beseit. A beautiful little village with a Romanesque bridge and cave paintings. There is a spectacular gully on the Matarranya river (known as "Gúbies del Parrissal"). It is in Terol province, 7 kms south of Vall-de-roures.

9

LLEIDA STEPPES

Large inland plains between 150 and 400 metres in height in the Catalan part of the Ebre Depression. It is the only area in Catalonia where the environmental conditions permit the birdlife associated with the Steppe habitat.
In 1987, a **Partial Nature Reserve** was created in the area and another one is planned.

Habitats: cereal crops, fallow land, barren and salt-affected lands, calcicole scrub, degraded ilex woods and riverside thickets.

Interesting species:
- *Present all the year round*: Peregrine Falcon, Red-legged Partridge, Pin-tailed Sandgrouse, Black-bellied Sandgrouse, Lesser Short-toed Lark, Calandra Lark, Thekla's Lark, Crested Lark, Sardinian Warbler, Black Wheatear, Blue Rock Thrush, Spotless Starling, Rock Sparrow.
- *Summer visitors*: White Stork*, Egyptian Vulture, Hobby, Lesser Kestrel, Little Bustard*, Stone Curlew*, Great Spotted Cuckoo, Scop's Owl, Red-necked Nightjar, Alpine Swift, Bee-eater, Roller, Hoopoe*, Short-toed Lark, Woodchat Shrike, Lesser Grey Shrike, Golden Oriole, Subalpine Warbler, Black-eared Wheatear, Penduline Tit*.
- *Winter visitors*: Merlin, Rock Bunting.
- *Migratory species*: Montagu's Harrier, Marsh Harrier.

*: individuals of these species are also present, in small numbers, in winter.

Description and habitat

The Lleida steppes are a habitat that has partly resulted from the degradation of scrub and continental Mediterranean maquis, and which can occasionally even be ascribed to the degradation of ilex woodland. Human activity, as well as the severe climate, the lack of rainfall and the regular presence of salty and chalky soils, are factors that all lead to the formation of open country, where grasses and scrub are predominant.

These large inland plains were formerly winter pastures for sheep and lands set aside for grain crops. There were also less extensive areas of vineyards, almond and olive groves. Low productivity and the lack of mechanization meant non-intensive farming methods, giving rise to a mosaic-like scenery, in which crops and fallow lands were interspersed with much barren land of various kinds.

At present, the steppe-like dry lands of Catalonia are only to be found in those areas of the Ebre Depression where no irrigation is available. Large areas of these steppes have been affected by a more intensive form of farming, however, made possible by the use of herbicides, chemical fertilizers and agricultural machinery.

In the itineraries described for the Lleida steppes and part of the Aragonese ones that are crossed by itinerary 9B, different kinds of scenery can be seen; from those that still conserve a lot of barren and fallow lands (itineraries 9A and 9B), to those where agricultural methods have now become much more intensified (itineraries 9C and 9D). Calcicole scrub and small patches of degraded ilex woodland are also encountered, as well as the odd riverside wood where species associated with this kind of habitat may be seen.

The **grain-producing steppe** consists of large plains where cereal farming is predominant, areas that have almost totally lost their original plantlife due to the action of herbicides. Barley is the basic crop here, and there are only occasional trees (generally almond) between the fields.

The grain-producing steppe has little variety and density of birdlife, especially from July to November, when vegetation cover is almost totally lacking. The highest density of birds coincides with period when the grain crops offer most cover (spring). At this time, some Euro-Asian grassland species such as Calandra Lark, Quail and, locally, Little Bustard, are to be found in good numbers.

The cereal fields undergo a series of transformations throughout the year. The "llaurat" or **tilled field**, when the soil is ploughed and ready for sewing. The field is called "sembrat" or **sown field** from the moment the seed is sown until the harvest. Lastly, the "rostoll" or **stubble** is what is left after the harvest, when only the stem base remains. A field of stubble or a ploughed field that are not sown in autumn become "guarets" or fallow fields.

The **fallow fields** are normally cereal plots that are left uncultivated for a year or more. Nowadays these fallow plots are still a regular feature in the south of Lleida and in the Aragonese "Monegros" region (cf. itineraries 9A and 9B). In the old days, they occupied very much larger areas, since only about half of the available land was actually cultivated. The more primitive form of agriculture that was practised in the past left large fallow zones. This was a necessary practice both as a period of recovery for the soil, as well as a way of ridding the land of weeds, which were eliminated by ploughing the field once or twice in the year sowing was to take place.

Fallow fields are also used as pastures in winter and spring. Their presence leads to the increase in the variety of species in an area, since they are a suitable habitat for the species that are adapted to barren lands and regions without much plant cover.

Barren or saline lands are uncultivated areas that are only used as pasture land. They normally have bushes and to a lesser extent, wide esparto grass or greybeard meadows. The flora of these meadows depends to a large extent on the soil, with an avifauna that one would normally associated with semideserts or places which lack vegetation. The sandgrouse and several of the larks clearly identify with this form of habitat. One particular form of barren land in the area is the **saline steppes** (Catalan: "salades"), which have a kind of vegetation to be found in shallow depressions and on ground with high chloride content only allowing halophytic plants (those which can stand high salinity levels) to survive.

In these barren lands there are also zones of **low bush** (in Catalan, "timonedes") which have very little vegetation cover, and are often associated with old fluvial terraces. Many of the plants on the "timonedes" are aromatic, and thyme predominates, thereby giving its name ("timoneda" in Lleida Catalan) to the habitat.

The **calcicole scrub** habitat is associated with basic soils and is normally to be found on rocky and rugged ground that has not been tilled. At the beginning of itinerary 9A there is a good example of this kind of habitat. It is difficult to make your way through this vegetation, which is thicker than on the "timonedes" and the barren lands, for you will come across plenty of prickly plants such as kermes oak and a species of buckthorn (*Rhamnus lycioides*) that normally grow alongside rosemary, which is the most characteristic species in the calcicole scrub habitat. The birds associated with this habitat are the scrub warblers, although plenty of other species are to be found. Their presence will very much depend on the existence of trees and vegetation-free crags in the vicinity.

Ilex woods are only to be found in the northernmost part of the Catalan Ebre Depression. The copses crowning the Serra Llarga (to be visited at the end of itinerary 9C) are what remains of the old ilex and Lusitanian Oak woods.

They are degraded ilex (subspecies *Rotundifolia*) woods and have a poorer growth than the typical Mediterranean ilex wood. Occasionally these woods are more like scrubland.

The **riverside woods** are to be found alongside water courses that run through these dry lands and are principally made up of poplar trees, elms and alders. Although these itineraries were initially designed to show visitors areas of steppe, riverside woodland may also be studied along the river Set, a small water course on itinerary 9A, as well as the rivers Cinca and Alcanadre, that are followed on large stretches of itinerary 9B.

Most of the roads joining up the different itinerary starting points pass through **irrigated farmland**, with abundant orchards and forage crops. In winter, Lapwing and finches (especially Chaffinch) are very common in these habitats. Several species of thrush, particularly Mistle Thrush, and Blackbird, are also very common here.

How to visit the area.

If you are coming from the Ebre Delta or from the Ports de Beseit, and wish to visit the Lleida steppe area, you must drive through Gandesa, Ascó and Flix. Follow the 233 local road (carretera comarcal 233) to Bovera, La Granadella, El Soleràs, and, finally, Albagés. The first itinerary (9A) begins at this latter town. If you are coming from other parts of Catalonia, you may also reach the Lleida steppes area by way of the A-2 motorway which goes from Barcelona to Zaragoza. Leave the motorway at the Les Borges Blanques and Mollerussa exit. Soon after the toll, the exit road becomes the 233 local road (carretera comarcal 233) which you should take to the left towards Castelldans and Albagés.

As against the itineraries in other regions, the Lleida steppe itineraries do not all start off from the same point, but follow on one from the other. Itinerary 9A, which starts off in Albagés, ends up at Artesa de Lleida. If you have carried out this itinerary in the evening, you may choose to wait in Artesa de Lleida until dusk. This will be the ideal moment to turn back on our tracks to watch the evening activity of Calandra Lark and Little Bustard, as well to hear the call of Stone Curlew and Red-necked Nightjar. From Artesa de Lleida you will take a local road to Lleida, a city where there are lots of hotels for night-stopping. On the itineraries you will also pass plenty of village bars where you will be able to get a snack, and maybe even find a bed.

To start itinerary 9B, you must take national road 2 (Carretera Nacional 2) towards Madrid and Saragossa. After **9 kms** you will come to Alcarràs, a village where you will be able to see the Stork's nest on the church tower. This village was the site of one of the last Lesser Kestrel colonies in Catalonia. You will come to Fraga **26 kms** further along the N-2 road, in the direction of Zaragoza. This town also has a Stork's nest, although not on the church tower as at Alcarràs. Here, the nest is on a civil building. After **36 kms**, following a long climb, you will come to the Aragonese Monegros plains. From this point on (although you are not yet on itinerary 9B), it is worth stopping occasionally to scan the surrounding area. It may well provide the odd surprise such as a flight of sandgrouse on its way to or from a drinking site. After **55 kms**, you will come to the village of Candasnos, where the itinerary starts. There are several restaurants and small hotels in Candasnos. This itinerary, which finishes in Fraga, will enable you to get a good idea of the Ebre Depression scenery. Here, farmland alternates with areas of fallow and barren lands. The second half of this itinerary passes through an interesting river valley and villages with White Stork nests. The farmland is less interesting from the point of view of sighting steppe-loving birds. From Fraga, you may care to return to Lleida along the N-2 national road on which you came to the area.

In Lleida you can visit the new cathedral, a building which has 1,200 House Martin nests on it. There are several hundred further nests on nearby buildings. The rare Wallcreeper is sometimes seen on the old Cathedral (cf.

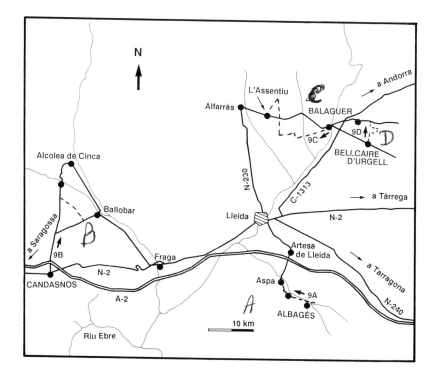

other places of interest) in winter, while Blue Rock Thrush and Black Redstart, as well as other interesting Medieterranean species such as Sardinian Warbler and Serin, are also to be seen there throughout the year.

The other two itineraries are to the north of Lleida in zones of cereal farmland, although some areas of chalky barren land and a few patches of degraded ilex woodland may also be visited. Both itineraries can easily be covered in one day. Itinerary 9D is complementary to itinerary 9C, but Little Bustard can be more easily seen. Both these itineraries are on tracks and it is not a good idea tó go on them in very wet periods (which are infrequent) since you may well get bogged down on some stretches.

You must go to Balaguer along the Corbins road to find the starting points of these two itineraries. This road is quieter than the 1313 local road (carretera comarcal 1313) which also leads to Balaguer, and subsequently goes on to Andorra. The Corbins road will not only enable you to get more out of the scenery, but will also allow you to stop and birdwatch with greater ease. It starts off at Lleida, leading off from Príncep de Viana street, near the station. You must take care at the junction on the way out of Lleida, and take the right-hand turning to Corbins. (The left-hand turning heads for Torreserona). At Corbins there is a stork's nest on the church tower. The inhabitants of Corbins look after this nest, and replaced it after repair work on the tower in 1986. Continuing along the road towards Balaguer, you will cross the river Noguera Ribagorçana, which used to have one of the finest riverside woodland areas in Catalonia, until a hydroelectric company destroyed the vegetation in 1988. Soon after you will pass by Torrelameu, and 4 kms later you will come to Menàrguens. In **Menàrguens** you will also find a stork's nest on the church tower. You will get a better view of the nest if you climb up a hillock there is behind the church. You will find your way to the hillock (on foot) by way of a narrow street leading off from the village square. This is also a good spot for distinguishing between the two species of starling, which both breed under the church eaves.

From Menarguens you must head for Balaguer. Soon after the first houses in the village, you should take the turning to Alfarràs which you will find on a bend. If you wish to go to the city centre, take the road to the right. If, on the other hand, you want to drive straight on to itinerary 9C, you must turn left on to the Alfarràs road. Itinerary 9C ends up at the village of Algerri, from where you must take the C 149 road (joining Alfarràs and Balaguer), back to Balaguer. Balaguer also has a stork's nest, as well as a Sand Martin colony within the city itself. They nest in holes in the partition material of a stone wall. The colony is to be found beside the Alfarràs-Balaguer road at the very point where it joins the riverside avenue (whether you are coming from Alfarràs or going in that direction).

To get to the starting point of itinerary 9D, you must cross the river Segre in Balaguer on the northernmost of the two bridges, on road C 148, and head towards Tàrrega and Barcelona. After about 8 kms, you will come to Bellcaire, the point at which itinerary 9D starts. This itinerary finishes on the Agramunt-Balaguer road, not far from the village of Assentiu. You must turn left on this road if you wish to return to Balaguer.

Two days is the shortest period of time you will need to cover the four steppe birdwatching itineraries: half a day for each itinerary. But it is better to spend at least two and a half days, or more, if you wish to visit any of the villages or towns along the way, especially in autumn and winter. You should distribute your time as follows: half a day for itinerary 9A; one whole morning, which can be extended to a full day, for the itinerary in the western part of the Aragonese Monegros area (itinerary 9B), and a full day for itineraries 9C and 9D. It is better to go on itinerary 9C in the early morning because most of the walking is done towards the west, and you will have the sun at your back. If you start out in the afternoon, the chances are you may get lost when it gets dark. If you do not have enough time for all four, you should choose the itineraries which cover the species you are most interested in. It will probably be best to combine one of the first two itineraries with one of the other two.

All four itineraries may be covered by car. You are however advised to stop off now and then (at places that are not specially recommended stopping places), and to take a walk in the surrounding area, above all in areas where habitats overlap. Remember to check your petrol and your spare tyre before driving into these dry areas. You are also advised not to dawdle in these drier areas at midday because the heat will be suffocating and the fauna will be very idle. The best time of year for these itineraries in the Catalan steppe areas is from April to June. In this way you can avoid the summer heat as well as the cold and fog of winter. Nevertheless, any time of the year is perfect for observing the beauty of this area.

Birdwatching

9A. Itinerary in the dry farming areas south of Lleida

Starting point: Albagés **End of the itinerary**: Artesa de Lleida **Time needed**: half a day **Means of transport**: by car and on foot (optional) **Observations**: best in the afternoon

The starting point on this itinerary is in the village of Albagés, at the Borges Blanques main road and Juncosa road crossroads. Take the Borges Blanques road, and after **2 kms**, you should take a track to the left (on a bend) which has a small signpost indicating the way to Cogul. The first part of the track leads through rugged country with slopes which are quite steep. This habitat is ideal for Red-legged Partridge, Sardinian Warbler, and, more locally, Rock Sparrow. Blue Rock Thrush can be found on the rockier ground. In the breeding season Bee-eater and Black-eared Wheatear are also common. A few pairs of Dartford Warbler breed in the area, becoming a good deal commoner in winter.

To the left of the track is the river Set, with riverside vegetation along its banks. At odd points where the river flows more slowly, there are larger patches of reeds where the boisterous Great Reed Warbler can be heard from May to July. In the clumps of riverside trees growing in the damper parts of the valley, you may see the shy Golden Oriole, if you are patient enough, as well as Turtle Dove and Melodious Warbler. On spring evenings you should also be able to locate Scop's Owl in the trees by listening out for their monotonous and repetitive call, although it will be hard to see this species.

At **km 6.5** of the itinerary, just after one of the lusher patches of riverside woodland, you will come to the site of the Cogul cave paintings (cf. other places of interest). You can also take advantage of this stop to inspect the clump of trees on one side of the track (which from now on will be tarmac), and the rocky slopes on the other side. Five hundred metres further on you must leave a track signposted to Castelldans to your right, and soon after, at **km 7.5**, you come to a crossroads with three possible roads to be taken. The turning to the left is the way into the village of Cogul; the central road is a track leading to Granyena and Alcanó, and the turning to the right, which is the one you should follow, is a tarmac road leading to Aspa. All the way along this route you will be coming across small stone constructions, some of which are in ruins. They are used as night-time shelters for sheep. The numerous holes in the stone walls are good breeding sites for species such as Hoopoe, Stock Dove, Jackdaw and Little Owl, the characteristic outline of which may be frequently spotted in full daylight perched on mounds or poles. Both species of starling can also be spotted in this area, since it is the point where their distributions overlap. In the breeding season, the Spotless Starling is commoner, but in winter, with the arrival of large numbers of birds from central and northern Europe, the Starling is more common.

After **11 kms** you will come to Aspa. At the entrance to the village, the road forks. Take the left-hand turning, and will soon be out of the village, winding your way down a steep road that leads to a small stream with riverside trees where all the typical species associated with this habitat are to be found. Soon after you will pass to one side of another track, leading to Castelldans, and a little further on, the road will begin to climb up. As you climb, the scenery will open up, and at **km 12.5**, you will come out on to a plain. It is a mosaic made up of cereal fields, fallow fields, barren areas and almond and olive groves. All these elements add up to a habitat rich in birdlife.

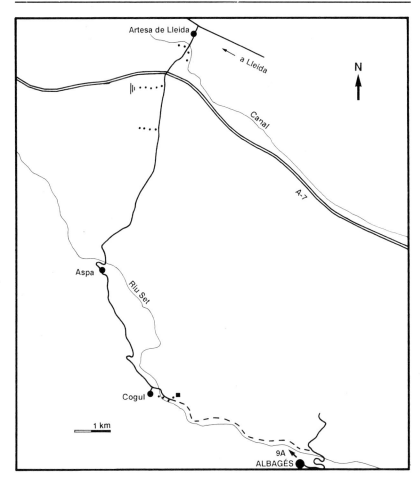

There will be plenty of Woodchat Shrikes on the tips of olive and almond trees in the breeding season. Keep a look out for Lesser Grey Shrike too, as there are a few pairs in this sort of habitat, though they will tend to be on small rows or clumps of almond trees rather than in the larger groves. You should observe the shrikes very closely because in this area, as against the Empordà area (cf. Itineraries 2A and 2B) - which is the only other place in the Iberian Peninsula where this species breeds - , the similar Great Grey Shrike is also present in spring and summer, although it is more abundant in winter, when it stays on as sole representative of its genus. The Great Grey Shrike prefers to breed in the copses or small clumps of wild trees found on some slopes and in rugged areas, but this does not mean that the species may not be seen as it looks for prey while perched on an olive or almond tree. You should therefore try and spot all the distinguishing features. Take care because some of the guidebooks are a little confusing on the subject in the context of southern Europe (cf. Specialities, page 276).

You will almost certainly have noticed that there are plenty of Magpies on the plain. In hot and dry zones, the presence of Mapgies almost certainly means there are Great Spotted Cuckoo around. The best way to find out is to listen for its cackling call that is produced on the wing in the months of March, April and at the beginning of May. In July you may also see young birds being fed by Magpies.

The best place to look for Roller is on the edge of almond groves, especially when the trees are quite tall, with adjacent open fields and barren areas. Olive groves hold a lot of thrushes in winter, especially Song Thrush, though Mistle Thrush and Redwing are also to be seen. Redwing are especially numerous in years when it is very cold in Central Europe.

In the course of this itinerary, you might make stops to inspect the different habitats. A good spot to do this is **km 16.3**. The road descends steeply and on a bend you will find a track leading off to the left. You can leave the car at this point. It is a rugged zone with plenty of barren ground that may conjure up interesting larks. The commonest is the Short-toed Lark. Before the beginning of the June harvest, this species gathers in good numbers on the barren plains and on fallow ground since it does not frequent ripening grain fields. As from the month of June until August, it may still be found on the fallow land, but in less dense numbers since it is also to be seen in the stubble. The Lesser Short-toed Lark is rarer and demands a more specialized habitat. It will only be found on old barren lands with taller vegetation, and is particularly fond of small flat-topped hillocks in these areas. Listening out for its call, which resembles the House Martin's call, is a good way of locating the species.

The Calandra Lark is one of the most regular species to be seen on this itinerary in the breeding season. It is the only lark to be found within the cereal fields, although it is also common on the barren and fallow land. Thekla Lark is also to be seen in the area. It can be told apart from Crested Lark because of its song, its smaller size and darker appearance as well as by the habitat. Thekla Lark is the only member of the Lark family to be found on steep slopes and on the most rugged ground that abounds on this itinerary. Crested Lark are much less common here than Thekla Lark, and will only be seen beside the tracks and on the roadside. Another interesting species to be looked out for on the barren and fallow ground is Pin-tailed Sandgrouse. You may be lucky enough to spot one scanning the uncultivated land, although you are more likely to see them fly over, especially if you listen out for the special call is makes on the wing. Stone Curlew are also common on the barren lands, especially on the rockier ground, although they may be seen in all the open habitats in the area, even in almond and olive groves. Its evening call is very common, and is sometimes accompanied by that of the red-necked Nightjar, a species that breeds in the same sorts of habitat as Stone Curlew.

The few trees growing on some fringe areas and on barren ground provide Green Woodpecker with enough breeding sites to keep up quite a reasonable population in the area. The open nature of the habitat enables you to get good views of this shy species. Ants are an important part of the Woodpecker's diet here, a factor you will be able to check out by taking a look at the many ant-hills that have been devastated in the barren areas.

Another very interesting bird that may be found in some barren areas is the Spectacled Warbler. This species has a very uneven distribution, but it is well worth looking out for on barren areas with very low bushes. Finally, Red-legged Partridge are very common in this area, and you will hear the male birds calling throughout the spring. The best time of year to see partridge is in August when the female birds are followed about by their young, which by that time will be fairly grown up. Partridge, however, are commonly seen throughout the year. The abundance of partridge and rabbits in this area makes it one of the principal gathering places in Catalonia for young and sub-adult

Pin-tailed Sandgrouse

(mature birds cannot breed here for lack of breeding sites) Golden Eagle and Bonelli's eagle. You must therefore do your homework on the juvenile plumages of these species! Other birds of prey to be seen in the area are Kestrel and Common Buzzard throughout the year, as well as Short-toed Eagle from March to August. This latter species doubtlessly benefits from the large amount of Montpellier Snake and Ocellated Lizard in the area. Merlin and Peregrine Falcon are winter visitors that feed on the large flocks of finches and larks wintering in the area.

A little further on in the itinerary, at **km 17.5**, there is another site where it is worth stopping. Just after a small hump in the road, and as you start to descend, you will find a tarmac road leading off to the right. Leave the car on one side of the road. The difference between this place and the former stop is that here there are good vantage points commanding excellent views over spacious grain fields. From where you have left the car you may cross the road and walk along a track, leading west, with large plains on either side. Before harvest time, you should see plenty of Calandra Lark singing on the wing over the ripe barley. You will also hear the typical call of Quail and Corn Bunting. Little Bustard is also to be seen in these fields, especially in winter. In the breeding season there is the odd pair, but it is more abundant on itineraries 9C and 9D. Montagu's Harrier stopped breeding here several years ago, but it can still be seen on migration, flying over the large expanses of barley, especially at the end of April and in May. Remember not to walk in the fields before harvest time (the crop would be damaged in this way). After the harvest you may do so, with the added interest that a walk in the stubble may result in good sightings of larks and Pin-tailed Sandgrouse. If you venture out on to the stubble, do be sure to wear protective footwear and socks to avoid cuts and scratches caused by the razor-sharp stubble. Once the fields are ploughed, a wealth of worms are made available to insectivorous birds such as wheatears, although the seeds are buried and the surface becomes uneven and unsuitable for typical steppe running birds. You are therefore unlikely to find larks and sandgrouse here once the fields are ploughed.

At **km 18**, you will cross a bridge over the A-7 Barcelona-Zaragoza motorway, and at km 19 you will come to Artesa de Lleida, final stage of the itinerary. Just as you arrive in the village, you will cross over a canal skirted by fair-sized poplar trees. Apart from Golden Oriole and Turtle Dove, Penduline Tit also breed here. Its presence is soon given away by the typical thin call it often makes and which aids us to locate the species moving about in the tops of the trees. If you are lucky, you may find one of this species's strange nests. It is a bag-shaped nest, having the whitish colour of the poplar fluff the tit uses to make it.

9B. Itinerary in the north-eastern part of the Aragonese Monegres

Starting point: Candasnos **End of the itinerary**: Fraga **Time needed**: one day (it can be covered in less time) **Means of transport**: by car and on foot (optional)

The starting point (km 0) for this itinerary will be at Candasnos, at the crossroads between the N-2 national road from Barcelona to Zaragoza and the road to Ontiñena and Alcolea de Cinca, which is the road that you are to follow. This road has very little traffic, and this will enable you to stop with greater ease. It crosses the north-eastern part of the Aragonese Monegros. The Monegros have large expanses of barren plains, and in this particular area, there are also plenty of small gullies. This factor makes the landscape more rugged and opens up the possibility of seeing rupicoline species. As soon as you leave Candasnos, you will immediately get an idea of the sort of landscape you will be seeing on the first half of the itinerary, with successive large grain fields and equally large fallow fields, as well as small grassy hillocks, largely covered in wild esparto grass. You are advised to motor through this area at less than 40 KPH so as to be able to identify the flocks of Carrion Crow, Magpie, Jackdaw, Chough, Raven and other species feeding in fields along the way. It is a good idea to stop off at regular intervals and to take a walk in fallow or barren areas. In summer this will enable you to see Short-toed Lark, Calandra Lark, Crested Lark, Thekla Lark and, if you are lucky, the odd sandgrouse. To see these latter birds it is advisable to listen for the distinctive call of the flocks that may be flying in the vicinity. In winter, Linnet, Goldfinch, larks and Meadow Pipit are very common in the area.

A good place to stop off is at **km 5.2** of the intinerary (shortly before the 47 kilometre road mark), at a place where the road ascends, there also being some signs indicating it is a restricted hunting zone ("Coto de Caza"). At this point you can climb up on to the hillock on the left-hand side of the road from where you will be able to command a view over the surrounding area, and take a walk. Scan all rocky vegetation-free slopes, where Black Wheatear may be seen. Once back at the car, if you are not too tired, you may stop again 600 metres further on (50 metres after the sign indicating a sharp bend to the left). A track to the right at this point, leads to a sheep water hole. This track is a good place to see Lesser Short-toed Lark, although you will later be passing through better sites for this species. You can complete this stroll by walking across a nearby barren or fallow area, where you may see Tawny Pipit. On barren and salty ground you might well see Dupont's Lark; however, you must be very careful not to confuse this species with young Tawny Pipits (see Specialities, page 270).

At **km 9** of the itinerary, a small tarmac track, signposted to Ballobar, leads off to the right. Follow this road (unless there have been heavy rains; if

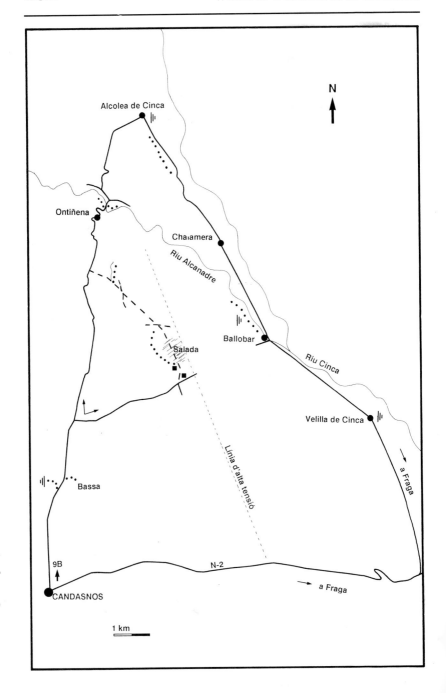

this is the case, go straight on to Ontiñena because the Ballobar road passes through some saltings that are easily flooded). On this stretch of road, and on the whole itinerary in general, you might well spot Buzzard and Kestrel at all times of year, as well as Merlin in winter.

At **km 15** you will see a crossroads sign, and soon after, a track to the right that is signposted to "El Campillo". You will see a small whitewashed building on the left, surrounded by an even paved surface. In front of this building there is a small path you should take. It heads north, and runs almost parallel with a high tension cable on the right hand side. It is worth keeping an eye on the piles of stones on the edges of the fields, where in summer you may see Black-eared Wheatear, Common Wheatear during the migratory period (which is long in autumn) and Black Redstart and Great Grey Shrike in winter.

The drive along these tracks should bring us into contact with Stone Curlew, partridge, Little Owl and Hoopoe. Look out for raptors, for Egyptian Vulture is to be seen on the whole itinerary in summer.

About one kilometre after leaving the road you will drive past a small farmhouse on the left, and 500 metres further on you will leave behind the farmland and begin to cross a large barren area with sparse vegetation, where salt-loving plants will be predominant, as you will be able to see by nibbling the shoots of any of the plants you pick. It is one of the typical Ebre area shallow saline depressions. This area is very good for Lesser Short-toed Lark, especially in the breeding season. It is the staple species in this habitat along with Short-toed Lark and Calandra Lark. Any point on the track is good for a stop. After taking a walk on the salting (heat or cold permitting), it is worth a further walk towards the plains that rise up to your left. This area has a lot of fallow land where you may well put up Pin-tailed Sandgrouse. Drive on and at the end of the salting you will come to a crossroads. The left-hand road climbs up to the aforementioned plains, though it is better to have covered the ground on foot. Drive straight on along the main track, which is in fairly good condition and still runs parallel to the high tension cable.

Soon after **km 18**, the track you are on branches off to the right. Keep on the track that curves slightly to the left. Fifty metres further on, another track in very good condition cuts across your track. Cross over and drive straight on along the track you should drive on in a north-westerly direction. The electric cable will now be getting progressively farther away from your track. You will still come to further crossroads and paths leading off on either side, but you are to drive straight on along the main track. At **km 21.3**, the track begins to descend and 800 metres further on you will skirt a small gully, with some small banks where rupicoline species may be seen, as well as Dartford Warbler. There are Bee-eater nesting holes on the bank. Once you are back at the car, continue along the track you were on until you reach the Candasnos-Ontiñena road, on the 59 km road mark. Turn right towards Ontiñena. If you wish, you can stop at the crossroads to take a look at the saltings on the other side of the road.

About 4 kms further on along the main road, you will come to Ontiñena, crossing through the village in the direction of Alcolea. On the way out of Ontiñena, you will soon cross the river Alcanadre, where you can stop to observe the riverside woodland species, as well as the birds there may be on a small patch of irrigated fields. Soon after, you will come to a signposted road. Turn left towards Alcolea de Cinca. About 600 metres further on, should take a turning to the right and drive up a road that leads to new plains. You will arrive in Alcolea de Cinca 8 kms after leaving Ontiñena. Here you will leave the steppe areas. The second half of the itinerary now begins. It is set aside for the observation of several Storks' nests and some magnificent clay river banks that skirt the river Cinca, as does the road itself.

On entering Alcolea de Cinca, you will find a crossroads with a road leading to Monzón on your left, the road straight on leading to Fraga and Albalate de Cinca, and, to the right, through the village, to Chalamera. You must take this last road. The road passes in front of the church, where there are three Stork nests occupied from February to July. Unlike in the rest of Europe, a few Storks often stay on in the area in winter. Keep on in the same direction,

Bee-eater

and once you have driven out of the village you will come across some large clay cliffs on the right. The river Cinca will now be on your left. You should be able to see a good deal of raptors and rupicoline birds in the area: Egyptian Vulture, Peregrine Falcon, Kestrel, Lesser Kestrel, Blue Rock Thrush, Rock Sparrow, Black Wheatear, Alpine Swift, Chough and Raven among other species. According to which month of the year you are visiting the area, Black Kite or Red Kite may be seen above the river Cinca, and most of the species associated with riverside woodland, such as Penduline Tit, Golden Oriole, Scops Owl and Nightingale are also to be seen here in spring.

After this stop, continue along the road to Chalamera and cross the village. Immediately after Chalamera you will come to the Sariñena-Fraga road, where you should turn left towards Fraga. Soon new cliffs will appear on your right. They may also be of interest, and will be with you as far as Ballobar. There is a Stork's nest in this town. You can get a really good view of it from the water deposit above the town. You may reach the deposit by way of a small path leading from the church square.

From now on the itinerary becomes duller since it passes through irrigated agricultural areas. You will drive hrough Velilla de Cinca, a village where there are still several pairs of Pallid Swift breeding, and soon after you will leave Miralsot to one side. There is a Stork's nest here. You will arrive in Fraga, the final stage of the itinerary, 31 kms after leaving Alcolea de Cinca.

9C. Itinerary on the Algerri plains

Starting point: Balaguer **End of the itinerary**: Algerri **Time needed**: half a day **Means of transport**: by car and on foot (optional) **Observations**: best in the morning

The starting point on this itinerary (Km 0) is the petrol station you will find on the left on the way out of Balaguer on the C-148 road to Alfarràs. You should only follow this road for 500 metres, where you will see some warehouses and silos on the right. Soon after, on the left, there are some more warehouses and silos alongside the "Sant Isidre" cooperative, as well as a wide track that you should take.

At **km 1.2** you will come to a junction. Take the left-hand turning along the main track in a south-westerly direction. Crested Lark and Magpie are common in this area, and Bee-eater nest holes are to be found in the small two foot banks on the side of the track. Stonechat, Black Redstart and Great Grey Shrike, species that often perch on the top of bushes or piles of stones, are present here in winter. At **km 2.3**, you will come to another junction. You should take the right-hand turning, signposted to Albesa. About 100 metres further on, a path will turn off to the right (keep straight on) and at **km 3.2**, at another junction, you should turn right on the track signposted to Albesa. Apart from Raven and Carrion Crow, which are resident birds in this and the plains to come, you should see Chough in winter. Flocks of Linnet and Goldfinch are also common in winter, more so than other species of finches. Skylark and Meadow Pipit are also common in winter. In spring these species are replaced by Calandra Lark (which is rare in winter) and Short-toed Lark, which are to be found on flat, uncultivated ground. Merlin is the main winter raptor, although Hen Harrier, Kestrel and Buzzard are also to be seen.

At **km 4.3**, you will drive past some large rocks and a small hillock on your right. It is the hillock (Catalan: Turó) of Mormur, the highest point on the large plain you are visiting. It is 327 metres high. Stop the car, and walk up to the top to get a good view of the surrounding landscape. Climb down the opposite side of the hillock, and keep an eye on the fields where Little Bustard are quite often seen. There is also a low ridge on the other side of the track. It extends to the south-east forming a great plain which is also worth visiting since it is a place where the last Catalan Black-bellied Sandgrouse can sometimes be seen. It is always advisable to climb the hillocks and higher ground. Not only do you get a better view, but you will also be able to spot flying raptors with greater ease.

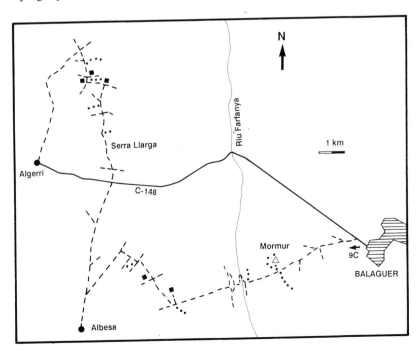

At **km 5.8** you will drive through some almond groves where a summertime stop might well reveal Woodchat Shrike, Roller and Orphean Warbler. After the almond groves, the road curves round to the right. Another track leads off to the left towards a *masia* (farmhouse). Your track, however, descends to a small valley which you will come to after a hairpin bend. The track leads to a small row of riverside trees and a small reedbed; it is the small river Farfanya, where, apart from Orphean Warbler and Roller (species that are constantly moving from the almond grove to the riverside area), you may also see Golden Oriole, Penduline Tit, Melodious Warbler, Great Reed Warbler and Green Woodpecker. Once you have crossed the small river, you may care to scan the slopes in front of you where Thekla Lark and several scrub-loving species such as Sardinian Warbler and Black-eared Wheatear will almost certainly be seen. At the foot of the slope there is a path leading off to the right that you should not take. Climb up to the plateau before you. Once you have climbed the slope and are on the plateau, you turn right on a path that is perpendicular to the one you have been coming along. You will be heading towards some sheds, but before arriving there (a short distance after turning on to this new track), take another smaller track to the left. This tracks heads towards the south-west (in the same direction as the original track), crossing large plains where in spring you should see plenty of Calandra Lark and Corn Bunting. This latter species likes to perch on prominent bushes and carry out its display song. Quail and Little Bustard calls may also be heard, although this species is rarer in winter. Keep on this same track, ignoring any subsidiary turnings, until you come to **km 9.3** where there is a small path leading off to the right. It is hard to see this path, though it may help to know that it leads to a small building. Do not take the path, but leave your car here and climb up onto the flat-topped hillock on your left. It should be quite visible from here. There is a small area of scrub on the hillock where in spring and summer you will almost certainly come across Short-toed Lark, as well as other species of larks. It is also a good site for observing raptors, as well as Little Bustard during their springtime display flights which are especially common at dusk.

At **km 9.5**, you will come to a crossroads where you should turn right, driving in a north-westerly direction. At **km 10.7**, you will cross a path and pass a house on your left. As on other buildings in this arid part of Catalonia, both species of starling are found breeding side by side, with Tree Sparrow and House Sparrow. At **km 11.4** you will come across some uncultivated hillocks on your right where you may possibly come across the odd Stone Curlew. At **km 11.7** you will come to a perpendicular path, skirted by a small stone wall. Take this path to the left. Twenty metres further on, turn right along another track that once again heads to the north-west. As soon as you are on this track, you will see a small arid area to your left. You may care to stroll through this zone to try and spot Stone Curlew, Short-toed Lark and Crested Lark. At **km 12.1**, a path leads off to the left which you must not take. Drive on up a sharp rise that you will see before you. At **km 12.6** you will once again come to a path joining the track at a perpendicular angle. Turn left along this track (on the right there is a pile of stones and a single nettle tree at this point). At **km 14.7** our track joins another one coming from the right. You must take this path, turning almost 180° round to the right. You will now head north towards the mountains. At **km 16** there is a track leading off to the right, but you should drive straight on. At **km 17.7**, at another junction, take the straight track to the right. At **km 19.6** you will cross the Balaguer-Alfarràs road, and, soon after the track will begin to climb up through almond groves towards some chalky hills. At **km 20.1** you will cross another track, and soon after you will begin to enter the Serra Llarga area on a relatively bad track. At **km 21.1**, you will come to some small plains where Stone Curlew, Little Bustard and Calandra Lark can all be seen. At **km 21.6** there is a small hillock on the right. Stop the car and climb up it. It will afford you an excellent view of the small surrounding plains, where you may see raptors such as Kestrel, Hobby, and, more rarely, Montagu's Harrier, Short-toed Eagle and even Griffon Vulture, Egyptian Vulture and Bonelli's Eagle. Drive straight on towards the north and at **km 22.6**, you will cross a track where there is an almond grove. In winter there are many Chaffinch and other finches in the groves, where the odd Rock Sparrow can also be seen.

At **km 23.3** there is a junction with turnings leading off on either side of a small clump of ilex trees. It is the first wood you will have come to, and you may care to start looking out for Subalpine Warbler and Bonelli's Warbler here. Wood Pigeon and Jay are also present here. Roller are to be seen quite frequently on the edges of the woods, and the most typical species on the small patches of barren ground is Black-eared Wheatear. At the junction, take the turning to the right that heads north. Do not take another path that leads off to the right here. Shortly afterwards, in front of a ruined house, your track curves round to the left, passing by a small path that again leads to the right. Head west along the small track that is skirted by stony verges on either side where lush trees grow. You will soon pass by a small pond with a washing-place and a fountain, where there are many nettle trees and typical riverside trees. It is a good spot to stop. On our right is the ruined village of La Figuera, which has been derelict since the Spanish Civil War. Blackbird, Short-toed Treecreeper, Golden Oriole, Turtle Dove and Orphean Warbler, among other species, are all to be seen here. Ortolan Bunting, Corn Bunting and several species of finches also visit this spot to bathe and drink on hot summer days. About 200 metres after the fountain you will pass by a house on your right, and 100 m further on the track comes to a junction. You should turn right, pass by a farm, a path that leads off to the left and another one to the right. Head north, passing by a small cemetery with cypress trees.

At **km 25** there is another junction beside a large rock on the right. Here you may once again leave the car and stroll through the ilex wood on your right. You may see Sardinian Warbler, Subalpine Warbler, Firecrest, Short-toed Treecreeper, and Cirl Bunting. You will see Ortolan Bunting if you climb a little higher up the hillock. Back in the car, you should drive straight on (on the left-hand track), passing by some small flat tracts where Stone Curlew, Little Bustard, Tawny Pipit and Wood Lark can all be seen in summer. In winter it is worth keeping an eye on the flocks of buntings for you may well come across Rock Bunting here. About 150 metres after the rock there is a turning off to the left that you should not take. Keep straight on a crossroads at **km 25.2** where your track is cut off by another more important one to the left that you should take. This track is in very good condition and leads straight to the village of Algerri. On the way down, however, you will once again come to interesting areas with similar characteristics to those that you came across on the way up. The crossroads may well be a good spot for stopping off and taking a walk in the ilex scrub before you, for this habit will become less frequent as you make your way down.

The only place at which you may now get lost is a junction at **km 26.8**, where there is a road leading off to the right. It should be obvious, however, that the track you must follow is the more important one. Another place where it is worth stopping, on the way into Algerri, is at a site where the road is enclosed by chalky hillocks and small cliffs. You may see Black Wheatear here. The itinerary ends up at Algerri.

9D. Itinerary in the dry farming area north of Bellcaire

Starting point: Bellcaire d'Urgell   **End of the itinerary**: Balaguer   **Time needed**: half a day
Means of transport: by car and on foot (optional)

This short itinerary begins at Bellcaire d'Urgell. If you are coming from Balaguer, you will find a turning off to the right to Linyola and Mollerussa. The turning is in the village itself, beside the Guardia Civil barracks. You should turn left here along the road that passes in front of the Guardia Civil barracks. This spot is the starting point (**km 0**) of the itinerary. The short road passes by the village school. At the end of the road, you should turn left towards the town hall square, which has a round fountain in the middle. Turn right at this point and follow the wide street with trees that leads to a track running past a clump of pine trees on your left. This track leads to tracts of arid land similar to the grain-growing steppes. It initially passes through an area of irrigation agriculture with alternate fruit orchards and grain fields. Mistle Thrush and Blackbird

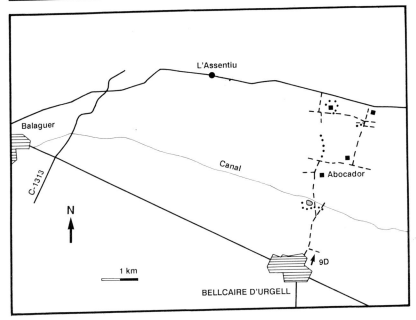

are two of the commonest species on this initial stretch, and Greenfinch are also very frequent in summer. In winter Chaffinch and other finches are also to be seen regularly.

Now drive on along the same track, and at **km 1.6** you will come to a small clump of poplar trees where there is a junction. Turn left here. In the trees, look out for Penduline Tit, Nightingale and Great Reed Warbler.

At **km 2**, just before you cross over a small canal, you will see a small pond with plenty of pine trees and riverside trees on the left. Try your luck once again at this pond, looking out for the species mentioned above, to which Cetti's Warbler, Golden Oriole, Melodious Warbler and Serin may now be added.

When you drive on, you will cross a bridge. Keep straight on along the track that heads north. You will now be able to see a small range spread at right-angles before you. It is made up of small chalky hillocks. At **km 2.5** the track begins to climb and you start to cross the ridge and enter the more arid zones. At **km 2.8** you will pass a small path on your left and a local rubbish tip on the right, where different crow family species can be seen. At this point on the road, Bee-eater are very common in spring and summer, as well as Little Owl throughout the year. Thekla Lark and Red-legged Partridge are to be found breeding on the thyme-covered slopes, where Black-eared Wheatear, Ortolan Bunting and Tawny Pipit are also present in less numbers.

At **km 3.**3 you will have entered the grain-growing areas, and you will come to a crossroads where you may leave the car and walk along the track that continues straight on from the road you were on before. Keep walking until the end of the hill in front of you. From here you will have a good view of the plain, where in spring you will see Calandra Lark and male Little Bustard on their display flight, especially at dusk. At this time of the year Quail and Corn Bunting are also frequent here. The good view you get from here (you will be able to see the Serra del Montsec (Montsec Range) in the distance) makes it possible to see raptors that could be flying at different altitudes above the plain. Hobby is one of the most regular raptors to be seen here, though many other non-breeding species are present in this zone, which they use as a feeding area. Marsh Harrier is an example of this phenomenon, and indeed, this site is one of the best in Catalonia for spotting Montagu's Harrier. Plenty of Magpie breed in isolated almond trees around here, providing Great Spotted Cuckoo with nests to deposit their eggs in. This latter species, however, migrates as soon as the female birds have laid their eggs. You may also spot the odd Roller in these almond groves, although the second half of itinerary 9C is the best place to see this species.

On returning to the crossroads where you left the car, take the track to the right which heads towards the east. At **km 4** there is a small stone hut on the left. You can stop here again and observe the plains from the roof of the hut, with the sun at your back. About 100 m further on, beside a hunting restriction sign ("Acotat de caça"), you should take a small path leading off to the left. Cross the plain and head towards a farm to the north. In winter, these grain fields have plenty of larks and Meadow Pipit, as well as several species of finch and bunting. At **km 5.3** there is a track leading off to the right and, shortly after, another path leading off to the left. Do not take either of them. You may care to take a walk on the small arid spaces to be found on this side. In spring and summer you should see Stone Curlew here, and if you are lucky, you might see Little Bustard calling from the ground. After this stop, drive straight on for a further 100 metres before coming to another crossroads, with one track leading off to the right, a second, heading straight for a farm, and a third, the one you should take, going off to the left towards a house in ruins. If you follow this path, you will find a small fringe of gypsophilous scrub where the species typically associated with this habitat (Thekla Lark, Black-eared Wheatear, Red-legged Partridge etc.) may be seen.

At **km 6.4** you will come to another derelict house. This is a good place to stop and have a walk about. Rock Sparrow are sometimes to be seen here. It is a reasonably rare and very local species on the steppe-like plains here. The vicinity of this building is a good place for awaiting nightfall, so that you may hear Stone Curlew, and possibly further afield, Red-necked Nightjar.

You should then continue along the same track for 200 m until you come to a crossroads where you must turn right towards the north. This track will lead you out of the arid lands onto a tarmac road which you should take to the left. It leads back to Balaguer, passing through L'Assentiu on the way.

Board and Lodging

The most important towns in the area are Lleida, Balaguer and Fraga. You should be able to get a room there without too much difficulty because they are not in a very touristic area. If you are looking for higher class hotels, the Hotel Parador Compte Jaume d'Urgell in Balaguer and the Hotel

Little Bustard

Residència Comptes d'Urgell in Lleida should meet all requirements, both being of four star rating. Besides these hotels, there is a wide range of establishments and full information will be given to you at the Lleida Tourist Office (Oficina d'Informació Turística) in Carrer Arc del Pont s/n, tel. (973) 24 81 20.

Those who wish to camp may do so at Càmping de les Basses, near Lleida, on the N-240 road to Huesca.

A good way of getting to know the dishes of this area is to go to the small restaurants in the market garden zones around Lleida, either in the Butsènit area (Can Rúbies or Cal Nenet), or at La Mariola (La Mina). If you prefer to stay in the city, you can go to La Huerta, to the San Bernardo restaurant or to the "Forn de Can Nastasi". However, there are many other restaurants in Lleida and the other towns where typical Catalan food is served, snails being a speciality of this part of the country. "Coca de Recapta" (a form of flat cake also known as "Coca d'Escalivada" or "Coca de Samfaina") is also very popular here. It may be bought at baker's shops in all the villages in the region.

As regards uncooked products, the importance high quality fruit has in these parts must also be mentioned. Pears, apples and peaches are especially good, as are the vegetables. The production of dry figs at Fraga should also be noted.

Other places of interest

- Seu Vella or Old Cathedral of Lleida. Built between the XIIIth and XVth centuries, it is the city's main architectural feature. It can be seen from afar on any route by which you may be approaching the city.

- Lleida commercial area. Situated between Sant Antoni and Carme streets, this is one of the major pedestrian areas in Catalonia, and the city's nerve centre. The Town Hall building, "La Paeria", was built in the XIIIth century, and is of architectural interest.

- Mercadal Square in Balaguer. One of the largest arched squares in Catalonia. With other nearby squares and arched streets, it offers an outstanding display of medieval architecture.

- Museu Comarcal de la Noguera (La Noguera county museum). Apart from the collection of architectural remains and sculptures, there is a collection of interesting objects that bear witness to the former importance of Moorish culture in Balaguer. It is on display in an old church in Sant Josep street, near the Plaça del Mercadal.

- Església de Sant Pere (St Peter's Church). Built on the site of an old mosque, the *Mudejar*-style church tower is still to be admired today. Part of the old Romanesque building is also conserved. In Fraga (cf. itinerary 9B).

- The Cogul cave paintings. One of the most important cave paintings sites in Catalonia. It is between Albagés and Aspa (cf. itinerary 9A).

10
THE MONTSEC RANGE
(SERRA DEL MONTSEC)

The Montsec Range is in the heart of Catalonia, and is the most important massif in the outer ranges of the Pyrenean foothills. It is also the best area for raptors in the whole country.

One part of the range, the Congost de Montrebei, was declared to be a Partial Nature Reserve in 1988. This step was taken in order to protect the otter. The conservation of the area is to be ensured almost immediately after the Catalan Parliament unanimously voted in favour of turning the whole massif into a Natural Park. Some of the reservoirs near the Montsec have sizeable populations of water birds and two of them (Sant Llorenç de Montgai and Cellers) will soon be officially declared Natural Wild Fauna Reserves.

Surface area: 100,000 hectares (Montsec and adjacent ranges and reservoirs).

Habitats: limestone cliffs, oak forests, ilex woods, pine woods, thickets, riverside woodland and reservoirs with wetland vegetation.

Interesting species:
- *Present all the year round*: Red Kite, Sparrowhawk, Goshawk, Buzzard, Bonelli's Eagle, Golden Eagle, Bearded Vulture, Griffon Vulture, Peregrine Falcon, Kestrel, Red-legged Partridge, Eagle Owl, Kingfisher, Great Spotted Woodpecker, Thekla Lark, Crag Martin, Great Grey Shrike, Cetti's Warbler, Fan-tailed Warbler, Sardinian Warbler, Dartford Warbler, Blue Rock Thrush, Black Wheatear, Penduline Tit, Crested Tit, Nuthatch, Short-toed Treecreeper, Dipper, Rock Bunting, Chough, Alpine Chough.
- *Summer visitors*: Purple Heron, Black Kite, Short-toed Eagle, Honey Buzzard, Booted Eagle, Egyptian Vulture, Hobby, Stone Curlew, Great Spotted Cuckoo, Alpine Swift, Bee-eater, Roller, Hoopoe, Wryneck, Short-toed Lark, Calandra Lark, Woodchat Shrike, Great Reed Warbler, Subalpine Warbler, Bonelli's Warbler, Rock Thrush, Black-eared Wheatear, Golden Oriole.
- *Winter visitors*: wildfowl, gulls, Alpine Accentor, Wallcreeper, Hawfinch.
- *Migratory species*: Osprey, Marsh Harrier, Hen Harrier, Merlin, waders.

Description and habitat

The Montsec is the largest of the ranges in the outer Pyrenean foothills. It is isolated and unique in its composition. In simple terms, it may be described as a vast, elongated limestone hump. It is about 50 kms long, running from east to west. Two large rivers, the Noguera Ribagorçana and the Noguera Pallaresa, run perpendicularly across the range through the two most impressive gorges in Catalonia called Montrebei and Terradets. These gorges divide the Montsec into three sectors. The central sector is called the Montsec d'Ares. It is the longest part, and rises to 1,677 metres at its highest point. To the east of the Noguera Pallaresa is the Montsec de Rúbies, which is shorter but fractionally higher (1,685 m). The westernmost sector, in Aragon (the Nogera Ribagorçana river is the frontier between Catalonia and Aragon) is the Montsec de l'Estall, which reaches a maximum height of 1,324 metres.

The south-facing slopes of the Montsec have huge breath-taking vertical cliffs, with smooth rock faces over 400 metres high. The north-facing slope, however, is less steep and is covered (in those areas where man has not destroyed the forest) in thick woodland. This combination of contrasting features (and other factors) is the reason for the large variety of raptor species that may be found here, giving the massif great importance from the point of view of the fauna. The presence of numerous cliffs and gorges enables vultures and large eagles to find breeding sites. The existence of large forests also does the same for tree-nesting species. The well-conserved state of the animal communities, with plenty of snakes, rodents, lagomorphs and birds of all sizes, provides raptors with ample prey. Extensive livestock-rearing, that still continues in the area, also provides necessary food for carrion birds such as vultures (the presence of artificial dead animal tips also helps). As a result of this, Bearded Vulture, Griffon Vulture, Egyptian Vulture, Golden Eagle, Short-toed Eagle, Goshawk, Sparrowhawk, Buzzard, Kestrel and Peregrine Falcon, as well as several owls including Eagle Owl, all breed regularly in the Montsec. If you now add the Montsec's surrounding areas, which are also visited on the itineraries given below, Booted Eagle, Bonelli's Eagle, Red Kite, Black Kite, Honey Buzzard and Hobby can also to be included in the list of breeding birds. To this, one can add five further species of non-breeding raptors which are seen in the area during migration.

As regards the vegetation, the almost geometrical east-west alignment of the massif, as well as the contrast in relief, results in major differences between one slope and the other. This gives rise to an increased botanical diversity, so that clearly Mediterranean species may be found as well as typically north Euro-Siberian ones. The north-facing slopes get almost twice as much rainfall as the south-facing slopes, and the sunshine on the former is much more limited, and almost nil in winter. The basic vegetation on the middle and high parts of these slopes is oak wood, made up of Pubèscent Oak and other typical Central European woodland trees. Human activity, however, has led to the degradation of the woods, which are only in good condition in the least accessible parts of the Montsec de Rubies. There are also patches of pinaster and odd Scotch pines. The presence of a beech wood, with mixed Durmast Oak in the Serrat de Fontfreda, on the north face of the Montsec d'Ares, is also an interesting feature. The basic vegetation on the south-facing slopes, which are much drier and sunnier, is the continental ilex wood, with occasional Lusitanian Oaks. In the more degraded areas, the woodland turns into kermes oak, with areas of calcicole scrub with box wood and other bushes.

When talking about the Montsec, it would be unpardonable not to mention the great paleontological importance of the area. The numerous Tertiary and Mesozoic fossil beds give a very clear picture of the flora and fauna in the area in previous geological eras. It was here that the oldest frog fossil in the world was found, as well as fossils of other amphibians, reptiles, birds, fish, insects, Crustacea and several species of plants.

Apart from the Montsec range itself, the itineraries in this chapter will also include smaller ranges and reservoirs to the south of Montsec. The mountains we shall refer to are the foothills that are to be found before descending to the Central Catalan Depression. These smaller ranges are not very high (500 - 1,000 metres) and they are covered in Mediterranean vegetation, basically continental ilex woodland with kermes oak scrub in the more degraded areas. There are grain-producing zones interspersed with a few almond and olive groves.

Sant Llorenç de Montgai and Cellers reservoirs stand out amongst the rest because they are surrounded by a rich belt of marsh and riverside vegetation. This phenomenon is possible because the water level of these reservoirs is very constant, thus allowing interesting water birds to thrive there. The belt of vegetation around the reservoirs is made up of reeds and bulrushes, and the riverside woodland is basically made up of poplars and elm trees.

How to visit the area

As previously mentioned, the two itineraries in this section are not limited to the Montsec itself, but also include a very large area between the reservoirs of Sant Llorenç de Montgai and Cellers. Between these two reservoirs, an ample area is covered, including not only the Montsec range, but a whole series of smaller ranges situated between the Montsec and the Lleida plain. These ranges are not too mountainous, but are interesting from an ornithological point of view. For this reason, the starting point for the itineraries is situated at Balaguer. For those wishing only to visit the Montsec range, however, it is better to choose a base nearer to the massif; Cellers, Àger or Vilanova de Meià are suitable points.

If you are coming to Balaguer from Barcelona, you should drive along the N-2 road as far as a point three kilometres after Tàrrega, where you turn off along the C-148 local road to Balaguer. You can also get here along the A-2 motorway as far as Lleida, taking the C-1313 local road to Balaguer from there. You can also use the Corbins road from Lleida to Balaguer. It is quieter and better for birds (as you can see in chapter 9, page 154). The Montsec can also be reached by train on the Barcelona-Lleida-Balaguer-La Pobla de Segur line. Those of you wishing to go on the Montsec itineraries immediately after completing itineraries 9C and 9D, will be ideally situated at Balaguer itself!

Itinerary 10A is perfect for getting to know the morphology of the massif since it crosses the very heart of the massif, climbing up the southern slopes of the Montsec d'Ares and descending on the northern slopes. It also includes a visit to the Montrebei gorge. This spot is certainly the most spectacular part of the Montsec and the place where you are most likely to spot Bearded Vulture and other large birds of prey. Itinerary 10B, however, shows us round the Montsec de Rúbies, where the massif's best forests are to be found. It includes the Camarassa, Sant Llorenç and Cellers reservoirs, the latter two having rich wetland vegetation on the banks. It therefore offers greater possibilities of observing water and forest birds, as well as being an itinerary on which Bonelli's Eagle may easily be spotted, in contrast with the rarity of this species on itinerary 10A.

Each itinerary requires a full day's outing, and even then, you will not be able to linger long at the various sites! If you want to get the best out of the day, do start off at daybreak. If you only have one day, itinerary 10A is the best choice, for it permits you to get to know the Montrebei gorge and is also better for raptors, the most remarkable feature of the Montsec birdlife. If you have two days for the itineraries here, do itinerary 10B on the first day because it is a circular route that brings you back to Balaguer at the day's end. Follow itinerary 10A on the second day because you will thus end up at Pont de Montanyana, from where you can drive on to the Aigüestortes-Sant Maurici National Park (itinerary 11A) or to any other area in the Pyrenees. Obviously, if you have more days available, more excursions can be made to get to know the area better. Both the itineraries given here can be split up into smaller excursions that can be combined with visits of a cultural nature. In this way your stay in the Montsec will be more relaxed and varied. For example, those lodging at Cellers can do the part of itinerary 10A that follows on from Ager by going to this village along the C-147 local road as far as the junction 8 kms south of Cellers and then taking the road to the right which leads straight there. Otherwise you can follow the Cellers-Vilanova de Meià part of itinerary 10B in the opposite direction to that described. In this way, you can get to know the more attractive parts of the itineraries in a much shorter space of time.

The Montsec is good for birds at any time of the year. In winter it is cold but snow is not common. In spring and summer, apart from the pleasant weather you will find, interesting birds such as Egyptian Vulture are an added attraction. For those wishing to see Wallcreeper, the winter period in the Montsec area is a good bet.

Bird-watching

10A. Itinerary in the Montsec d'Ares and Mont-rebei ravine

Starting point: Balaguer **End of the itinerary**: Pont de Montanyana **Time needed**: one day
Means of transport: by car and on foot · **Observations**: wear thick-soled sports shoes

You must begin the itinerary at Balaguer, in Portalet street, where there is a small colony of Sand Martin (see page 154). Follow this street to the north, that is to say, with the river Segre on your right. Once you get to the end of the avenue, instead of crossing the bridge, drive straight along the road to your left which is sign-posted to Les Avellanes and Tremp. The starting point (**km 0**) of the itinerary is at this point. After barely 300 m there is a junction where you should turn right towards Gerp. At **km 3.2**, you will arrive at the village where you take a road, signposted to Vilanova de la Sal, leading to the left. After Gerp, you will pass through an area of clay and chalk hillocks with low scrub where you may see Dartford Warbler, Thekla Lark, Black Wheatear, and, on rockier ground, Blue Rock Thrush.

After **km 6**, grain fields become predominant in the landscape, although there are also almond groves and patches of ilex woodland, especially on the hills, which in places have unfortunately been replaced by pine plantations. This mosaic of habitats should result in sightings of Roller, Cuckoo, Great Spotted Cuckoo, Bee-eater, Hoopoe, Turtle Dove, Wood Pigeon, Green Woodpecker, Woodchat Shrike, Great Grey Shrike, Red-legged Partridge, Sardinian Warbler and Subalpine Warbler. Raptors may also be seen: Kestrel, Buzzard, Hobby and Long-eared Owl, all of which breed in the ilex woods and hunt in the fields. In the grain fields, as well as hearing Quail, you may well come across typically steppe-loving species such as Stone Curlew and several species of lark such as Calandra, Short-toed and Wood Lark. This latter species is found where the woodland and the fields merge.

At **km 11.8** you should turn left and take a good track signposted to the Monastery of Santa Maria de les Avellanes (Monestir de Santa Maria de les Avellanes). To the left there is a good view of the foothills of the Pyrenees before you; in the foreground the Montroig range (Serra de Montroig); to the left, behind this range, is the Sant Mamet range (Serra de Sant Mamet) which has a rounded form; lastly, in the background, is the Montsec de Rúbies, followed by the Montsec d'Ares on its left. At **km 15.4** you will cross over a tarmac road and enter the town of Les Avellanes. Drive straight through on a tarmac road, and head for Vilamajor and Àger.

At **km 19.6** you will drive through Vilamajor and after **km 23**, soon after passing the "Fontdepou" housing estate on your left, you will see how the chalky hills gradually give way to limestone. The road begins to climb steeply up to the Port d'Àger (Àger mountain pass), which is 912 m high. There is a

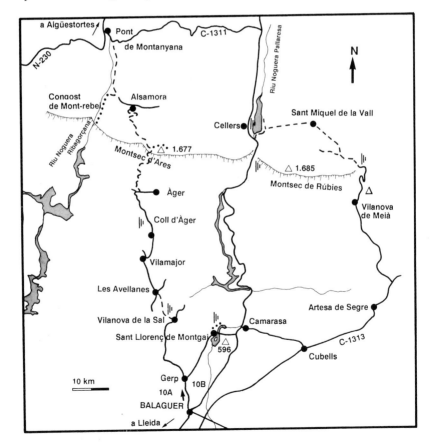

small hotel here and it is worth stopping to admire the magnificent view of the three Montsec sectors. In summer, a good many delta-wing enthusiasts from all over Europe can be seen flying here, for the south-facing cliffs of the Montsec d'Ares greatly favour the formation of thermal currents, as well as blocking out the north wind, making this area perfect for this sport.

Drive on to the north, and at **km 29.8** you will come to a junction. The left-hand road leads to Agulló but you shsould turn right on to the road to Àger and Tremp. You will soon come to a small plain with grain fields and almond trees. As it is a very productive area for these crops, a lot of the olive groves are progressively being uprooted. At **km 32** you will see Àger ahead of you with its prominent Romanesque collegiate church. A little before the village name sign, on the left, there is a track to "Coll d'Ares. Pista forestal" (Ares pass. Forestry track). Take this track, unless, of course, you first wish to visit the village (cf. other places of interest). You will be able to check you are on the right track if you see the cemetery's cypress trees ahead of you. The track is in good conditions because it is done up yearly.

About 500 m after the beginning of the track, at **km 32.5**, you will come to a junction where you are to turn left. In the centre of the cliff you will be able to see the Pedra hermitage (Ermita de la Pedra). In winter, Wallcreeper are to be seen on the cliffs around it. Blue Rock Thrush is present here all the year round, especially on bare rock on the lower parts of the cliffs. On this southern part of the Montsec which receives a lot of sunshine, ilex woods are to be found up to quite considerable altitudes. Typically Mediterranean species such as Dartford Warbler, Sardinian Warbler and Subalpine Warbler are to be seen in this habitat, along with good numbers of rabbit and wild boar. Groups of Vultures are frequently seen flying in the vicinity. Their numbers decrease in summer, once the breeding season is over, for many of these birds make their way to the Pyrenees, where the presence of summer flocks provides more food for them.

At **km 42** you will come to an area which is quite flat. It is called "L'Esglaó del Montsec" (The Montsec Step), and forms a small saddle or intermediate valley between the lower and higher cliffs. The odd field is still cultivated here, and Black-eared Wheatear, Cirl Bunting and Black Redstart should be seen near these agricultural patches. Mistle Thrush are also common, as are Red-legged Partridge, a very common species on the whole itinerary, especially in August when family groups are about. Above the saddle there are some pine plantations and odd oak trees which higher up the mountain give way to thickets, mainly composed of box-wood and different species of plants, such as hedgehog broom, a species which is associated with windy areas.

At **km 46.8** you will come to the summit. The track continues and at a spot where there is a fire prevention sign, there is a track leading off to the left you should take, leaving the main track which follows along the crest of the range as far as the highest point on the Montsec d'Ares. Before, though, it is worth taking a walk on the highest part of the range. Apart from raptors (Griffon Vulture, Egyptian Vulture, Bearded Vulture, Golden Eagle, Peregrine Falcon, Kestrel, Sparrowhawk etc.), you may also see Common Wheatear, Rock Bunting, Skylark, Wood Lark, Alpine Accentor (in winter only), and , with a bit of luck, Rock Thrush. Rabbit become rarer up here, giving way to hare. At this point, there should be wild boar tracks all around.

Once you are on the track just mentioned (it is not quite in as good condition as the track you came on), you will start to descend the northern slope of the Montsec. The view of the Pyrenees, when there is no mist, is breathtaking. Large sectors of this zone were converted into terraces with a view to planting pines here, though many of the trees did not survive. This part of the north face is the one with gentlest slopes, and is thus accessible from all parts of the Montsec. This explains why it is the area where the natural forest of oaks is in worst condition.

At **km 50.3**, soon after crossing a small gully, there is a small not very clearly marked path leading to the right. It climbs up a gorge where there are about ten pairs of Alpine Chough breeding. A small sign with an arrow will indicate the way, if a gust of wind has not done away with it! If you cannot find it, it is best to go back 300 or 400 metres, and look for the path with your binoculars from the other side of the gorge. There is a black cross half way up the gorge which will help you to identify the path and it will thus be easy to locate the place where it starts. The climb up to the cave's entrance will only take you about 5 minutes, and is not at all difficult. In the breeding season (the young take to the wing in July) you should be able to see Alpine Chough flying a few metres away from you. In contrast with the Common Chough (also common in the Montsec) which breeds in the mountains of the Iberian Peninsula, the Alpine Chough is here at its southernmost breeding quarters. In the old days, when hunting was practised to provide food for peasant families, the inhabitants of the Montsec mountains used to eat this species, although Common Chough were considered to be inedible. This gorge, known as the Graller del Boixaguer (in the Montsec, gorges are called "grallers" ("Chougheries") because of the presence of breeding Chough), is about 156 m high, and has a lake on its inner side.

Later, take the car and continue driving down the track. At **km 51.5** there is a wooden hut on the left-hand side of the track. It protects a natural rainfall deposit, where you can take a drink. As you descend, the oak woods are in better condition, and a few ilex and the odd plantation of pinaster will begin to occur. In all these woodland zones you are sure to find various species of tits, Short-toed Treecreeper, Mistle Thrush, Jay (much more numerous than on the south-facing slopes), Green Woodpecker, Great Spotted Woodpecker, Tawny Owl, Sparrowhawk and the odd Goshawk.

At **km 57.**2, at a place where an electric cable passes overhead, your track will come to a transversal track where you must turn sharply round to the left. One kilometre farther on you will reach Almasora, a village with a Christian look-out tower that brings to mind the period during which the Montsec was the frontier between the Moorish and Christian lands. At **km 62.**2 you will arrive at the ruins of *mas* El Pinell (farmhouse), a site that is often used by hikers for night-spending. From here, you will now be able to see the Noguera Ribagorçana at the point where it joins Canelles reservoir. In this mosaic of cultivated fields and small Lusitanian Oak woods you may see Red Kite, and, in summer, Honey Buzzard.

Leave your car at **km 63.4**, at a point where a track leads off to the left and descends sharply to the Montrebei gorge. This will be the starting point for the excursion on foot to the Montrebei gorge, one of the places where you are most likely to see Bearded Vulture as well as other species of raptors. It will take you about three hours to complete the walk, excluding time taken bird-watching. Walk along the path that goes down to the river, and follows along its course. This stretch of water was made into a Partial Nature Reserve for the better protection of the main otter colonies in Catalonia, although it is still not known what effect the rise in the water level (caused by the repair work on the dam) will have had on this aquatic carnivore. From here you will be able to see the silhouettes of the two cliffs on either side of the gorge, which is the administrative border between Catalonia and Aragon. The Catalan cliff, on the left, seems to have the face of a girl known as the "Donzella de Montrebei" (The Montrebei Maiden). Her nose is the first protuberance and her lips the second. The Aragonese cliff, on the other hand, has the outline of a rather coarse man. This difference between one side and the other gives rise to a wealth of jokes among the inhabitants on either side of the river. Further downstream, the path crosses over a metal bridge and heads towards the gorge that cuts its way across the rock. It sometimes seems that it will be impossible to go on, but the truth is that you can walk along the path without any form of difficulty. A pair of light boots is all that is needed to make your way through the gorge. The view is truly spectacular. It is the last important gorge that is still unspoilt in Catalonia. There was a strong defence campaign some years ago for there was a project to construct a road along the gorge. Luckily, it seems that this plan has now been dropped. At the narrowest part of the gorge, you should see plenty of Crag Martin, Alpine Swift, both species of Chough, Raven, the odd Blue Rock Thrush. It is also one of the best places for seeing Wallcreeper close at hand in winter. Raptors, however, are best observed at the point where the gorge starts to widen out on the southern side of the massif. You should then keep walking until you can get a good look at the reddish cliffs that will begin to appear on either side of the river. From this point you may well see Bearded Vulture as well as Egyptian Vulture, Griffon Vulture, Golden Eagle, Peregrine Falcon and Kestrel. Eagle Owl also breed here, and may be heard in January and February. It does not usually nest on the higher cliffs. The presence of the reservoir may also permit the observation of the odd water bird such as Grey Heron, Great Crested Grebe or Mallard.

Once you have made your way back to the car (along the same route), you must take the track you came on which runs parallel to the river, although you will now be moving upstream. About 600 metres after the turning, you will come across a large *mas* (farm), the lands of which were larger than those of many town councils. At some points, the river branches off into minor streams where several species of waders such as Common Sandpiper and Little Ringed Plover can be seen, especially during migration. In summer, local Booted Eagle, Black Kite and Red Kite are to be seen flying overhead in this area, and they are sometimes joined by large flocks of migrating Black Kites and Honey Buzzard. At **km 64.6** of the itinerary (1.2 km from the Montrebei turning) you will come to a better track. The signpost indicates La Clua to the right, though you should keep straight on. A little over 3 km farther on, you will come to a tarmac road that you should follow as far as **km 70.4**, when you will reach the C-1311 local road, very near to Pont de Montanyana, which is the final stage of this itinerary. From here you can easily reach the Aigüestortes National Park (Itinerary 11A).

10B. Itinerary in the Montsec de Rúbies and the Sant Llorenç, Cellers and Camarassa reservoirs

Starting point and end of the itinerary: Balaguer **Time needed**: one day **Means of transport**: by car and on foot

The starting point for this itinerary (**km 0**), is the same as for itinerary 10A. You should even take the same road as far as Gerp (**km 3.2**). In Gerp, however, you must take the road to Vilanova de la Sal, cross the village and drive on in the direction of Sant LLorenç de Montgai. As you leave Gerp, you will already be able to see the majestic Montsec cliffs, with the outline of the Serra de Montroig in front of them.

Soon after, you will come to the Sant Llorenç de Montgai reservoir, where there are interesting birds to be seen. At **km 8.2**, a small wood of pines and cypress trees appears on your right after some fields. Bonelli's Warbler, Subalpine Warbler, Firecrest, Long-tailed Tit, Great Tit and Blue Tit breed here. In passage, many passerines stop off in this wood, and Wryneck and Great Spotted Woodpecker can be seen quite frequently.

Egyptian Vulture

At **km 8.5**, you can stop beside the reservoir, leaving your car at the closed-off entrance to the dam area. Before you are the open waters of the reservoir, with Great Crested Grebe (up to 10 pairs breed here) and several diving ducks such as Common Pochard (about 200 birds winter here), Tufted Duck (between 10 and 40 birds), or the very much rarer Scaup or Ferruginous Duck. Odd birds of these last two species turn up yearly. It is also a common sight to see Kingfisher flash past, flying in a straight line over the water. On the left-hand side, the banks are covered in reedbeds, which become thicker towards the head of the reservoir. Purple Heron breed in these reedbeds, where the following reed-loving passerines are also to be found: Cetti's Warbler, Fan-tailed Warbler, Reed Warbler, Great Reed Warbler, as well as Reed Bunting in winter. In the nearby waters there are Coot, Moorhen, Little Grebe and numerous waterfowl, mainly consisting of Mallard (with numbers around the 1,500 or 2,000 mark every winter), though Gadwall, Shoveler, Wigeon, Teal, and even Garganey and Pintail on passage, may all be seen in small numbers. It is also common to see Grey Heron perched in one of the dead trees that emerge from the waters of the reservoir. This is one of the only sites where this species breeds in Catalonia.

On the other side of the lake you can see the Monteró cliffs, the patient scanning of which will probably reveal a Bonelli's Eagle on the wing. It is also common to see Short-toed Eagle, Kestrel, Peregrine Falcon and the odd off-course Griffon Vulture flying about there. Eagle Owl also inhabit those cliffs, and in January and February, its call is to be heard from any point in the village of Sant Llorenç. The abundant cliffs and rocky areas explain why there are so many Crag Martins and Alpine Swifts flying over the zone, as well as large flocks of Chough.

Take the car once again and drive towards the village which you will enter at **km 9.3** of your itinerary. At this point there are several good vantage points for observing the reservoir and the cliffs opposite. One of the best is the belvedere beside the Cultural Society ("Societat Cultural"), 300 metres after passing the village's first houses, at the highest point reached by the road within the village. As you can see, the reservoir is surrounded by riverside woodland, which in places is very fine. The shy Golden Oriole and Penduline Tit are to be seen there. In winter, Hawfinch are sometimes seen too, especially feeding on the fruit of the nettle tree. Areas affected by human presence (buildings and fields before entering the village) are the last of the habitats to be found making up this very varied environment. Indeed, in the vicinity of the station, Stock Dove, Black Wheatear, Cirl Bunting, Linnet and Sardinian Warbler are all to be found breeding.

Take the car once again, and drive on out of the village in the same direction, until you come to a small bridge which crosses over the reservoir at

km 11.7. In winter it is well worth scanning the rock cliffs on the right-hand side between the village and the bridge for here it is common to see Wallcreeper. The small surface area of these cliffs make it easy to spot this climbing bird, as well as Blue Rock Thrush which is present all the year round. Opposite the bridge, the waters of the reservoir are very much shallower and it is here that up to a hundred Teal winter. It is also quite a common sight to see the pair of Bonelli's Eagle from Sant Llorenç flying above the road here.

At **km 12.9**, you will come to the C-147 local road (carretera comarcal), which you should take to the left towards Camarasa, which is 500 metres farther on. Drive into Camarasa on the first of the turnings leading into the village, just before the houses. Drive along a tarmac road with a gully on the right-hand side and the last part of the town on the left. After a 600 metre upwards climb you will come to a crossroads where there is a pillar in honour of a local saint. If you turn left, you will return to the village (where the region's finest *coca de recapta* (a type of cake) can be bought in the baker's), but you must turn right and head for Cubells. It is not sign-posted, but you can ask the way for greater safety (Catalan: "A Cubells, si us plau?"). The north-facing landscape after Camarasa is a combination of dry grain fields, vineyards, almond groves, olive trees and a few hillocks with a covering of ilex trees, or oak trees. From the car, you may well see Red-legged Partridge, Bee-eater, Hoopoe, Little Owl, Woodchat Shrike, Turtle Dove, Wood Pigeon, Carrion Crows, Magpies, Stonechat, Crested Lark, and almost certainly, the odd rabbit too. This road has a tarmac surface on all but one short section, and leads us, at **km 22.8**, at a point where Cubells can be seen ahead of you, to the C-1313 local road, where you should turn left to Artesa de Segre.

At **km 32.5** you will reach Artesa de Segre, where good *coca* and Clua goat's cheese may be bought. The road enters the town, in which you should look out for a turning to the left to Tremp and Isona. Drive out of the town along the valley of one of the main tributaries of the Ebre, the river Segre, which you will cross at Pont d'Alentorn. Soon after, at **km 37.1**, you should leave this road and turn left on to a narrower road sign-posted to Vilanova de Meià.

This is the road that comes closest to the Montsec de Rúbies, although the surrounding hills obscure any view of the south-facing cliffs until you come very near to them. At **km 48.7**, you will come to a junction where you should turn right into Vilanova de Meià. Keep on straight and at **km 51** you will arrive at the Font de l'Edra (Edra spring), beside which there is a plain with poplars where it is possible to camp. If you stop here and take a look at the waters of the spring, you should soon see Pyrenean Brook Salamander, an endemic species in the Pyrenees, as well as the odd water snake. When you drive on, you will immediately be able to see the Roca dels Arcs, the main cliff on this mountain. It is a favourite mountain-climbing site. From here on you must keep an eye on the sky, as Golden Eagle, Peregrine Falcon and Kestrel are not rare here. The road begins to climb and the forests start to look finer as you proceed. At **km 53.4**, after a small bridge, you will come to the Font de la Figuera (Figuera spring) and a parking area on the right where it is also possible to camp. About 2 kms later you will drive through the Congost del Pas Nou (Pas Nou gorge) which separates the Montsec de Rubies from the Serra de Comiols. It is smaller than the two gorges that divide the Montsec, but also has a wealth of raptors.

At **km 58** the tarmac road comes to an end and there are two tracks to choose between. You should take the left-hand one. In a little under 2 km, you will come to the Hostal Roig pass. From here you suddenly come across a marvellous view of the northern slopes of the Montsec de Rúbies and the Montsec d'Ares. As may very well be appreciated from here, the northern slopes are far less steep than the almost sheer cliffs on the south-facing slopes. The gentle nature of the slopes and the fact that they face north have given rise to much finer forests on this side. Oak woods predominate, but are in quite bad condition on the lower slopes, as is demonstrated by the presence of many Scotch pine, since in the old days the more accessible forests in the Montsec were intensively exploited for the production of charcoal. Further up the slopes, though, the relatively steep gradient (when compared with the north slopes of the Montsec d'Ares) made it impractical to exploit the forests. It is for this reason that there are magnificent century-old forests of Pubescent Oak, where most of the trees have trunks that are over a metre and a half in perimeter.

At **km 61.3**, where the track you are on turns sharply to the right alongside some small fields, there is a gravel track leading off to the left. This track is narrower than the track you have been following up until now, and if it has been raining, it may be in a bad state. In that case it is preferable to keep to the original track which will pass through Sant Miquel de la Vall and eventually lead to the Cellers reservoir. In dry weather, it is worth taking the gravel track that passes very close to the forest. You can be sure you are on the right track if you come to a pig farm after about 50m. After the farm, any suitable stopping place will do for a stop to observe forest birds. Goshawk, Sparrowhawk, Buzzard and Short-toed Eagle are all present here. Great Spotted Woodpecker, Short-toed Treecreeper and Nuthatch may all be seen on the tree trunks. Nightjar, Mistle Thrush, Song Thrush (somewhat rarer) and a host of small forest passerines such as Robin, Wren, Bonelli's Warbler, Firecrest, Long-tailed Tit, Great Tit, Blue Tit and Crested Tit all breed here. Among the winter visitors, the following stand out: Bullfinch, Hawfinch, and Chaffinch (which is especially numerous and also breeds in small numbers). If you want to take a stroll, remember that the higher you climb, the better the condition you will be finding the forest in. On the lower slopes, though, the presence of farms and small fields, as well as the less dense vegetation, all contribute to making the habitat more varied, thus attracting birds that are fond of more open and humanized areas such as Green Woodpecker, Cirl Bunting, Subalpine Warbler or even Red-legged Partridge.

About 400 metres after having taken the gravel track turning, there is a path leading off to the right and another one to the left. You should drive straight on. Blackbird, Jay or even squirrel may well cross the track in front of the car. At **km 68.2**, when you are starting to see ilex trees once again (due to the lower altitude), there is a path off to the left, leading up the mountain. This path, or any of the ones leading off to the left farther on may be followed on foot to bring you nearer to the better conserved areas of forest.

At **km 69.7**, once you are out of the forest, you will come across two white houses on the left-hand side of the road, and a track to the right leading to a camping area with a fountain and other facilities. About 200 m farther on, you will cross the river Barcedana, and soon you will be seeing the Cellers reservoir with the town of the same name on the other side. At **km 72.4** you will come to a tarmac road. If you turned left, it would lead you (at **km 74** of the itinerary) to the C-147 local road. This will indeed be the road to take on the way back, but for the moment, time permitting, you may choose to investigate the tail end of the Cellers reservoir, which is also called "Terradets". In this case you will have to take the C-147 local road to the right and go over the bridge that crosses the reservoir. The rock wall on the left of the bridge has a colony of Jackdaw. You will soon come to the village with the Hostal del Llac on the right. This hotel is very much the haunt of hikers and it is the perfect place to put up if you really want to get to grips with the Montsec area. There is a belvedere beside the hotel and from there you can observe the lake's waterbird species, which largely coincide with those seen at Sant Llorenç de Montgai. One special feature about Cellers is the arrival of large amounts of Black-headed Gull and Herring Gull, which flock to Cellers to moult after the breeding season. In order to get a closer look at reed-dwelling birds it is better to drive on for a further 3 kms to the tail end of the reservoir. It is a very thick reedbed, and Marsh Harrier and Bittern have been seen there in the breeding season. Several species of wader, including Black-winged Stilt have also been seen on small beaches on the banks and islands in the reservoir. It is not too unusual to see Egyptian Vulture feeding on dead fish on these very beaches! When the road starts to lead away from the reservoir, it is time to turn round and make your way back to the other side of the bridge crossing the reservoir, unless you want to go on to Castell de Mur (cf. other places of interest): you will be back at **km. 74** once again if you subtract the 10 kms you will have covered in this optional trip to the reservoir. You must now take the Balaguer road (clearly sign-posted) whether you have done the Cellers trip or not. The road passes through several tunnels and leads to the Terradets gorge, which is as spectacular as the one at Montrebei, though quite different on account of the ecological disturbance the road here causes. To the impact caused by the road, which is to be "improved" soon, one must add that caused by the railway line, the dam, the hydroelectric station and the high tension electric cables. It can only be hoped that Montrebei never looks like this!

At **km 76** it is worth stopping to take a close look at the Barranc del Bosc (Bosc Gorge). In front of you there is a small entrance on the left-hand side of the road where you may leave the car. But if there is a lot of traffic, you will have to be careful carrying out this manoeuvre. If you look down into the gorge, you will see the Roca Regina (Regina rock) to your right. It is very sheer and one of the most difficult faces to climb in the whole Montsec. You will also notice that there are two paths. The one on the right is for the mountain-climbers, and the one on the left makes its way 3 kms up the gorge. If you have time, you can take this path. It is good for observing typical Montsec massif birds of prey, for the road will offer little more than Crag Martin from this point onwards.

Once you are out of the gorge you will see some plane trees at **km 77.5**. It is the sign that you are approaching the Font de les Bagasses (Fountain of the Whores). This fountain owes its name to the times when prostitutes used to offer their "services" here at the time the road was being built through the gorge. The view of the Terradets cliffs is much better from the fountain.

At **km 80.5** there is a turning to the right towards Àger, which you should not take. From here on the road skirts Camarasa reservoir, which is much less interesting than Cellers and Sant Llorenç from the point of view of seeing water birds. However, you may well see Dipper on the river beneath the dam, as well as plenty of birds of prey on the hills around the reservoir. You must be careful though because there is a tunnel just before the dam and it is difficult to find a place to leave the car.

The road will eventually lead you to the village of Camarasa, at **km 106**, and twelve kilometres later you will come to Balaguer, the point you started off from.

Board and lodging

If you decide to spend the night at Balaguer, the starting point for the two itineraries described here, you have various hotels to choose from. From the excellent Hotel Comte Jaume d'Urgell to less luxurious ones (that also offer good facilities) such as the Hotel-Restaurant Mirador del Segre, Hotel-Restaurant Urgell and Hostal Solanes. The Hostal el Pont is the cheapest option.

If you want to spend the night nearer the Montsec itself, you can go to Cellers (Hostal del Llac) or Vilanova de Meià (Hostal Pissé). There is also the Hotel Juan Ramiro at the Fontdepou housing estate (Urbanització Fontdepou, km 26 on the Balaguer-Tremp road). Bed and breakfast establishments are also available at Àger, Pont de Muntanyana and Les Avellanes.

For those wishing to camp (the text mentions several free camping areas), there is the Badia camping site at Àger and, 2 kms from the Baronia de Sant Oïsme on the Cellers road, the Zodiac II camping site, with bar, restaurant and supermarket facilities.

Other places of interest

- Balaguer (cf. page 173).

- Àger collegiate church. One of the most interesting church-fortresses in Catalonia. An XIth century Romanesque church within a castle, it has a XIV-XVth century Gothic cloister and is now being restored. There is a project to convert the collegiate church into a museum. The building is to be found on a hillock above the village of Àger, on km 32 of itinerary 10A.

- Castell de Mur and Santa Maria collegiate church. The main historical monument in the whole of the Tremp valley. The majority of the murals decorating the basilica apses are in Boston Museum (U.S.A.). The 10th century castle has 3 metre thick walls and a graceful tower. It is near Guàrdia de Tremp. You can reach Castell de Mur by taking a road to the left off the continuation of the C-147 local road, about 4 kms north of Cellers (cf. itinerary 10B).

- Vilanova de Meià. A typical village with old buildings and a charming square. The church has a beautiful Gothic arch.

11

AIGÜESTORTES AND
SANT MAURICI LAKE NATIONAL PARK

The Park is in the Pallars Sobirà and Pallars Jussà *comarques* (Central Pyreneean region). It is the only national park in Catalonia, although the I.U.C.N. does not recognize it as a park because of the hydroelectric activity taking place there.

Inaugural date: 21st October, 1955.

Area: at present, 10,230 hectares. Including the future enlargement: 22,396 hectares.

Park offices: Parc Nacional d'Aigüestortes i Estany de Sant Maurici,
      Serveis Territorials del Medi Natural
      Camp de Mart, 35
      25004 Lleida.

Habitats: Subalpine mountain pine and fir trees, Scotch pine and beech woods, heaths, Alpine meadows, scree and rocky areas, rivers and high mountain lakes.

Interesting species:
- *Present all the year round*: Goshawk, Golden Eagle, Bearded Vulture, Ptarmigan, Capercaillie, Tengmalm's Owl, Black Woodpecker, Great Spotted Woodpecker, Ring Ouzel, Crested Tit, Treecreeper, Short-toed Treecreeper, Dipper, Citril Finch, Crossbill, Chough, Alpine Chough.
- *Summer visitors*: Griffon Vulture, Woodcock, Crag Martin, Rock Pipit, Red-backed Shrike, Dunnock, Alpine Accentor, Garden Warbler, Whinchat, Rock Thrush, Marsh Tit, Nuthatch, Wallcreeper, Yellowhammer, Bullfinch, Golden Oriole.

Description and habitat

The National Park of Aigüestortes and the lake of Sant Maurici are situated in the axial Pyrenean range and are an exceptional area for nature-lovers, be they hikers, geologists, botanists, ornithologists, etc.

This high mountain park is partly in the *Comarca* of Pallars Sobirà and partly in that of the Pallars Jussà, between the rivers Noguera Pallaresa and Noguera Ribagorçana. In simple terms,the area may be said to be divided into two major valleys: the valley of Sant Nicolau, which faces west, and which may be reached via Boï village, and the valley of the Escrita which faces east, with Espot as its central point. The heads of these two valleys meet at a col 2,423 metres high. It is called Portarró d'Espot. The highest summit is Peguera, 2,982 metres high, although Els Encantats, two immense granite peaks 2,747 metres high overlooking Sant Maurici lake, are more famous and are also symbols of the Park.

One of the foremost features about this whole region is that it has been shaped by glacial phenomena. Dozens of small lakes (gouged out by ice), waterfalls, streams and peat bogs mixed in with forests of mountain pine, fir tree, Scotch pine and beech, Alpine meadows, scree and summits form the terrain where a wealth of interesting plants and fascinating animals live, all of them typical high mountain species.

As both valleys are orientated in an east-west fashion, there is a great contrast between the vegetation on the sunny side and that on the shady side. The peripheral zones of the Park (the areas that suffer the greatest amount of human disturbance) are basically made up of **grass meadows and pasture**, with areas of **woodland** composed of deciduous trees such as hazel, alder, mountain ash tree, birch tree, poplar, ash and willow. These areas contain species more often associated with hilly or Mediterranean areas whereas the entire Park is above the 1,600 metre mark, at Subalpine and Alpine altitudes.

On the way into the park there are **forests of Scotch pine**, a conifer with a special bluish hue and an orange coloured trunk. This forest is on the sunny slopes of the Escrita valley and ascends as far as the 1,800-2,000 metre mark.

In Sant Nicolau valley, above the La Llebreta lake, there is a forest called Bosc de Llacs, which is especially interesting. It is a **mixed forest** with beech trees, birch, poplar and is the only forest in the Park with such characteristics. It is very damp, with very varied vegetation and abundant fauna, especially birds and amphibians.

Between the 1,600 and 1,900 metre mark there are **fir woods**. The largest fir wood in the Park is the Bosc de les Raspes, south of the Espot-Sant Maurici road. It is very richly wooded with huge trees covered in goat's-beard spiraea (a lichen that gives them a mysterious appearance). This wood is a refuge for many species of animals in winter.

As you climb up the mountain, there is a species of tree that becomes more and more predominant: **mountain pine**, a species which is very resistent to the cold, snow and strong mountain winds. The undergrowth beneath the mountain pine is usually composed of Wortle-berry and rhododendron.

On sunny Subalpine slopes there are **heaths** of juniper, bearberry, laburnum, and rhododendron.

At about the 2,200 metre mark you enter the Alpine area where there are no trees because of the harsh climate. From 2,200 up to 2,800 metres the scenery is made up of **Alpine meadows**, that in July and August are covered in Alpine flowers. Both the animals and the plants living here are adapted to a very rapid life-cycle, because the snow is present here almost up until summer and begins to fall again soon after that season comes to an end.

As you climb up farther, the meadows give way to **scree, summits and other rocky parts**, that have no vegetation. Only a few species of lichen and animals can survive here, and are generally very interesting: Ptarmigan, Alpine Accentor, Stoat, Wild Goat and Snow Vole.

The **lakes** (estanys) in the Park are not very attractive for the birds because they lack aquatic vegetation. The odd Grey Wagtail, Dipper, and sporadic Common Sandpiper may occasionally be seen there. The only lakes which have aquatic vegetation are La Llebreta, Ratera and Dels Barbs.

How to visit the area

To reach the area from Barcelona, you should take the A-2 motorway as far as Martorell. Proceed along the N-2 road to Tàrrega and take the C-148 local road to Balaguer and Alfarràs. In Alfarràs you must turn on to the N-230 road, pass through Benabarre, and continue as far as the Pont de Muntanya turning, where itinerary 10A finished. Then you drive on the N-230 towards the Vall d'Aran. Soon after entering the village of Sopeira it is worth stopping in a lay-by on the right-hand side of the road before entering a series of tunnels. On the right you will see some fine cliffs where interesting birds such as Bearded Vulture, Griffon Vulture, Egyptian Vulture, Golden Eagle, Short-toed Eagle, Peregrine Falcon, Kestrel, Raven, Alpine Chough and Blue Rock Thrush may all be seen. In winter it is also worth stopping after the tunnels at the Escales dam, where Wallcreeper may also be seen.

Keep driving north and 3 kms after Pont de Suert, you should take the L-500 road in the direction of Caldes de Boí. Less than one kilometre after the Erill-la-vall turning, you will come to the Boí road on your right. Boí will be your base for the Aigüestortes itinerary (11A).

To go from Boí to Espot, where itinerary 11B to Sant Mauici begins, there are two possible routes. Both these routes are quite long because there are no direct roads despite the short distance between the two villages as the crow flies.

The first of these two routes (122 kms across areas of Pyrenean foothills) takes you back to Pont de Suert. From there you must take the winding C-144 road to La Pobla de Segur acroos the Port de Perves (mountain pass). It is a very interesting route because along the way you can see Short-toed Eagle, Golden Eagle, Griffon Vulture and Egyptian Vulture. The pass is a good area for spotting Rock Thrush, Red-backed Shrike, Great Grey Shrike, Common Wheatear, as well as the rather rarer Tawny Pipit. Once you have arrived in La Pobla de Segur, you should take the C-147 road to Sort. Before reaching Sort you will pass through the impressive Congost de Collegats

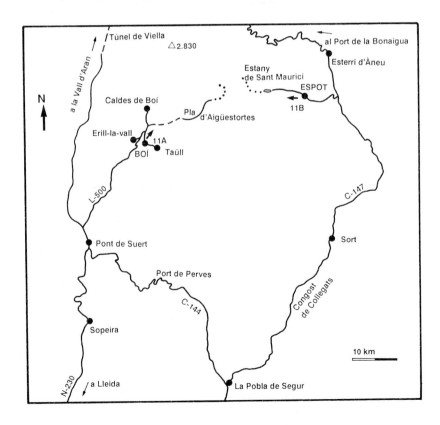

(creek), which was officially declared to be a Nature Reserve and Picturesque Spot. After passing through Gerri de la Sal, with its saltpans and old XIIth century monastery, you drive on through Sort, Llavorsí, until, just before La Guingueta d'Àneu (with its reservoir where Mallard, Cetti's Warbler, Kingfisher, and, in winter, Grey Heron may all be seen, as well as other species), there is a narrow, twisting road (LV-5004) to the left that leads to Espot. On the way up, Red-backed Shrike are common, and may be seen perched on the bushes beside the road.

The second option (108 kms across much more northern European and Alpine landscapes) involves taking the N-230 road towards the Vall d'Aran through the Viella tunnel. The entrance to the tunnel is in a beautiful high mountain area. In Viella (where there is a petrol station), you should take the C-142 local road to Salardú, following along the valley (which is famous for its Romanesque churches) as far as the Bonaigua mountain pass. On your way over the pass, look out for Alpine Chough, Golden Eagle, Rock Thrush (on the scree beneath the Mare de Déu de les Ares sanctuary), Crag Martin, Whinchat, Rock Bunting, Linnet and other passerines in the bushes beside the road. In winter the road may well be closed because of the snow. Before leaving the Vall d'Aran, do enquire about the state of the roads!

As you make your way down from the Bonaigua pass, you will enter one of the largest fir and mountain pine forests in the Pyrenees, the Mata de València. There are plenty of forest species to be seen here: Black Woodpecker, Capercaillie, Goshawk, Woodcock, Tawny Owl, Tengmalm's Owl, Treecreeper, etc. The river is a Nature Reserve for the protection of the otter, and also forms part of the Peripheral Protection Area of the National Park. Even if you decide to drive to Sant Maurici via Pont de Perves, you should devote any time you have available to a visit to this zone, because in the National Park itself there is no forest like it. Once you are on the road again, you will arrive in Esterri d'Àneu, where there are plenty of food shops. You should now drive along the C-147 road. Once you have driven past the petrol station (the only one in the area), you will arrive at La Guingueta, and soon after, at the Espot turning.

If you wish to get to the National Park on the public transport facilities, there are regular bus services from Barcelona and Lleida to Boí and Espot, where there are also four-wheel drive taxis for hire.

It is best to start off in the early morning if you are to cover the full programme on these two itineraries. Remember that the drive from Boí to Espot will take a good half day, whichever of the routes you choose. A sensible way of organizing your visit would be to spend a full day on the Aigüestortes itinerary (11 A), the following morning on the famous Romanesque churches at Taüll (cf. other places of interest), and, at midday, to drive to Espot. The next full day could be set aside for visiting the Sant Maurici-Ratera area (itinerary 11 B). The National Park can be visited at all times of year, but in winter it can be very difficult because of the heavy snow on the roads the itinerary follows. However, winter visits are worthwhile if only to see the snow on the mountains and the frozen lakes. The perfect time of the year to visit the Park is from the end of May to the beginning of July. After that, the presence of thousands of tourists makes observation of the shyer species quite difficult. Nonetheless, the Park itself continues to offer all the charm of the preceding period.If you rise early in the morning, you will be sure to find almost no one around even in summer. Summer storms are quite usual, so be sure to take a raincoat in case a shower catches you out in the open. From September to November birds are not so easily spotted, but the autumn colours in the trees and the gentle light make the landscape very attractive.

Birdwatching

11 A. Aigüestortes itinerary

Starting point and end of the itinerary: Boí **Time needed**: one day **Means of transport**: by car and on foot **Observations**: tricky in winter

You begin the itinerary in the Boí Valley which is famous not only for the National Park but for its many Romanesque churches. If you visit these fine old monuments, do not forget your binoculars because old buildings are often good places for birds such as Swallow and House Martin, Tree Sparrow, White Wagtail and Black Redstart, with its typical call. In areas with trees and vegetation around the churches it is easy to hear Nightingale, Garden Warbler, Blackcap, Golden Oriole, Chaffinch and Serin, and you might also see Cirl Bunting, Yellowhammer, Goldfinch and Linnet. Western Whip Snake are also to be seen in this zone, and you must be on the look out for Griffon Vulture and Golden Eagle flying above you or on the surrounding ridges. In the evening you should also listen for the repetitive whistle of the Scop's Owl. There is one of the Park's small Information Centres in the square here. Unfortunately it is only open in the months of July and August. You will be able to get maps and a guidebook to the Park. Nearby there are shops where you can get food.

To start the itinerary itself you should take the forest track sign-posted to the Park. You will find it 2 kms above the village of Boí. This track is in bad condition and it is difficult to make your way along it in a normal car because of the loose rocks. If you do not want to risk it with your car, you can leave it and continue on foot, although you must remember that it is 5 kms from this point to the entrance to the Park. You can also arrange to be taken in a four-wheel drive taxi from Boí, although this system is not too convenient as it will be the driver who decides where and when to stop! It is worth having a go with your own vehicle. Drive slowly and take good care. The good news is that this run down track turns into a fine tarmac road once it enters the Park! If you decide to go up on foot, be sure to wear sensible walking shoes (to avoid twisted ankles on the rocks) and to start off in the early morning so as not to arrive in the Park too late on in the day.

The climb passes through meadows and small patches of deciduous trees, ash and hazel trees where you will see more or less the same birds as in the village's surrounding area. When you come to the Sant Nicolau stream at the bottom of the valley, however, you may care to look out for Pyrenean Brook Salamander, an endemic amphibian in the Pyrenean range.

Just before entering the Park, in some meadows on the left, you will find the only free camping area on this side of the park. You can camp here, but there are no facilities.

The tarmac begins soon after, and will continue as far as the Aigüestortes plain. You will suddenly come to a plain at the altitude of 1,600 metres. In the plain is the peaceful **Llebreta lake** (Estany de la Llebreta), which is surrounded by meadows. On the left-hand side of the road there is a steep slope with scree and scattered Scotch and mountain pines, as well as box-wood and wild rose bushes. On rocks beside the road, you may well spot Common Wall Lizard sunning themselves or hunting for insects. Red-backed Shrike breed in

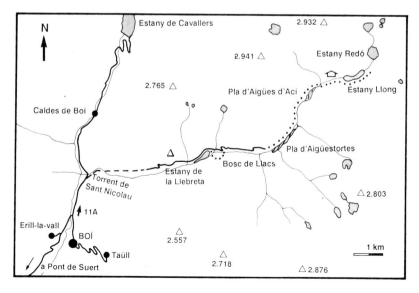

the wild rose bushes, as do Crag Martin on the small crags up above. Kestrel, Bearded Vulture, and in summer, Griffon Vulture, may all be seen on this slope.

The Llebreta lake lies to the right. It is surrounded by a bog where there are plenty of Common Toad and Grass Frog. In summer, the young of these two species can be counted in their thousands on the dry land.

Beyond the lake there is a slope with a mantle of rich mixed woodland - the most profuse in the Park. At lower levels the woodland is made up of Beech, Poplars, Birch and other deciduous trees, but farther up, firs and mountain pine predominate. It is worth wandering off the road for a moment, and following the path across to the far side of the lake where there is a pleasant meadow with birch trees and mountain ash trees. Here Rock Bunting are to be found breeding among the rocks, Dunnock in the rhododendron bushes and Goshawk, Jay and Green Woodpecker may be heard calling from the forest. Mistle Thrush, Wren and Firecrest can also be seen in this region.

Take the car again (or keep on walking if you have come up on foot) up the winding road and look down on the beautiful view of the lake and the surrounding plain from above. A river crashes down on your right. The beautiful waterfalls are known as "**Toll del Mas**". Just before you reach the car park (where you should leave your car), the road passes through an area with huge boulders where Black Redstart breed. The warden in the small wooden hut will give you a sheet of paper with the regulations that must be observed within the National Park.

You have now arrived at one of the most fascinating spots in this Pyrenean Park, and one to which the Park owes its name: **Pla d'Aigüestortes** (Aigüestortes Plain). Unfortunately, in the summer season hundreds of visitors flock here all at the same time, and the area loses most of its peaceful nature. This is one of the best reasons for coming up in your own car: you will be able to get there very early in the morning, before most of the tourists arrive.

The plain is an old Ice Age lake, which has nowadays become filled up with silt. It has turned into a plain where the river branches out into several courses which wind their way around islands full of fir and mountain pine trees. Amongst the rhododendron bushes there are plenty of attractive mountain flowers. In the crystal-clear waters of the river you can see large trout, and the quieter reaches of the river are a good place to see Dipper.

If you follow the footbridges leading from island to island, you can take a pleasant walk that will bring you into contact with plenty of forest species such as Coal Tit, Crested Tit, Long-tailed Tit (the former two species are especially common in all the Park's forests), Goldcrest, Short-toed Treecreeper, Crossbill, Song Thrush, Blackbird, Mistle Thrush, Jay and

Carrion Crow. Some of the tree trunks have woodpecker holes in them. You may well see three species of woodpecker here: Green Woodpecker, Great Spotted Woodpecker and the spectacular Black Woodpecker. The latter two species breed in old birch and fir trees that grow among the rocks on the south-facing side of the mountain to the left of the track. Here you can also hear the cooing of Wood Pigeon, and, in the early morning, the call of the Goshawk. You may also be surprised to see, side by side, two finches that are associated with different habitats: Serin and Citril Finch. Above the south-facing slope there is a sheer cliff that is often visited by birds of prey such as Kestrel, Griffon Vulture, Bearded Vulture and Golden Eagle.

You may now choose between extending your walk in the surrounding area, or continuing along the track if you have the time.

If you opt for this latter suggestion, you will be able to observe how the wood thins out as you climb, thus affording you glimpses of birds such as Dunnock, Black Redstart and Raven. After a while, you will come to the **Pla d'Aigües d'Ací** (Aigües d'Ací plain), an old silted up lake which is very similar to the one at Aigüestortes. Once you have crossed the plain, the climb up to the **Estany Llong** (Llong lake) now begins. You will cross a forest of mountain pines where you will once again be seeing typical woodland species.

At the 1,980 metre mark you will come to the Estany Llong refuge, and, soon after, the lake itself. Alpine Chough and Chough are often seeing flying above this area. On the right there is a wood of mountain pines where Capercaillie and Black Woodpecker are to be seen.

On the way down (especially if you have only gone as far as Aigües-tortes), it is worth taking a walk in the **Bosc de Llacs** (Llacs forest), crossing the river at the Toll del Mas. It is interesting to descend through this wood as far as the Llebreta lake. This may well offer you the opportunity of observing woodland birds of a different kind from those seen in the more Alpine woods: Firecrest, Chiffchaff, Marsh Tit, Nuthatch, Green Woodpecker and Goshawk.

11 B. Sant Maurici itinerary

Starting point and end of the itinerary: Espot **Time needed:** one day **Means of transport:** by car and on foot **Observations:** tricky in winter

The itinerary begins at the point where Espot village ends and the tarmac road leading to the National Park starts. One of the last houses in the village, before the Romanesque Capella bridge, is one of the small Information centres (only open in July and August, from 9 am to 1 pm, and from 4 pm to 8 pm). In the shop "Esports Roya", however, you can find maps and guide-books, as well as camping gas and change. It is open all the year round.

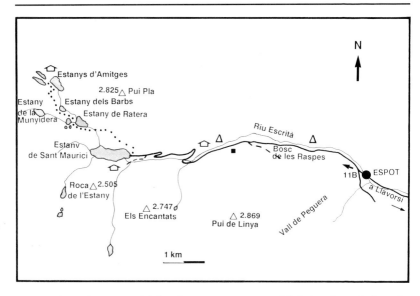

If you have no vehicle of your own or your visit is in winter (when the access road is usually snowbound), the 8 kms from Espot to Sant Maurici is a pleasant hike, as well as a good walk for forest birdwatching. If you have your own vehicle it is worth stopping off along the way and strolling into the forest (or simply standing around at the roadside for a while) to observe interesting species.

The itinerary is along a glacial valley. On the left-hand side of the initial sector of the track there is a steep slope which is covered with Scotch pine. On the right there is a series of grass meadows fringed with bushes and birch trees, where birds associated with open ground, such as Whinchat, Yellowhammer, Blue Tit or Whitethroat may be seen. Keep an eye on the opposite slope which in places is quite craggy, for large raptors such as Griffon Vulture, Golden Eagle, and sometimes even Bearded Vulture, may be seen flying over the ridge. At **km 1.2** (from the beginning of the itinerary), a track leads down to some meadows on the right. You may camp here if you have previously obtained permission in the village.

At **km 3**, the road enters the forest which is composed of fir and birch trees. This prolific forest (the best in the whole National Park) has varied flora and fauna. It is easy to observe all kinds of forest birds here: Blue Tit, Crested Tit, the noisy Chaffinch, Firecrest, Goldcrest, Blackbird, Mistle Thrush, Song Thrush, the pretty Bullfinch, Nuthatch, Robin, Jay, Treecreeper (both species), Sparrowhawk and many other species. Birds such as Capercaillie, Woodcock and Tengmalm's Owl - all interesting, though difficult to spot - take refuge in the highest and least accessible parts of the forest.

At **km 3.**6 you will come to a signpost indicating the Park limit. In summer a forest warden will issue you with a leaflet listing basic regulations to be followed during the visit. The height here is 1,620 metres and the impressive stone peaks of Els Encantats is for the first time to be seen on the horizon above the forest. On the left there is a track (in very bad condition at the beginning and cut off further on) leading to the Peguera valley. On the right there is a small hut which is always open. It is a perfect shelter for those caught by sudden showers, which are especially frequent in summer.

The road passes through an area of old forest where the trees are covered in goat's-beard spiraea (filament lichens of the *Usnea* genus), giving the area a mysterious air. From here you may well see or hear Black Woodpecker flying above the forest. After another kilometre, there is a bend in the road which crosses the river Escrita on the bridge known as "Pont de Pallers", where there is another refuge hut. It is not always open.

There is then a hairpin bend in the road. If you are on foot, you can avoid it by walking through a meadow with birch trees, juniper bushes and hazel trees on the left, approximately parallel to a line of electricity pylons. Other than shortening the route, this detour enables you to walk in among the trees. Rock Bunting is to be found here, and if you listen out for its strange call, it will be easier for you to spot it. If you keep on along the road (not taking the short cut), you will come to a path leading off to the right to the free camping area. You must remember, however, that there are no camping facilities here!

If you took the path up through the meadow, you will come out on to the road once again near a small hut. From here, you will have an excellent view of the U-shaped glacial valley beneath you. You are now at quite a height and the roads proceeds on the right-hand side of the river, that tumbles noisily down the valley. The forest becomes sparser on this slope, but the trees (Scotch pines and fir trees) are larger. Further on, mountain pine, birch and mountain ash trees start to appear. As you proceed along the track you will hear the characteristic call of the flocks of Crossbills. At **km 7**, on a sharp right-hand bend, there is a track leading off to the left to the Ernest Mallafré refuge hut and a short cut to **Sant Maurici lake**. The road cuts back a little, and a short distance beyond another bend, the lake opens up before you, framed between the Els Encantats and Roca de l'Estany peaks. If you are in a car, you will have to leave it here.

In summer, there are normally a lot of people here, but it is always worth stopping off a while, because the crumbs and refuse attract birds such as Chaffinch, Jay, Carrion Crow, Citril Finch and Black Redstart. It is also a good spot for Rock Bunting. In winter you may well see the odd flock of Siskin here. Around the Els Encantats peaks there are flocks of Chough and Alpine Chough to be seen, as well as Raven, Swift, House Martin and Crag Martin. You must also keep your eyes on the Pui Pla ridges north of the lake, for they are one of the best sites for observing Bearded Vulture, Golden Eagle and Griffon Vulture.

After resting awhile, you can continue on foot along the track skirting the right-hand side of the lake and leading up to the Ratera and D'Amitges lakes. If you wanted to go straight to the top you could hire a four-wheel drive taxi in Espot, a necessary step because it is forbidden to go up in private cars. But the charm of this marvellous itinerary would then have been lost!

This track is often particularly boggy and it is a good idea to wear Wellington boots if you do not want to end up with sodden feet! The route you are now on passes through mountain pine, sallow, birch and mountain ash trees. The vegetation is lush with plentiful mountain flowers (remember it is forbidden to pick them!) , among which the *Dactylohiza* and *Gymnadenia* genus orchids and the magnificent yellow martagon stand out. This first sector of forest is perfect for Crested Tit, Citril Finch, Firecrest, Wood Pigeon and Crossbill.

Tengmalm's Owl

Further on there is an old Guardia Civil post, where there are lots of birds to be seen. The view is also good from this point. Higher up, the forest begins to give way to an area which has a magnificent view of the whole valley, with Els Encantats, La Roca de l'Estany and the Sant Maurici Lake in the background. In the bushes and trees along the way there are Dunnock, Citril Finch and Mistle Thrush, as well as the spectacular butterfly *Parnassius apollo*.

At the 2,100 metre mark, the track crosses over a stream leading out of the **Ratera lake**. Soon after, you will see the lake. While not the biggest of the lakes, it is certainly one of the most beautiful in the Park. You should stop for a good while here, for there are sure to be plenty of Subalpine forest birds in the vicinity: Crossbill, Crested Tit, Coal Tit, Citril Finch, Short-toed Treecreeper, Chaffinch, Wren, and even the odd Red Squirrel. There are Capercaillie in the forest on the left of the track and in the trees beside the waterfall cascading down from Coma de l'Abeller. This species can sometimes be seen flying across the lake in the evening or at dawn.

There may be Black Redstart among the rocks on the left of the track, and Great Spotted Woodpecker usually breed on the hillock that separates the lake from the Ratera ponds. Grey Wagtail are to be seen on the banks of the lake, and maybe Common Sandpiper, Grass Frog and Pyrenean Brook Salamander too.

You should also keep an eye on the crags around you, for there are often large raptors, Chough and Alpine Chough about. Wallcreeper can sometimes be seen on the rock faces, although they are difficult to spot if you do not hear their whistle first.

If you follow the path a little farther up the mountain, you will soon come to the **Basses de Ratera** (Ratera ponds). It is an old lake which has been almost entirely silted up and covered in Bog Cotton. Dipper sometimes visit these ponds and the nearby Ratera lake.It is also a good place to listen out for the call of the Ring Ouzel. Two paths lead off from this point: the one on the left which leads to the Munyidera lake and the one you should follow straight ahead, which leads up to the D'Amitges lakes after skirting the small Dels Barbs lake. If time is running short or the weather is not too good, however, you may finish off the itinerary at the Ratera ponds, returning to the car on the track you came up on. If you decide to venture on, though, you will arrive at a fully Alpine habitat after ascending steeply.

One the way up, you will probably hear Dunnock singing. This species breeds in the rhododendron (*Rhododendron ferrugineum*) bushes. If you keep on as far as the **D'Amitges lakes** (where you may spend the night in a refuge hut with a fabulous view of the surrounding crags and rocky peaks), it is possible that you will see chamois, the tame but rather scarce Alpine Accentor and Rock Pipit. If you want to see Ptarmigan, you will have to take a long walk in the higher parts of the mountains, although this species is very difficult to spot.

Board and lodging

On either side of the National Park there are villages with plenty of restaurants and bed and breakfast lodgings where you can dine and sleep in the manner best suited to your budget.

In Espot you can eat at Ca la Palmira or Restaurant Juquim, and sleep at the Saurat, Sant Maurici and Roya hotels. There are also rooms to be rented in private homes. If you wish to camp there are two camping sites, El Sol i Neu and La Mola. They are both on the Espot access road. You can also camp on the free camping sites mentioned in the text. In the Park itself, you can only sleep at the Ernest Mallafré refuge hut at Sant Maurici (the only hut open all the year round) and at the D'Amitges hut in the D'Amitges region. There are also camping sites, hotels and bed and breakfast lodgings at La Guingueta and Esterri d'Àneu. If you go to the Mata de València forest in the Bonaigua valley, it is worth trying the food at the Hostal la Bonaigua at València d'Àneu.

In the Boí valley there are also plenty of restaurants, especially at Boí and Erill-la-vall (Hostal Fontdevila, Hostal Beneria, Residència Pey...). In summer, however, it can be difficult to get a table. The same may be said for hotel rooms which should be booked well in advance at that time of year. Camping is possible at the free camping area at the entrance to the Park (without facilities) or at the Boneta cmping site at Barruera. The only refuge hut on this side is the one you come to before the Llong lake.

Other places of interest

- The Boí valley has one of the best selections of Romanesque churches in the Pyrenees, many of them with beautiful bell towers, and often decorated with XIth and XIIth century friezes. Sant Feliu in Barruera, Sant Joan Baptista at Boí, Santa Eulàlia at Erill-la-vall, and, above all, Sant Climent and Santa Maria at Taüll, are all well worth a visit. The last two are National Monuments, although the original paintings are in the Art Museum of Catalonia in Barcelona.

- Sant Pere del Burgal. An old IXth century Visigothic monastery, later transformed into a Benedictine abbey. Cross the river Noguera Pallaresa on the bridge opposite Escaló (before arriving at La Guingueta d'Àneu), and take a track to the right. You will arrive at the ruins of the abbey in one kilometre.

12
ANDORRA

The Principality of the Valleys of Andorra (Andorra) is a small Catalan-speaking country in the Pyrenees between the states of Spain and France.

Area: 468 km^2.

Habitats: Subalpine mountain pine and fir tree forests, Scotch pine and ilex woods, heaths, Alpine meadows, scree and rocky terrain, rivers and high mountain lakes, grass meadows and agricultural zones.

Interesting species:
- *Present all the year round*: Golden Eagle, Bearded Vulture, Capercaillie, Partridge, Ptarmigan, Black Woodpecker, Great Spotted Woodpecker, Dipper, Nuthatch, Short-toed Treecreeper, Treecreeper, Alpine Chough, Chough, Alpine Accentor, Crested Tit, Rock Sparrow, Snow Finch, Citril Finch, Crossbill, Rock Bunting.
- *Summer visitors*: Griffon Vulture, Alpine Swift, Crag Martin, Rock Pipit, Melodious Warbler, Ring Ouzel, Rock Thrush, Sardinian Warbler, Dartford Warbler, Bonelli's Warbler, Wallcreeper, Red-backed Shrike.

Description and habitat

By reason of its situation on the southern slopes of the Pyrenees, Andorra is a very mountainous country with an average height of almost 2,000 metres. There are two main valleys which are quite steep-sided (especially the one to the west). The rivers Valira d'Ordino and Valira d'Orient run along these valleys, which converge just above Andorra la Vella, the capital of Andorra. It is in these two valleys that most of the villages are to be found. There are plenty of secondary valleys with clear streams. Some of these valleys have lakes of a glacial origin at their heads. The highest peaks are amost 3,000 metres high.

Until the second half of this century, the economy of Andorra was very similar to that of other Pyrenean valleys, being based on livestock-rearing and mountain agriculture. In the last few decades, however, there has been a tremendous boom in commerce and tourism, as well as the more recent development of the winter sports industry, which has completely revolutionized the social and economical structure of the country. Urban growth snowballed anarchically as a consequence of deficient territorial planning policy and shortcomings in environmental legislation. This led to the partial destruction of the country's natural and scenic wealth. Despite this, these Andorran valleys still retain elements of remarkable biological interest.

In the lower areas, and though this may seem surprising, there are Mediterranean-type ilex woods that rapidly turn into mountain forests as the altitude rises: first there are Scotch pines, and further up Subalpine forests made up of firs and, above all, mountain pine forests. Above the tree-line, where the harsh climate makes it impossible for trees to survive, there are Alpine thickets and meadow land, as well as areas of scree. In many places, there are birch copses or thickets (box-wood, laburnum heath and rhododendron), many of which have been severely cut back in the past. The flowering in spring of the rhododendron (red flowers) and the laburnum (yellow) is particularly spectacular, as is the abundance and variety of Alpine flowers. On the banks of the rivers you will come across riverside woodland. Birch is predominant in the higher zones and alder and willow in the lower parts.

From the point of view of the fauna, the areas which perhaps conserve most interest are the Subalpine woods and the high mountain meadows. Mammals such as Pine Marten, Stoat and Wild Cat are still common, although Chamois are now rare due to excessive hunting. Bear were common in former times (the Pyrenees' largest bears were hunted here), but now this species only appears rarely in Andorra. The birdlife is basically made up of mountain and high mountain species, although lower areas are also inhabited by Mediterranean species.

The fields used in agriculture are mainly on the valley bottoms. In the last few years, traditional activities have lost ground and this has lead to a serious decrease in agricultural and ancient nomadic shepherd practices. From having been a vital industry before, forestry has also become less important. This phenomenon, however, will lead to the gradual recovery of the forests.

How to visit the area

From Barcelona, the shortest route to Andorra is Manresa-Berga-Cadí tunnel (toll)-La Seu d'Urgell and then across the southern frontier into Andorra along the C-145 local road. If you are heading there from the Lleida steppes (Itineraries 9C and 9D), from the Montsec (Itineraries 10 A and 10 B) or from the Aigüestortes and Sant Maurici Lake National Park (Itinerary 11B), you should take the C-1313 local road to La Seu d'Urgell. The only other frontier pass (in the north-east) is on the N-20 road from France. You can reach Andorra by bus from Barcelona (Alsina Graells company, with buses leaving from the Ronda Universitat) or Lleida. You can reach the areas where the itineraries start off by car, and, in the case of itinerary 12 A, by the regular bus line that links up the villages of Andorra.

The official language in Andorra is Catalan, but French and Spanish are also used. The official currency is the peseta and the French franc.

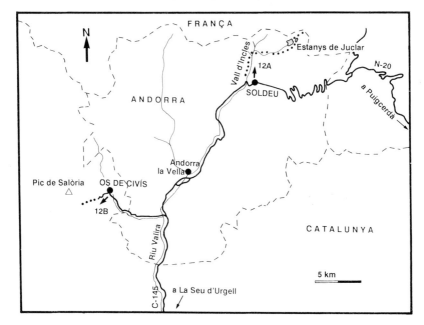

The two recommended itineraries should be covered on foot. Itinerary 12 A is the longer of the two, and will take you 5 hours (there and back). The itinerary climbs 500 metres to an area of lakes and calls for a certain degree of fitness. Itinerary 12 B is much gentler, and takes less than two hours (not counting additional options described at the end of each itinerary).

The best time of year to visit is between the end of spring and autumn. The first part of itinerary 12A is very much visited by tourists in July, and especially in August, so it is necessary to start off early in the morning in those months. A good pair of thick-soled mountain boots is recommended, especially on itinerary 12A, and you must also beware of the very intense high-mountain sun. You must also be ready for cold and rain, for the weather, even in summer, can change from sunshine to rain in minutes. In winter the birdlife loses a lot of its interest, and most of the tracks covered in the itineraries are snowbound, especially on the higher ground where the snow may remain for six or seven months of the year. On some stretches, the track may be impassable if you do not have the right gear. It is not too advisable to follow the itineraries in winter. Waterproof mountain boots, legging and a good overcoat (as well as a certain degree of experience of mountain hikes in winter) are vital requirements if you venture forth!

Although in summer it is nòt strictly necessary, you are advised to get hold of maps of the area, especially if you want to go on excursions other than itineraries 12A and 12B. The best maps are N°7 (Haute Arriège/Andorra) in the "Randonées pyrénées" series which is published by the French Institut Géografique Nationale (in French and Spanish) and the maps called "Andorra" and "Sant Joan de l'Erm" which are published by the Alpina publishing company (in Catalan and Spanish).

Birdwatching

12A. Itinerary in the Incles and Juclar valleys

Starting point and end of the itinerary: 1 km from Soldeu **Time needed**: about 5 hours **Means of transport**: on foot **Observations**: best in the morning. Mountain boots. Tricky in winter

The starting point for this itinerary is at the foot of the Incles valley, at the point where the valley makes contact with the CG.2 road, about 1 km below the village of Soldeu. If you are coming from the south, you will find the access road into the valley about 5 kms beyond Canillo, after passing a petrol station. It is on a very sharp bend at a point where the road crosses over the river that flows down the Incles valley.

There is a track along the left-hand side of the river. It is quite passable by car, and leads along the bottom of the valley to a camping site. You should leave the car here, though, and continue the itinerary on foot. You are in the wide and glacial Incles valley. The landscape is made up of meadows with the odd shepherd's hut. On the higher slopes there are mountain pine forests. Continue along the track, which for the moment proceeds along the left-hand side of the valley. You should be seeing Song Thrush, Skylark, Yellowhammer, and in parts where the laburnum scrub approaches the track, you may also see Dunnock, Whinchat and Rock Bunting. In autumn you may sometimes see species such as Redwing, Fieldfare and Brambling. You must also keep an eye on the sky, where there may be Golden Eagle, Sparrowhawk and Kestrel. In places where the track comes close to the river, you may well see Dipper and Grey Wagtail.

You will come to a signpost indicating "Port d'Incles" to the left and "Estany del Juclar (1.50')" to the right. You should take the right-hand road. You will immediately cross the river and arrive at the camping site. Keep straight on along the track, which now crosses a small clear mountain pine wood with a few birch trees. This will be the most forested area on the whole itinerary, and it is worth taking your time to look for Coal Tit, Crested Tit, Goldcrest, Citril Finch, Crossbill, Chaffinch, Bullfinch, Great Spotted Woodpecker, Mistle Thrush and Ring Ouzel, which may also be seen on the south-facing slopes of the valley, as well as Kestrel.

In the vicinity of a small picnic area the ground is clearer and Tree Pipit, Whinchat and Yellowhammer may be encountered. As on all the various stages of the itinerary, you should look out for Golden Eagle, Raven, Chough and Alpine Chough on the high ground.

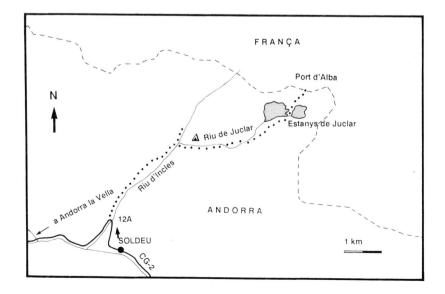

Snow Finch

You will cross a small bridge over the river at the picnic area, and should look for a small path which is marked with white and red paint on the stones. The path begins to climb steeply between great blocks of stone, laburnum bushes and scattered pines on the left-hand side of the river. Here you may see Dunnock, Wren, Citril Finch, Rock Bunting and you may even put up the odd covey of Partridge. About half-way up the path between the picnic area and the lakes, you will once again find a bridge over the river. You can see Grey Wagtail and Dipper on the river here.

From this point onwards, the trees begin to disappear and meadows and low bushes become the predominant form of vegetation. On the rockier slopes you may have the chance to spot Alpine Accentor and the rare Wallcreeper. The path crosses over to the left-hand side of the river and a little farther on, after passing by a ruined house and a rain gauge, you will come to another bridge which once again leads you to the right-hand side of the valley. The areas of meadows and rocks are good for Wheatear, as well as for Black Redstart, which will become more frequent as you continue on up. You will also be able to see Chough, Alpine Chough and Raven in this zone.

You will arrive at the Juclar lakes (2,299 metres high) about three hours after starting the itinerary. There are two glacial lakes, the first of which has been enlarged with the aid of a dam. The habitat here is made up of meadows and rocks. To the birds mentioned for the last part of the itinerary, Rock Pipit and Ptarmigan (if you are very lucky) may now be added.

To the north is the mountain range that marks the frontier between Andorra and France. To the north east you may see two mountain passes: El Port de Juclar and El Port d'Alba, which is to the right of the Juclar pass and a little higher up. You may care to climb up to these two passes, thus increasing your chances of coming across Ptarmigan. To reach them, you must take the path that skirts the first lake on the right-hand side and then climb up the slope towards the passes. From each of the passes you will have a view of a different French valley. The return route is the same as the way up, but now you will cover the ground in less time (2 hours).

12B. Itinerary in the Salòria valley

Starting point and end of the itinerary: Espot **Time needed:** one day **Means of transport:** by car and on foot **Observations:** tricky in winter

To reach the starting point of this itinerary, you must first get to the village of Os (or Aós) de Civís. This village is within the Spanish State, but is best reached from Andorra because it is situated at the head of a valley that is in Andorra on its lower reaches.

A few kilometres after leaving Andorra la Vella on the Seu d'Urgell road (CG.1), you should turn right in Aixovall and follow the signposts to Aós (8 kms away). You will cross over the river Valira and see that the road continues along the valley of the river Aós (a tributary of the Valira), which will be on your left-hand side. The valley is very narrow, and on either side you will see very steep and rocky slopes. The north-facing slopes are more forested, especially with Scotch pine, and on the sparser south-facing slopes there are ilex trees, giving a Mediterranean environment which permits certain species such as Sardinian Warbler and Dartford Warbler to get a foothold in these valleys. Although the valley is very narrow and limits your view of the higher slopes, you may choose to stop off and birdwatch at one of the picnic sites on the left-hand side of the road (the larger ones 2 kms beyond the village of Bixessarri and just before entering the Spanish State are the best places to stop). Other than the afore-mentioned warblers (which are quite shy and may sometimes only be pinpointed by their call), you may see Crag Martin, several species of tit, Firecrest, Jay, Great Spotted Woodpecker and perhaps even hear Black Woodpecker. Raptors such as Peregrine Falcon, as well as Chough and Alpine Chough are also to be seen here. Grey Wagtail and Dipper are common on the river.

The valley opens up as you reach Aós de Civís. There are meadows with scattered juniper bushes as well as the odd birch and Scotch pine tree. Cross through the village on the tarmac road and over two rivers. The road begins to wind its way up to the Borda La Plana. The tarmac comes to an end and you now continue along a track. About one kilometre from the large house, on a sharp bend, you will come to a turning. The main track continues climbing up to the left (as far as the Conflent pass), and on the right there is another track, which is the one you should take. Leave the car here and start the itinerary on foot.

You may care to spend some time birdwatching in the meadows around the small group of houses and on the edges of the forest, where Tree Pipit, Dunnock, Mistle Thrush, Blackbird, Red-backed Shrike, Carrion Crow, Chaffinch and Yellowhammer are to be seen.

Once you are on the track, you will immediately come to a young wood of mountain pine and fir trees. You are now in the north-facing side of the valley of Salòria. The south-facing side is much more sparse in vegetation and rockier, with scattered Scotch pine trees, bearberry heath and meadows on the lower slopes. After about 150 metres you will come to a turning to the right that leads down to the river, but you must keep straight on, as you should also do when you come to paths leading off to the left further on (they are old forest tracks used for timber extraction).

You may well hear the typical call of the Black Woodpecker, and come across the odd Great Spotted Woodpecker, Goldcrest, Wren, both species of treecreeper, Coal Tit, Crested Tit, Jay, Chaffinch, Bullfinch, Crossbill and

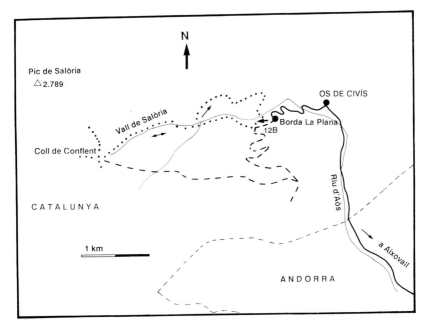

Siskin. This latter species has population booms in some years. In this wood there are also Capercaillie to be seen, but they are rare and very shy. To increase your chances of seeing one (almost wishful thinking!), you can take the track leading off to the left (to the Conflent Pass) from the place you left the car.

It is worth keeping an eye on the south-facing slope, which further up the valley begins to become covered in laburnum heath. Raptors such as Golden Eagle and Kestrel may be seen there. You should also take note of the small parallel paths that run along its lower part, for it is along these paths that you will have to return later.

Remember to keep walking straight along the track until you reach the end of the track, that leads to the river. Do not take any notice of the paths leading off on either side.

The Conflent pass, with the Salòria peak and large tracts of meadowland (where you have the chance of seeing raptors such as Griffon Vulture, Bearded Vulture and kestrel) is at the head of the valley. You will get a much better view of the region if you climb up the mountain towards the pass, as is explained in the final section, which is recommended at the end of this itinerary.

To continue the itinerary, you should cross over to the south-facing slopes by crossing the river and taking one of the paths leading down the valley. Be sure to take a path that passes through the meadow rather than one that goes through the laburnum bushes (which are more difficult to negotiate). You should make your way down without wandering away from the river. This bushy zone, with scattered pines and old terrace stone walls, is ideal for seeing Black Redstart, Whinchat, Dunnock and Rock Bunting. Cross the stream and you will come to a small shepherd's hut. The path then descends to the river. Once you have reached the river, do not take the path that leads away on the other side, but follow the left-hand bank of the river. You will soon come to the path you have to follow. In this area, there are meadows with juniper and wild rose bushes, and pines on the higher slopes. Dipper may be seen on the river, and Black Woodpecker inhabit the north-facing forest slopes (listen for its call on the wing). Raptors such as Sparrowhawk will still also be seen.

At a junction in the path, you should take the right-hand turning. Once Borda La Plana comes into view, look out for the area where there have been landslides into the river. Here you must descend to the river and take the path (it is quite visible) which leads away from the right-hand side of the only black-coloured landslide (consisting of dark materials). Take the path that leads down to the river and cross it when you are opposite the afore-mentioned path. It will lead you back to the track you came on in the car, which will be about a hundred metres further on to the right.

There is also the option of going up to the Conflent pass (about 1 hour 15 mins.). To do this you should take the path that leads off at the end of the track, at the river. The path winds up through an area of meadows with the odd patch of woodland. Citril Finch, Black Redstart, Partridge, raptors, Raven, Alpine Chough and Chough are all to be seen here, as well as Rock Pipit and Alpine Accentor at the summit. From the pass you may care to climb up the Salòria peak (2,789 metres high), where there is a chance of seeing Ptarmigan. This last climb, however, will make the walk a good longer and more tiring.

Board and lodging

The touristic and hostelry offer in Andorra is remarkably wide. Hotels and restaurants of various tariffs and categories can be found in almost all the towns in Andorra. At the height of the skiing and holiday season, as well as at weekends, it may sometimes be difficult to find free places. There are several camping sites and mountain refuges. The refuges are far from the roads and can only be reached on foot.

You can find lodging near the beginning of the recommended itineraries. For itinerary 12A, you will be able to find hotels at Encamp (25 hotels), Canillo (13 hotels) and Soldeu (9 hotels). There is also a camping site in the Incles valley (cf. itnierary 12A). The camping site is open from June to September and has a restaurant service. For itinerary 12B, there are 21 hotels at Sant Julià de Lòria. At Borda La Plana (cf. itinerary 12B), there is a hotel (hostal d'Aós) with a restaurant service.

If you want to start the itineraries early in the morning, it is worth bearing in mind the time you might waste on the stretch of road between Andorra la Vella and Les Escaldes, where there are often traffic jams. It might well, therefore, be worth finding a hotel nearer the itinerary area.

There are also plenty of high standard restaurants, the prices of which will be commensurate with the quality of the food being served. The following restaurants may be mentioned: La Borda del Rastell at Sant Julià de Lòria, La Borda de l'Avi at La Massana and the famous Restaurant 1900 at Les Escaldes.

Other places of interest

- Romanesque church of Santa Coloma. This has a very original cylindrical bell tower. Between Sant Julià de Lòria and Andorra la Vella.

- Encamp and Sant Joan de Caselles Romanesque churches. Between Canillo and Ransol.

- Casa de la Vall (Andorra la Vella). A XVIth century rustic, mountain-style house. It is the seat of the Andorran Government (Consell General de les Valls). It may be visited from 10 am to 1 pm, and from 3.30 pm to 6.30 pm. On Saturdays it is only open in the mornings. On Sundays it is closed all day.

- La Seu d'Urgell (Catalonia). There is a large Romanesque cathedral here as well as the Urgell Diocesan Museum (Xth-XVIIIth century religious art). It is 10 kms away from Andorra's southern frontier.

13
CADÍ-MOIXERÓ NATURAL PARK

This Park is in the eastern Pyrenees, at the place where the *comarques* of Cerdanya, Alt Urgell and Berguedà meet. It forms part of the inner ridges of the Pyrenean foothills. The Cadí-Moixeró Natural Park and the Aigüestortes and Sant Maurici Lake National Park are the two most important high mountain reserves in Catalonia.

Inaugural date: July 1983.

Area: 41,342 hectares, of which 1,671 belong to the Pedraforca Natural Landscape Area of National Interest.

Park offices address: Parc Natural del Cadí-Moixeró
Avinguda Reina Elisenda, s/n,
08695 Bagà.

Habitats: cliffs and rocky areas, Subalpine forests of mountain pine and fir trees, Scotch pines, beech woods, heaths, grassy meadows, Alpine meadows, agricultural land.

Interesting species:
- *Present all the year round*: Bearded Vulture, Goshawk, Golden Eagle, Peregrine Falcon, Capercaillie, Tengmalm's Owl, Black Woodpecker, Great Spotted Woodpecker, Crag Martin, Dipper, Rock Pipit, Alpine Chough, Chough, Bonelli's Warbler, Crested Tit, Nuthatch, Short-toed Treecreeper, Red-backed Shrike, Crossbill, Rock Bunting.
- *Summer visitors*: Short-toed Eagle, Griffon Vulture, Alpine Swift, Wryneck, Rock Thrush, Alpine Accentor, Wallcreeper, Ring Ouzel, Citril Finch, Bullfinch.
- *Winter visitors*: Snow Finch, Brambling.

Description and habitat

The Cadí-Moixeró Natural Park is one of the best-known and admired mountain regions in Catalonia. Its landscape is very spectacular and it is also fairly close to Barcelona. The first reference to the need to conserve the area dates back to 1931, when the Generalitat (Catalan autonomous Government during the Republic) took steps in this direction. There were then further protection plans until the year 1983, when the Generalitat (reinstated in 1979) officially declared the Cadí and Moixeró ranges, as well as the Pedraforca, Cadinell, Tosa d'Alp, Puigllançada and Rus massifs (which form part of the same mountain system) to be a Natural Park. The Park extends from west to east over about 30 kms, following the mountainous barrier of the Cadí-Moixeró.

This Natural Park is a high mountain area because its altitude ranges from the 900 metres in the valleys to the south, to the 2,647 metres of Puig de la Canal Baridana, the highest peak. There are basically seven kinds of different habitats: cliffs, traditional meadows and agricultural land, deciduous woodland, Scotch pine woods, mountain pine and fir tree woods, Alpine meadows and heath.

The **cliffs** are entirely composed of limestone and may appear in the form of scattered crags or long imposing cliff-faces. The northern slopes of the Cadí are a good example of this latter characteristic, being about 15 kms long, with rock faces over 500 metres high in places. The southern face of the Moixeró range is not as long, but its rock faces are equally high. The latitude and the characteristics of the area are two features which combine to make the north-facing cliffs quite different from those facing south. The north-facing ones are covered in snow and ice for about 7 months of the year. Those facing south have a warmer, more favourable microclimate for the fauna, giving rise to a greater variety and density of birdlife. The limestone substratum also contributes to this circumstance because the limestone cliffs absorb and give out a greater degree of warmth. Furthermore, the special physical characteristics of these cliffs, which are full of caves, fissures, holes and ledges, make the area perfect as a refuge and breeding site for a good many birds of prey and rupicoline species.

Traditional-style meadows and agricultural land occupy the lower areas of the park. These zones are basically made up of grassy meadows (which are regularly harvested) and fields where fodder crops are grown for the livestock. The combination of these crops with strips of woodland or bushes between fields makes the area very attractive for many species, especially in autumn and winter. Food is to be found here because there is usually no snow and because the crops are normally composed of forage plants. The species normally associated with this kind of habitat are also to be found here. Particularly noteworthy are those species associated with Central European birdlife such as Yellowhammer and Red-backed Shrike, as well as other much more ubiquitous species such as Skylark and Stonechat.

The **deciduous woods** may be classified in two groups: those principally made up of beech and oak, which are to be found on the southern slopes at the eastern end of the park; and those on the lower parts of the north-facing slopes, below the coniferous forests. The latter group is made up of a wide variety of species (poplars, alders, willows, sycamores etc.). Apart from the vegetation, these woods also differ in that those facing south are large and continuous areas of woodland, whereas those facing north are really patches of woodland found scattered among the crops and meadows on the lower slopes. The birdlife in the two areas is basically the same (essentialy Central European woodland species), although the greater variety of habitats to be found in the lower woods gives these a greater density and variety of birdlife than in the beech and oak woods.

The **Scotch pine forests** are the most widespread habitat in this natural park. On the lower slopes, these forests intermingle with areas of crops and beech or oak woods, although they also reach up as far as the lower parts of the mountain pine and fir tree forests, often forming areas of mixed woodland. The Scotch pine forests are to be found both on south-facing slopes and on those facing north. This series of circumstances means that the birdlife to be seen depends very much on the situation of each particular site. It is in the most concentrated parts of these forests that you will see this habitat's most characteristic (but not very numerous) range of species. The following are among the most typical: tits, Firecrest, treecreepers (both species), Jay, Chaffinch, Crossbill, as well as Great Spotted Woodpecker, Sparrowhawk and Goshawk.

The **mountain pine and fir tree forests** are to be found between 1,600 and 2,400 m on the south-facing slopes, and between 1,600 and 2,100 m on the north-facing slopes. This kind of forest is generally in good condition in the park, and there are even some tracts of virgin forest. The best parts are on the north-facing slopes of the Cadí range. Their inaccessibility and the park's current protection plan (forbidding any form of commercial felling) have led to the conservation of truly impressive forests. Despite the fact that Pyrenean Subalpine forests are only made up of two species of conifer (in contrast with the Alps, where the variety is greater), the birdlife here is of great interest. The Pyrenees are the only zone in the Iberian Peninsula where species associated with Boreal-Subalpine systems are to be found. Many north European species are indeed missing here, but other species associated with different ecosystems such as European high mountain, Central European woodland and even Mediterranean areas, are to be found here.

The **Alpine meadow areas** are on the higher slopes of the mountains above the forests of mountain pine and fir trees. They are known as Arctic-Alpine ecosystems, and are associated with the Arctic tundra and European high mountain areas. These meadows, however, are singular in that they lie on calcareous soils, and are therefore generally quite dry, supporting a kind of vegetation that does not permit the presence of some species of birds typical of Alpine meadow areas. One example would be Ptarmigan. On the other hand, this circumstance does open the door for some Mediterranean species such as Red-legged Partridge. There are also several species that are normally associated with European mountain systems: Alpine Accentor, Snow Finch or Alpine Chough.

The **heaths**, areas of low bushes, are mainly composed of box-wood here, although this is sometimes mixed with other species such as bearberry. The heaths occupy large tracts of the south-facing slopes, especially in the Cadí range. They are normally to be found among rocks in areas with not too much soil. In some north-facing areas, the heath is composed of rhododendron, although it is normally limited by the fact that this species prefers acidic and not calcareous soils. The dry nature of the box-wood heaths, in south-facing areas, makes it possible for a few Mediterranean species to breed at quite considerable altitudes, as occurs with several species of warbler and bunting. These zones are also suitable for European high mountain species, especially in the highest parts where the heath is to be found among crags and cliffs. In rhododendron heath areas, the same species may be observed as in the mountain pine and fir tree forests, for the rhododendron bushes, which rarely occupy extensive areas, normally grow in among these trees.

How to visit the area

If you are coming from Barcelona, you should first head for Manresa. The A-2 motorway is the road to take (as far as Martorell) if you wish to leave the city on its south side. At Martorell you must turn off on to the C-1411 local road. If you prefer to drive north out of Barcelona, you must take the Terrassa motorway. The road to the Cadí is clearly marked at both exits. From Manresa you must head north on the C-1411 road until you arrive at Bagà, the point where itinerary 13A begins. From here you can visit the southern part of the Cadí. If you are coming from the north, from Andorra or France (the frontier post is at Puigcerdà), you should take the C-1313, which goes from La Seu

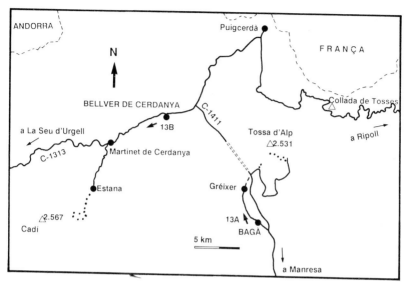

d'Urgell to Puigcerdà and which leads to Bellver de Cerdanya, the starting point for itinerary 13B in the northern part of the Park. In either case you may go from one side to the other of the Cadí range by way of the Cadí tunnel.

You can also reach Puigcerdà by train, and from there you can proceed on local buses along the northern edge of the Park.

Information about the Park, as well as maps and brochures, may be obtained in different languages at the information centres situated at the service area of the Cadí tunnel or in the town halls of the towns of Bellver de Cerdanya or Tuixèn. The Park Reception Centre is expected to be completed in 1990. It will be dependent on the Park Management Board, and will be in the town of Bagà (in the "Districte Forestal" Avenue).

The minimum amount of time needed to carry out each one of the itineraries described here is one day. Itinerary 13A may be covered by car and on foot. It is better for seeing raptors such as Bearded Vulture, and rupicoline species such as Wallcreeper, for example, and also takes in a greater range of habitats. Itinerary 13B, which is mostly covered on foot, visits better Subalpine woodland areas of mountain pine and fir tree, and is therefore better for observing forest species such as Capercaillie and Black Woodpecker.

The best time of year to visit the Park is basically from May to July, but September, October and November are also interesting months. Winter months (from December to April) are less recommendable because of the weather conditions, while August is the time of year there are most visitors in the Park.

Birdwatching

13A. Itinerary on the southern slopes of the Moixeró range

Starting point and end of the itinerary: Bagà Time needed: one day Means of transport: by car and on foot Observations: tricky in winter

The starting point of this itinerary is the Bagà Town Hall square. You should take the tarmac road to the Coll de Pal. At **km 7.6**, you will find a turning to the left to a *mas* (farm) called L'Hospitalet. The turning is just before the bridge over the Gréixer river. Leave your car at this point and take the first birdwatching stroll of the itinerary. Take the forest track that follows along the Gréixer river (little more than a stream here). You will be able to see birds that are associated with this habitat such as White and Grey Wagtail and Dipper. You will also see typical Scotch pine woodland and bush-loving species such as Chaffinch, Firecrest, Nightingale, Jay, Blackbird, Song Thrush as well as several kinds of warbler and tits such as Crested Tit. Having walked approximately 1.5 kms along the track, there is a sharp bend to the right before a bridge that crosses over the river. Here you must leave the track and head for a meadow on your left. From this meadow you take another track, often used by cows, which climbs to another meadow (Camp del Teixó). From here you will get a marvellous view of the cliffs and it is a perfect place for observing raptors (Bearded Vulture, Griffon Vulture, Golden Eagle, Peregrine Falcon and Kestrel), Chough, Alpine Chough, Ravens and other species such as Wallcreeper, Alpine Swift, Crag Martin and House Martin, which breed in natural caves in the cliff faces. Behind you, to the south, you may also see a south-facing Scotch and mountain pine wood where Black Woodpecker breed, although the magnificent forests on the north-facing slopes of the Park (itinerary 13B) are the best site for this species. In the Camp del Teixó area you will also see typical meadow and heath species such as Tree Pipit, Red-backed Shrike, Stonechat, Cirl Bunting, Rock Bunting, Ortolan Bunting and Mistle Thrush.

Returning along the same track to the car, continue along the road towards Coll de Pal. At **km 8.5**, just before a bend to the left, stop again in a place where you can leave the car. There is a path leading off from this point. After crossing the Les Rovires water course it leads to an abandoned house called Casa de Millares. In the area between the water course and the neighbourhood of the house you may see the bird species associated with all the different kinds of woodland in the Park as well as other typical beech wood and deciduous forest species: Marsh Tit, Bullfinch, Nuthatch, Whitethroat, Garden Warbler, Wryneck and Honey Buzzard.

Once again back at the car, you should follow the road in the same direction until you come to a belvedere at **km 12.3**. From here you will have a marvellous view of part of the Pyrenean foothills. You will also be able to see the different members of the crow family present in the area, among which Alpine Chough are to be counted. In this zone it is not in the least difficult to see Alpine Accentor, and you may even catch a glimpse of the odd Wallcreeper on the stone wall on the other side of the road.

Take the car once again and drive up to the Coll de Pal, which you will come to at **km 20.5**. Leave the car in the parking area on the other side of the road at the very spot where there is a signpost that reads "Coll de Pal 2,080 m". From this point begin climbing up to the left, in a westerly direction, towards a small pass that is clearly visible from here. You must remember that it is a high mountain walk and that basic precautions must be taken, especially in the colder months. Once you get to this first pass, which is only about 300 metres from the Coll de Pal, you should take the path leading to the west, which after a further 800 metres comes to the Coma Floriu pass. On this part of the

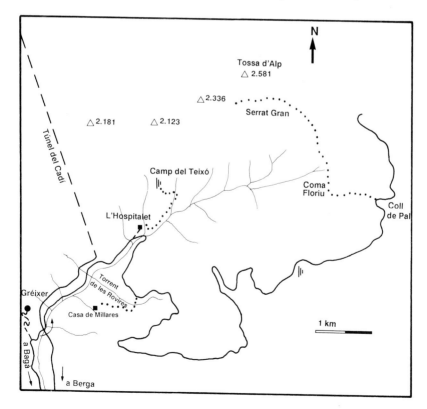

itinerary, and in the vicinity of he Coma Floriu pass you will be able to see Alpine meadow species such as Rock Pipit, which is very abundant, and Common Wheatear. Snow Finch is normally seen in winter whereas Alpine Accentor are to be seen here throughout the year, as long as there is no snow. You can also see Rock Thrush, Black Redstart, Partridge, Alpine Chough, as well as several species of raptor such as Kestrel, Peregrine Falcon, Golden Eagle, and, in summer and autumn, Griffon Vulture.

From the Coma Floriu pass you should head north following along the ridge known as "Serrat Gran". There are several paths continuing at an unchanging height along the slope. They lead to the area of high cliffs you are interested in. From here onwards, the path becomes a little more difficult because the slope you are walking along becomes steeper and there are now occasional scree falls to be crossed. If inexperience, lack of suitable equipment or the presence of snow or ice make you feel a little unsafe on this ground, it is better not to carry on. You are also recommended not to continue if it looks as if it might thunder because storms in this area are usually quite alarming! If the conditions are favourable, however, you will reach the cliff area in about three quarters of an hour. It is at the same height as the Coma Floriu pass. Hare and Chamois are very common in this area. You will be seeing all the aforementioned Alpine meadow species along the way, as well as the odd Dunnock in the few bushy areas you will come across. The path ends up at the top of a cliff, from where you can enjoy a splendid view of the same cliffs you could see at the beginning of the itinerary from the Camp del Teixó. The species you can see are also the same as those you could see from below. The advantage is that from here you can really make contact with them. Wallcreeper, for example, may be seen only a few metres away if you are patient and conceal yourself quietly in a suitable hiding place.

The return to the car will be along the same path you came on. Be sure to have had a good rest before making your way back, for it is often fatigue that causes those silly accidents!

13B. Itinerary on the northern slopes of the Cadí range

Starting point: Bellver de Cerdanya **End of the itinerary**: Estana **Time needed**: one day **Means of transport**: by car and on foot **Observations**: tricky in winter

You begin the itinerary at Bellver de Cerdanya by driving along the N-1313 road towards La Seu d'Urgell. Once you have driven through Martinet de Cerdanya and just before coming to the Hotel Boix you will find a tarmac road leading off to the left. It is sign-posted to "Montellà". You must take this turning, cross over the river Segre and take a forest track on the right to

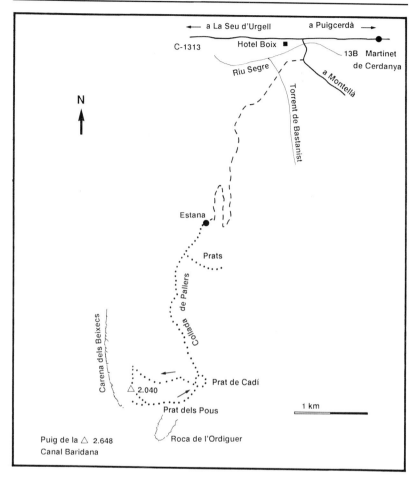

"Estana" 200 m further on. Most of this track's 6.5 kms has no tarmac surfacing (other than in the village of Estana), but it is quite a good track. It passes through large areas of box-wood heathland. As has already been described in "Description and habitat", there are several Mediterranean species living here, despite the high altitude and the cold temperatures. Among other species, you may see Red-legged Partridge, Turtle Dove, Little Owl, Woodchat Shrike, Great Grey Shrike, Cirl Bunting, Dartford Warbler, Corn Bunting, Bonelli's Warbler, Stonechat, Goldfinch, Ortolan Bunting and Woodlark (in the small patches of pine and oak wood along the way). You may also see raptors flying above the area, notably Short-toed Eagle, Buzzard and Sparrowhawk, all of which breed in nearby woods.

Once you have arrived in **Estana** (1,483 metres high), you can look out for the species typically associating with man, such as Common Starling, House Sparrow, Swallow and Swift. Leave the car here and begin the itinerary on foot. You should follow the forest track to the Pallers pass (**Collada de Pallers**). From here, you will have to climb up to Prat de Cadí, although it is first worth walking in the meadows in the vicinity of the pass. For instance, you may care to go along the path that heads east towards an oak wood. This walk might well reveal Central European species which, from a point a little before Estana, will have begun to substitute the species associated with more temperate zones. You can therefore see Greenfinch, Bullfinch, Red-backed Shrike, Garden Warbler, Whitethroat, Melodious Warbler, Song Thrush, Robin, Dunnock, Tree Pipit, Skylark, Wryneck, and, in the oak wood itself, Great Spotted Woodpecker, Nuthatch and Chiffchaff, as well as more ubiquitous species such as Blackbird, Wren and Goshawk.

About half way up you will come to a pass where there is a boundary

Once you have finished this ramble and are back at the Collada de Pallers pass, you should begin the climb up to Prat de Cadí. At the pass itself there is a large sign which indicates the beginning of the nature trail in the Natural Park and gives details about the area. It will take you about one hour to get to Prat de Cadí, and the path is very clearly marked out with yellow rhombi which have a red circumference within them.To begin with you will pass through very young Scotch pine woods. As you climb up further, the woods become more mature. The density and variety of the birdlife also increases, the msot common species being Jay, Mistle Thrush, Wood Pigeon, Blue Tit, Crested Tit, Chaffinch, Wren, Short-toed Treecreeper and Firecrest.

About half way up you will come to a pass where there is a boundary stone in the area. Here, Scotch pine begins to be substituted by mountain pine. From here on up, you will be in a zone of typical Pyrenean Subalpine woodland, with mountain pine mixed in with fir trees. The woods have rhodedondron bushes as their undergrowth, suggesting that the area is completely snowbound in winter. This wood has interesting birdlife, although it varies from area to area in acordance with the predominant forest species, the altitude and the composition of the undergrowth. You will not come to the best woods for birdlife until you get as far as Prat de Cadí, and the further up you go, the more birds you should see: Crossbill, Siskin, Coal Tit, Goldcrest, Ring Ouzel, Black Woodpecker and Partridge. Citril Finch is one of the commonest species here and is easily seen in the sparsest wooded tracts in the meadows.

The **Prat de Cadí** appears suddenly as you climb up a small summit. It is a very beautiful sight. The plateau is about 3 hectares in area. It is covered in meadows and surrounded by thick mountain pine forest. The region is overlooked by the impressive north-facing Cadí cliffs that suddenly appear before you all of a sudden from behind the trees. After a short rest, it is worth wandering across the Prat de Cadí for nearly all the typical mountain pine species, except for Capercaillie and Woodcock, can be seen here. These two species normally stay in the quieter areas of the forest. At times you will be able to hear the impressive drumming and the various strident calls of the Black Woodpecker, and if you are lucky, you may even see one. Three pairs of Tengmalm's Owl have recently been found breeding in the Prat de Cadí area. It is a difficult bird to hear for it only sings from January to May, a time of year this area is snowbound. Over the rest of the year it only makes the odd call in the evening just before it starts its activity. During your ramble on the Prat de Cadí it is a good idea to keep an eye out for raptors such as Golden Eagle, Bearded Vulture, Griffon Vulture, Short-toed Eagle, Kestrel, Goshawk or Alpine Chough, Chough, Carrion Crow and Raven in the sky and on the cliffs.

After visiting Prat de Cadí, you may care to take a final walk to the forests higher up the mountain in search of shyer species such as Woodcock, and, above all, Capercaillie. You should take a path that leads from Prat de Cadí on the opposite side of the plateau to where you arrived. Head west towards a summit covered in forest. Once you have reached the top, you should follow a level path leading west into the forest. It is a good zone for seeing Capercaillie. Walk stealthily through the forest without making a sound, keeping your eyes skinned on the branches and the ground to try and spot the bird before it flies off. It is much more frequent to see Capercaillie crashing off through the trees after first hearing the heavy flapping of its wings. This is also the breeding area of Woodcock, a species that is only easy to spot at dawn and dusk when it carries out its display flight over its territory. Other than birds, you may also come across the odd Roe Deer, Pine Marten, and abundant Red Squirrel.

Continue walking along the path, and after a while you will notice that the wood becomes sparser, and eventually you will come to a point overlooking a large area of scree. Here you should head up the mountain on the southern side through an area of sparse woodland that still bears the scars of former felling operations. The track the trunks were dragged along will be your path. Keep an eye out on the way up because in summer and autumn you may well come across family groups of Capercaillie. Once you have reached the top of this summit, which is 2,040 metres high, you will come to a meadow (Prat dels Pous) situated beneath a south-facing slope which in mountain pine. Head towards the meadow making your way down the small wooded slope, which has more birdlife than other forested areas because of its milder microclimate.

When you reach the meadow you will see the ridge known as "Beixecs" to the south-west. It descends to the north and has rocks at its base. You should

Wallcreeper

approach this area for it is ideal for seeing Wallcreeper in summer and early autumn. You may well see Chamois there too.

There is a path leading off from the eastern end of the **Prat dels Pous**. It heads north-west and will lead you back to the Prat de Cadí once again. This path passes through an area of north-facing slopes with sparse mountain pine woodland with small trees. The region is typical of mountain woodland zones near the tree limit. When you have reached Prat de Cadí, make your way down to Collada de Pallers and Estana village (where you left the car) along the same path you came up on.

Board and lodging

Bagà and Bellver de Cerdanya are the two best points to head for to visit the Cadí-Moixeró Natural Park. They are indeed the starting points for the itineraries described here. There are boarding houses and hotels (Cal Batista, La Pineda and Ca l'Amagat boarding houses at Bagà and the Maria Antonieta and Bellavista hotels or Mas Martí, Pendís, Vianya and Maties boarding houses at Bellver de Cerdanya). You will also be able to find other villages in the region with hotels at varying prices. The skiing resorts of La Molina and Alp have the best hotels in the area. In La Molina there is the four-star Palace Hotel as well as several three-star hotels (Adserà, Roc Blanc, La Collada). In Alp there is the three-star Hotel Alp. Remember that in August and during the skiing season you may have difficulty getting a room there.

If you wish to camp, you will find the first class "Solana del Segre" camping site at Bellver de Cerdanya, as well as further sites at Prullans and Tuixén that are only open in the summer months. In the Park itself there are nine mountain refuges where you may spend the night. You can get information about their location and the services they offer at the Park's information centres (cf. How to visit the area).

If you want to taste local cooking (the *comarca* of the Cerdanya is really famous for the variety of its local dishes), there are various restaurants you might try: the Hotel Boix and the Hotel Cadí in Martinet de Cerdanya, where you may also find a room; the Hotel Bellavista at Bellver de Cerdanya or the Hotel Ca l'Eudald and the Les Lloses restaurant at Alp.

Other places of interest

- Bagà. An important village in medieval times, it conserves part of the old walls and a beautiful arched square where the market is held on Wednesdays. It is the starting point for itinerary 13A.

- Sant Llorenç Monastery, near Bagà. A splendid Romanesque church with three aisles built on top of a wide crypt. Between Guardiola de Berguedà and Bagà.

- Talló church (Bellver de Cerdanya). An important Romanesque building which is known as "La catedral cerdana" (The Cerdanya Cathedral). It is 2 kms south of Bellver de Cerdanya.

- The Llobregat springs. Source of one of the best-known Catalan rivers with springs and waterfalls that are much visited. In Castellar de N'Hug, 23 kms from Bagà, on the Guardiola de Berguedà-La Pobla de Lillet road.

- Llívia. A village under Spanish administration, though enclosed by French-governed land. There is a museum containing interesting pharmacy utensils. The pharmacy is considered to be the oldest in Europe. It is 5 kms north of Puigcerdà.

14

NÚRIA AND FRESER-SETCASES NATIONAL RESERVE

The Freser-Setcases National Game Reserve is in the *comarca* (county) of the Ripollès in the eastern Pyrenees. It was created for the protection of Chamois and high mountain fauna.

Inaugural date: 1966.

Area: The National Hunting Reserve covers 20,000 hectares in all.

Habitats: Subalpine mountain pine forests, Scotch pine forests, oak woods, beech woods, riverside woodland, grassy meadows, Subalpine meadows, scree and rocky areas, rivers and high mountain streams.

Interesting species:
- *Present all the year round*: Golden Eagle, Bearded Vulture, Goshawk, Ptarmigan, Partridge, Great Spotted Woodpecker, Dipper, Snow Finch, Short-toed Treecreeper, Treecreeper, Alpine Accentor, Chough, Alpine Chough, Crested Tit, Nuthatch, Crossbill, Rock Bunting.
- *Summer visitors*: Short-toed Eagle, Honey Buzzard, Hen Harrier, Peregrine Falcon, Dotterel, Alpine Swift, Wallcreeper, Crag Martin, Rock Thrush, Ring Ouzel, Rock Pipit*, Bonelli's Warbler, Red-backed Shrike, Citril Finch*.
- *Winter visitors*: Meadow Pipit, Brambling.

* : a few birds of this species are also present in winter.

Description and habitat

The Freser-Setcases National Game Reserve was created in 1966 for the protection of chamois and high mountain fauna in general, at a time when chamois populations were getting desperately low. This step led to the very satisfactory recovery of the chamois and also had an excellent effect on the situation of other high mountain species, such as Ptarmigan, Capercaillie and Golden Eagle. The Núria area is better known to the public at large for the Sanctuary and its skiing stations than for the natural attributes it possesses.

The whole reserve (and the Núria area) is of glacial formation. There are many glaciated valleys and cirques on the higher ground. At the point where the rivers Núria and Freser come together, there are a lot of cliffs with sheer rock faces where signs of the weathering process caused by the descending glaciers can be seen. The higher areas are very eroded and have very gentle contours. Altitudes here vary from 1,000 metres to 2,913 metres at the top of Puigmal, the highest peak, and there are several peaks over the 2,800 metre mark. The more craggy peaks are surrounded by areas of scree.

The Núria zone has more human disturbance because of the skiing station and the Sanctuary. It is a traditional pilgrimage centre and may be reached by cable car. The tarmac road climbs as far as Queralbs, but there is a fine forest track as far as Fontalba.

Various mountain and high-mountain habitats are encountered along the way: woods of different kinds, meadows, water courses, scree, cliffs and areas with human influence.

Oak woods (especially the Durmast Oak woods of the Valley of Ribes), are of medium size, and have fern undergrowth. These areas are to be found near Ribes de Freser and on the way to Queralbs. They have been very much tampered with by man, and a lot of felling has gone on in order to produce meadows and arable land. Proof of this can be found in the fact that there are oaks mixed in with the pines and standing alone.

Beech woods are to be found in the Ribes de Freser area alone. Some of these woods are of great size, especially those on the right-hand side of the slopes of the Sant Amand massif, on the way into Ribes de Freser. The wildlife variety is increased as there are Scotch pines, oaks and birch trees mixed in with the beech. It is the habitat where Short-toed Eagle and Honey Buzzard breed.

Scotch pine woods are very widespread in the Valley of Ribes. On your way up to Queralbs, you will be finding this habitat on either side of the river Freser. These forests look very young because they are over-exploited by the local councils. This is very negative factor for the Capercaillies, which are scarce at the best of times. On the other hand, there are good numbers of Buzzard, Great Spotter Woodpecker, Treecreeper and Crossbill.

The **mountain pine woods** are basically small patches of forest areas struggling against the severe climate and human exploitation. The best areas of mountain pine are be found in the least accessible spots, as may be seen on the Fontalba track. You will be passing through this kind of habitat once you get to Núria and on almost all of itinerary 14B.

The **riverside woodland areas**, which have abundant birdlife, are to be found from Ribes de Freser to near Pont del Cremal, above Queralbs. The altitude further up the river is too high for this kind of woodland. In many zones, these woods have been felled because of the river canalization scheme, floods and riverbank plantations.

Other less widespread woodland types include ash and poplar groves. They may be found at any point in the Ribes valley, mixed in with pines and oaks, and are a form of transitional habitat that is very good for birds.

The **meadows** are a good exponent of the vegetation of this area. There are grazing and hay-harvest meadows on the lower parts of the valleys up as far as Queralbs. In the high mountain areas **Alpine** and **Subalpine meadows** are commoner, forming areas of turf studded with Fescue and gentians. These areas can be encountered beyond the Pla de Sallent up as far as the summit of the Puigmal and also at Fontalba.

Springs and **streams**, as well as odd patches of **bog**, with pretty flowers, mosses and saxifrages are very typical in this area. Dipper, wagtails and Rock Pipit are very common here.

Scree areas are to be found on both itineraries because the terrain is very rough and the high ground is quite free of vegetation. There are large tracts of scree beneath the Puigmal with abundant Alpine Accentor, Rock Thrush and Ptarmigan. The **cliffs** in the area also have Wallcreeper, Black Redstart, Alpine Chough and Chough.

The **man-affected areas** (**crops, tracks and villages**) must also be mentioned because it is here that a lot of the more adaptable species find food and shelter: Swallow, sparrows, Carrion Crow and several species of finch.

How to visit the area

To visit this area you should first drive to Ribes de Freser. If you are coming from France or from the Cadí area, you can come along the N-260 road via Puigcerdà (following the signposts in the direction of Ripoll). If you are coming from the Costa Brava area via Olot and Ripoll, you will also reach Ribes de Freser on the N-260. If you are coming from Barcelona, you should take the N-152 road as far as Ripoll, where you should take the turning to Ribes along the N-260 road. You must be careful with the numbers of the roads in this area because some of them have changed and your map may have the old ones!

You can also reach Ribes de Freser by train on the Barcelona-Puigcerdà line. There is a small train from Ribes to the Núria Sanctuary with a half-way stop at Queralbs. You can also drive up as far as Queralbs.

If you wish to go on the three recommended itineraries, you must be sure to have a full day and a half free (half a day per itinerary). More time will be needed if you do not want the itineraries to be merely ornithological. The situation of the itineraries and the possibility of taking the small train opens up the possibility of making all kinds of different combinations. You will have to choose among these according to your own priorities. The Ribes-Queralbs sector, the initial part of itinerary 14A, may be covered in the small train, although it is preferable to go by car, if you have one. This will enable you to stop off at interesting places along the way. You may cover the climb from Queralbs to Núria either by following the remaining part of itinerary 14A or along itinerary 14B. In either case you may also link up this part of the itinerary (if you are not too tired and time permits) with itinerary 14C, the principal interest of which lies in the good chances it offers of spotting Ptarmigan on one part, at least, of the walk. In spells of good weather, when the days are long enough and there is no snow or ice about, you may link up itineraries 14B and 14C in a circuit so that no part of the walks will have to be covered twice. It is a long excursion (it can be covered in a single day, but you will not be able to dawdle!) which passes through high altitude areas on the second half of itinerary 14C. If you wish to do this walk, be sure to take all necessary high mountain precautions and have an ordinance survey map of the area with you. As regards the Queralbs-Núria section of itinerary 14A, you may climb it on foot, as described in the text, or else leave it for the descent (which is easier) and go up to Núria on the small train.

The best time of year to visit this area is spring (end of April), summer and autumn. Weekends in July and August are not recommended because of the flood of tourists that flock to the area. Whatever time of year you choose, it is advisable to start off in the early morning. Not only will it make your itineraries quieter, but you also coincide with the time of day the birds are most active.

If you wish to see Ptarmigan in their spectacular winter plumage, you should do part of itinerary 14C at the beginning of winter (November and first fortnight in December). Be sure to go well-equipped. It is also at this time of year that the Mouflon and Chamois are looking their best. After mid-December (depending on the year) there is too much snow and ice there, and several stretches of the itinerary are very dangerous.

If you wish to see Rock Sparrow (a species you are most unlikely to encounter on the itineraries described here), you can visit one of the colonies

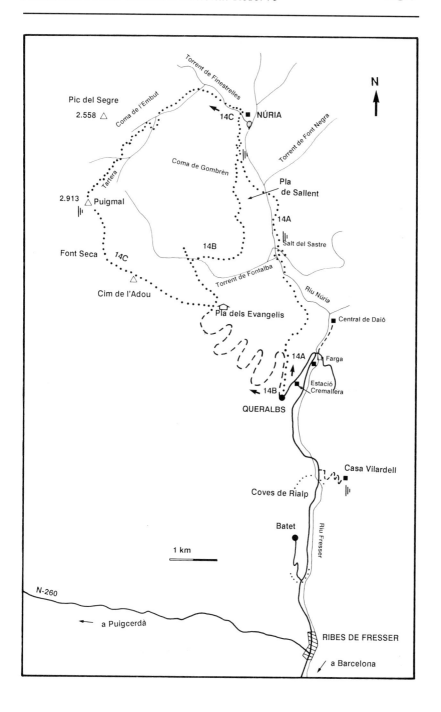

this species has on the way to the nearby village of Ogassa. In Ripoll you should take the N-260 road up the valley of the river Ter (where Common Sandpiper are common) towards Camprodon. At the very entrance to Sant Joan de les Abadesses, take a turning to the left to Ogassa. After about 2 kms you will start to see derelict factories. Rock Sparrow breed in some of these old buildings.

Birdwatching

14A. Itinerary in the Freser and Núria valleys

Starting point: Ribes de Freser **End of the itinerary**: Núria **Time needed**: half a day **Means of transport**: by car, on foot or by small train **Observations**: tricky in winter

Drive out of Ribes de Freser in the direction of Queralbs (those of you coming by train must take the small train (Catalan: "cremallera") up to Queralbs. On the way out of Ribes you may care to stop off for a moment opposite the **S.A.I.D.A. factory** and scan the river, for it is the only site on the whole itinerary where you might see Kingfisher in summer. Dipper are also to be seen here, especially in the early morning, although this species can also be seen at many other places along the itinerary. Wryneck also breed in the small copse above the houses.

On the section of the itinerary that is covered by car you should keep an eye on the sky because Short-toed Eagle may well be visible at any point between Ribes and Queralbs. Kestrel and Buzzard are almost certain to be about too. In spring it is also common to see flights of Honey Buzzard migrating through the area.

Drive on for 1 km and you can stop near the turning that leads off to the left to Batet. Here there are usually plenty of finches (among which Siskin are common in autumn on the alders). Kestrel are also present here all the year round, and, with a little bit of luck, you may see Common Sandpiper on the river.

You might stop off again at the **Rialb caves**, about 3.5 kms from Ribes, leaving the car on the esplanade on the left immediately after the bridge. There is a Scotch pine wood on the left above the caves, and several grass meadows surrounded by poplars. Chough and Crag Martin breed all around the cave area (cf. other places of interest). Spotted Flycatcher and Stonechat are also common. Meadow Pipit (in winter), Tree Pipit (in summer), as well as numerous thrushes and finches, may all be seen throughout the year in this region of meadows and woods. The rare Hen Harrier, which has its principal Catalan breeding area here, may also be seen, although it breeds in meadows higher up the mountain. At night you may often hear Tawny Owl hooting, and Eagle can occasionally be heard too. Nightjar are also present in summer, although it is not often heard. There is a pair of Dipper here all the year round on the river. In winter they may often be seen emerging from under the ice! About 100 metres beyond where you left the car, there is a track off to the right. It is not in a very good state, but it leads to a fine poplar grove. You may care to wander along it and follow the stream, where you might be lucky enough to see Woodcock flying about in the evening. The track on the right climbs up to Vilardell house, where there is a thousand year old oak tree and a fine view of the Serra d'Estremera. Goshawk can often be seen flying above the woods, especially at the beginning of spring when the birds perform their display flights. Honey Buzzard can also be seen here.

Take the car once again and drive on up. The fine view and the variety of habitats you will come into contact with on the next 2 kms of road make this a good stretch for spotting all these typical mid-mountain species.

At km 6 you will come to **La Farga**, a children's summer holiday home surrounded by lush vegetation which holds plenty of birds, especially in spring and summer: House Sparrow, Tree Sparrow, Dunnock, Blackbird, Song Thrush, Black Redstart, Chiffchaff, Bonelli's Warbler, Nightingale, Cetti's Warbler, tits, finches and buntings. From here you may also care to go to the bridge beside the bend on the Queralbs road. Here you can see White Wagtail, Grey Wagtail and Dipper in the river, as well as Siskin in the trees along the bank. There is a track to the left leading to the Daió hydroelectric station, just before the Freser Gorges (Gorges del Freser), and a narrow tarmac road also leads off to the right to the villages of Serrat and Fustanyà.

Further on along our itinerary you will come to **Queralbs** at Km 7. You can leave the car in the small train parking area or in the square at the entrance to the village. From here you continue on foot up to Núria on the traditional path, which follows the GR-11 (Grand Route) and is marked with red and white markings. The first part of the path heads right above the public washing place. It is wide and well paved to begin with, passing close to houses and pastures, and is an interesting spot at all times of year for the variety of birds that may be seen. Citril Finch, Rock Bunting, Short-toed Treecreeper, Treecreeper, Nuthatch, Firecrest, Red-backed Shrike and the occasional Sparrowhawk are all to be seen here. About 250 m from the village you will come to a junction; here you should take the turning to the left.

Keep climbing up the mountain along the winding path with stone walls on either side, where Chiffchaff, Black Redstart and Wren breed. About 700 m after the village, the path crosses the track to Fontalba. It then passes through a rather overgrown zone near the small train line. Part of the path has fallen away in a landslide but the GR-11 red and white markings are clear at all times. Occasionally, the path passes through large tracts of scree.

About 2 kms after Queralbs the path crosses the small train line above a tunnel and descends gently to the river Núria. The vegetation changes a little; you leave the copses behind and come to areas with birch and ash trees and raspberry bushes.

About 700 m further on, you will cross the **Pont del Cremal** (Cremal bridge). The railway and the impressive Dent d'en Rosell cliff face will be on your left. You should continue on the other side of the the river, climbing up a steep path with nettles and raspberry bushes on either side. In autumn you will be able to see Alpine Accentor, and, with a little bit of luck, the odd flight of Snow Finch. Between here and Núria you must be on the look-out, for it is the best area in which to see Golden Eagle and Bearded Vulture at all times of year. Bearded Vulture do not breed here but visit the area very often. There are always groups of Chough, Alpine Chough, and occasionally odd Kestrel pestering these large raptors. In summer Swift and Alpine Swift are very numerous because of the wealth of breeding cliffs all around.

Once you have reached the top of **Salt del Sastre**, 500 metres further up, you must stop to get a look at the magnificent view of Fontalba stream on the other side of the river. It is worth scanning all lichen-covered cliffs on the right-hand side of the stream, for a pair of Wallcreeper usually breed here. You can also see the Fontalba wood above the Dent d'en Rosell cliff.

The itinerary now continues on the right-hand side of the river, having large boulders on either side. On stretches of path affected by landslides you may have to clamber up a few metres, but this should not be too difficult. You will soon pass the **Cua de Cavall** (Horse's Tail), a beautiful waterfall where Dipper and Crag Martin breed. There is also a small cave here which is a useful shelter in bad weather.

About 5 kms after Queralbs, you will come to **Pla de Sallent**, a meadow beside which there is a mountain pine wood. Apart from seeing the odd chamois or mouflon, especially in winter, you may also see Citril Finch, Ring Ouzel and Crossbill. Citril Finch can be encountered in any of the small woods in this area, but the place to get the best sight of them is in the Bosc de la Verge (Virgin's Forest) at Núria itself, on the right-hand side of the sanctuary. At Pla de Sallent there is a small bridge, the Bridge of the Three Mills (Pont dels Tres Molins), and on the right-hand side of the mountain, the Font Negra stream cascades down impressively. On the left there is a large gash in the forest caused by winter avalanches.

At Pla de Sallent, the itinerary continues through woodland and climbs up a stony stretch of path to Agulla de l'Estany (Lake "Needle") where there is a splendid view of the **Núria Sanctuary**, the lake itself and the surrounding mountains. At the sanctuary esplanade you can see flights of finches (Citril

Finch, Linnet and Chaffinch) as well as House Martin, Crag Martin and Dipper and Grey Wagtail by the stream.

14B. Itinerary on the Fontalba and Gombrèn mountain valleys

Starting point: Queralbs **End of the itinerary**: Núria **Time needed**: half a day **Means of transport**: by car and on foot **Observations**: you can go on to itinerary 14C. Tricky in winter

After passing the Queralbs small train station you must take a turning to the right where there is a small signpost indicating the route to Fontalba, and drive along a mountain track leading to the Fontalba pass (Collada de Fontalba), which is 2,100 metres high. This track is 11.5 kms long. It rises very steeply, but it is wide and has a good surface. Along the way you are sure to see a lot of Song Thrushes, the odd Jay, and, maybe, a flight or two of Cross-bill. The landscape is a mixture of pastures (sheep and cows graze here) and occasional patches of pine wood. There are also some stone constructions that mark the boundary between meadows, as well as some shepherds' huts.

Once you have reached the top, park the car on the esplanade known as **Pla dels Evangelis**. There is a forest refuge hut (El Pinetar) which is not in a very good state, although you can spend the night or take shelter there if the weather is bad. In front of the refuge hut there is great glaciated valley covered in Subalpine meadows and scree. The Puigmal peak (2,913 metres high) towers above this valley. From here you will have to take the path that skirts the valley. After 2 or 3 hours, at a birdwatcher's gait, you will have covered the 4.5 kms of flat ground that lead to the Núria Sanctuary. You can return to the car back along the same route, or, time and weather permitting, you may care to do itinerary 14C (cf. How to visit the area).

Before beginning the walk though, it is worth having a close look at the meadows on the south-facing slopes (the glaciated valley will be in front of you to the left), for it is here that you may see Hen Harrier, Hobby and Peregrine Falcon. All three species breed nearby, and during the breeding season they are seen quite regularly. Hen Harrier skim over the land on the long flights that are typical of the harrier family, and it is not uncommon to see Hobby perched on one of the many boulders in the area. Peregrine Falcon are more irregular, and are only occasionally seen flying past.

In summer, once you are on the path (the most clearly marked one leading off to the left from the esplanade), you will see a lot of Rock Pipit, Skylark and Rock Bunting, as you will indeed in all meadows along the way. Skylark and Rock Pipit breed in holes in the tufts of grass, and if you stroll through the meadows, you are sure to put some up.

When you get to the far end of the valley (near the source of the **Fontalba stream**, where you can at all times drink its cool and clear water), you should see great flights of Chough and Alpine Chough and the odd Raven. You might also see flocks of chamois on the slopes before you. The flocks may even be quite large, especially in winter.

When you have walked about 1 km, you will come to a mountain pine forest. It is neither dense nor large, and has a lot of clearings with rocky areas. Beneath you there is a steep drop down to the river Núria. Ring Ouzel breed in this forest, and you should be able to see this species with ease between here and Núria, except in winter when it migrates or moves down to lower mountain areas. You should also see and hear Crossbill, Citril Finch, Goldcrest, Short-toed Treecreeper, Crested Tit and Coal Tit. In the forest clearings you may see the odd Partridge, a species that is hard to see, unless you happen to come across it and put it up. This particular zone is excellent for this species, but, as happened with the hare, uncontrolled hunting has cut down its numbers severely.

You will have no problems continuing along the path, and you will come to fine natural belvederes over the valley of Núria. From any one of them, a patient wait is almost sure to result in sightings of Golden Eagle on the wing, as well as the rarer Bearded Vulture. On the second half of the itinerary (on foot), at about 3 kms from the esplanade where you left the car, you will come across occasional patches of scree, in which you may well see Alpine Accentor, Black Redstart, and, in summer, Common Wheatear. The path skirts a broken down shepherd's hut, and continues to rise and fall through a very stony area. There will still be mountain pine forest tracts about you, and the forest species mentioned earlier should still be visible in the vicinity.

When you are very near the Núria Sanctuary, you will pass through **Coma de Gombrèn**, an open space with meadows and rocks where there is a shepherd's hut in which you can shelter if the weather is bad. On the last stage, you have to descend by a stony path leading to the sanctuary along which you will get a good sight of a fair-sized patch of mountain pine where chamois sometimes hide.

14C. Puigmal itinerary

Starting point and end of the itinerary: Núria **Time needed**: half a day **Means of transport**: on foot **Observations**: you can go on to itinerary 14B. Tricky in winter

Start out from the Núria Sanctuary and climb up the Finestrelles stream valley in a north-westerly direction. This stream is the one to be found to the left of the front part of the Sanctuary building. Walk beside the stream for about 500 metres, and turn left into the glacial valley known as the **Coma de l'Embut**. Here you must leave the path that continues parallel with the

Finestrelles stream, and turn left on to the path that runs alongside the Embut stream. Keep on in the direction of the source of the stream (which keeps appearing and disappearing because of the karstic nature of the ground).

About 800 metres from the Sanctuary you will come to the **Pla dels Eugassers** (Mare Shepherds' plateau), an area with a liquorice-covered slope full of Rock Pipit, Skylark, Common Wheatear, where, if you look carefully enough, you might see the odd Rock Thrush too. From here you have a steep one kilometre climb up to the great **Puigmal and Pic del Segre scree areas**. This is an excellent place for the magnificent Ptarmigan. You may find it very easy to see this species here, but you may have to be patient if you are not lucky enough to see them immediately. The best time of year to see them is in spring and early summer, for in winter (when Ptarmigan indeed have that spectacular snow-white plumage) the route is dangerous unless you come equipped with climbing irons and ice-axe. There is no particular spot for seeing Ptarmigan since the scree area is very spacious and offers this species endless cover. In your search for Ptarmigan, you may also come across the shy and beautiful stoat.

In the whole of the Embut valley zone you are also quite likely to see chamois and Golden Eagle. On the ridgetop, and on all the crags, you may also

Ptarmigan

spot the butterfly-like flutter of the Wallcreeper. It is only present here in summer, and when the cold comes, this species heads for the very rocky and milder regions of the Pyrenean foothills. You can pinpoint this species by listening out for the soft warbling song it makes as it climbs, as well as by the whistling alarm call it makes as it flies off. The area is also excellent for Snow Finch at any time of the year. They can either be seen individually or in flights. No nest has yet been found in the area, but flights of adults and young fledglings have been seen in summer near the top of the ridge. In winter and spring, large flights of Snow Finch look for seeds in the snowdrifts, producing spectacular flashes of white as they fly off. In the skiing season, Snow Finch can often be seen on the terraces of bars at the skiing resort, along with Alpine Accentor, picking up the crumbs that fall from the tables!

You will see a rain gauge on the left-hand side of the lower part of the scree slopes. Beside it there is also a path leading up to the **Puigmal** peak. If it is not too late, you can get to the top, for the ascent will only take you about one hour. Puigmal is the second highest peak in the eastern Pyrenees (after Pic Carlit in French Catalonia). From the top there is a magnificent view of the Cerdanya, the mountains of Andorra, the whole of the Ripollès, and, in the distance, if it is not too misty, Montserrat, the Montseny massif and the Costa Brava. On the way up, you will be seeing Alpine Accentor, which are sure to come close to you if there is the possibility that bread crumbs may be had. If you are on your own and are feeling patient, they will even eat out of your hand!

You can call it a day whenever you wish and make your way back to the Sanctuary. If you are combining this itinerary with 14B (cf. How to visit the area), you will have to leave the Puigmal summit and follow along the top of the ridge in a south or south-easterly direction, passing Font Seca and the Adou, peak until you reach the Fontalba pass. It will take you at least three hours to get from Puigmal to Fontalba. It is a good idea to keep on the top of the ridge all the way. If in doubt, take the more easterly of the options, that is to say the ridge is furthest to the left. The last half hour will present no problem because you will be able to see the car down below in the Pla dels Evangelis car park.

Board and lodging

The villages that offer the widest scope for lodging are Ribes de Freser (Catalunya Park Hotel, Hotel Balneari Montagut, Hotel Residència Catalunya, Hotel Sant Antoni and the Prats, Moliné, Fanet and Cazadores boarding houses) and Queralbs (Hostal Rialp and Hostal Residència l'Avet), although Ripoll, the *comarca* (county) capital, only 14 kms from Ribes, should also be borne in mind.

You can also spend the night at Núria. If you have left the car at Queralbs, you can go up on either of the first two itineraries (14A or 14B), spend the rest of the day visiting the area or covering part of itinerary 14C, and come down the next day on the other itinerary. There is a hotel (Hotel Núria), a mountain refuge and a Generalitat youth hostel that may be visited all the year round by International Youth Hostel Association card-holders. The most difficult times of the year for finding rooms are in July and August, over the Christmas holidays, and winter weekends during the skiing season.

There are no camping sites on the itineraries, but there are free camping areas in the vicinity of Queralbs and Núria itself. The nearest camping sites are at Planoles and Ripoll.

In so far as food is concerned, there is excellent meat (especially roast lamb) and sausage (Catalan: "embotits") to be found, as well as trout and mushrooms in autumn. The following restaurants are among the best known: Restaurant Els Caçadors at Ribes de Freser, and Grill el Gall, a stone's throw from Campdevànol. There are two restaurants at Núria.

Other places of interest

- Ripoll Monastery. Xth century Romanesque building. The XIIth century doorway arch is considered to be the most important example of Romanesque sculpture in Catalonia. It is in the town of Ripoll, 14 kms south of Ribes de Freser.

- Ripoll Museum and Archives. A remarkable collection of articles on the life of the shepherds and the industry of the *comarca*. Next to the Monastery.

- Queralbs - XIth century Romanesque church. Its square tower is particularly outstanding.It is in the higher part of the village and is better reached on foot because of the narrow streets (cf. itineraries 14A and 14B).

- Núria Sanctuary. An old hospital and confraternity. The Sant Gil chapel and the sanctuary with the pot and the image of the Virgin of Núria are particularly interesting. At the end of itineraries 14A and 14B and the beginning of itinerary 14C.

- Rialb caves. Prehistorical human remains were found here. They are between Ribes and Queralbs, at km 3.5 of itineraries 14A and 14B.

15

PUIGSACALM AND GARROTXA VOLCANIC ZONE NATURAL PARK

This Natural Park is in the *comarca* (county) of the Garrotxa in the region of the county capital, Olot. It is the best example of volcanic landscape in the Iberian Peninsula and one of the most interesting in Europe. The nearby **Serra de Puigsacalm-Santa Magdalena** (Mountain Range) is also included here, despite the fact that it does not form part of the Natural Park. It is a mountain system that links up the Pyrenees with the Serralada Pre-litoral (pre-coastal mountain range), and is the southernmost distribution point of many plants and animals associated with the Euro-Siberian, Central European and Atlantic mid-mountain regions.

Inaugural date: 3rd March 1982.

Area: 11,908 hectares (of which 887 are Natural Reserves).

Park office address: Parc Natural de la Zona Volcànica de la Garrotxa
Casal dels Volcans
Avinguda de Santa Coloma s/núm.
17800 Olot.

Habitats: Beech woods, oak woods, ilex woods, scrub, meadows, volcanic cones, cliffs, cultivated land.

Interesting species:
-*Present all the year round*: Goshawk, Peregrine Falcon, Red-legged Partridge, Collared Dove, Great Spotted Woodpecker, Dipper, Dartford Warbler, Sardinian Warbler, Crested Tit, Nuthatch, Bullfinch, Rock Bunting.
-*Summer visitors*: Short-toed Eagle, Hobby, Bee-eater, Hoopoe, Alpine Swift, Wryneck, Crag Martin, Bonelli's Warbler, Golden Oriole, Red-backed Shrike.
-*Winter visitors*: Alpine Accentor, Brambling, Hawfinch, Alpine Chough.

Description and habitat

The Garrotxa Volcanic Zone Natural Park was created on 3rd March 1982, when the Catalan Parliament enacted the Volcanic Zone Protection Bill after a vigorous campaign headed by the most prestigious social and political groups, with the support of scientific organizations throughout the country. The Garrotxa Volcanic Zone thus became the first natural area to be protected by the newly-restored Catalan Government (the "Generalitat de Catalunya").

The Garrotxa volcanic zone is without doubt the largest exponent of this kind of geological phenomenon in the Iberian Peninsula. There are about thirty volcanic cones of strombolian nature (Croscat, Montsacopa), some of an explosive type (Cairat), other mixed strombolian and explosive combinations (Santa Margarida, Garrinada) and over twenty basaltic lava flows with quite exceptional morphological features. Most of the cones to be found in small groups between 450 and 900 metres in height (above sea level) either have well-conserved central craters situated above the cone or craters that are slanted to one side. The cones are between 10 and 160 metres high, between 300 and 1,500 metres across at the base, and are made up of volcanic slag and cinders with volcanic lava bombs scattered here and there. They were all created as a result of a single series of explosions that must have lasted a period of between several days and a few months. The rocky masses of the lava flows cover the valley bottoms, and lie over the old river beds and water courses. These rocks descend as far as Sant Jaume de Llierca in the Fluvià river valley, and as far as El Torn in the Ser river valley, being up to 16 kms long and several dozen metres thick. The eruptions took place at intervals over the course of the Mindel-Riss interglacial period, 350,000 years ago, up until the Epipalaeolithic period, with volcanic activity recurring about every 10,000 years. The last eruption one can put a date to must have occurred at the Croscat Volcano 11,500 years ago. The area can therefore be considered as being volcanically inactive now, but it cannot be regarded as completely volcanically extinct. The vegetation in the area is very varied because Mediterranean and Submediterranean flora converge here with Central European vegetation of an Atlantic nature. The latter form of vegetation, uncommon in our country, can be found between the altitudes of 400 and 500 metres. This is made possible by the high rainfall rate (the annual average is above 1,000 mm) and human presence, which leads to thermal inversion. This phenomenon affects the local birdlife by making these lands unsuitable for the more Mediterranean species, which are nonetheless very much present in neighbouring *comarques*. However, 1,500 superior plant species have been identified in the Park, which may thus be considered to have a wide variety of plant life.

The Puigsacalm-Santa Magdalena range belongs to the Catalan Transverse Range (Serralada Transversal Catalana), a mountain range that runs from the north-west to the south-east, linking up the Pyrenees with the Serralada Prelitoral (pre-coastal range) and separates the inland plains of the Central Depression from the Empordà plain. Geologically it is made up of Eocene period materials and its basic characteristic is the high rainfall (1,200 mm) and high atmospheric humidity. These factors enable many mid-European and Atlantic plant and animal species to thrive in the area. Plants with high hydrogen content and seasonal activity (because of the low winter temperatures) are predominant in the area.

Woodland covers almost 75% of the Natural Park's surface area. The lower, drier ground is normally covered with mountain ilex, although those woods growing on a substratum of siliceous soils differ in that plants preferring acidic soils are much more abundant. The Submediterranean vegetation zones mainly comprise dry Pubescent and Durmast oak woods. The Atlantic vegetation areas have various kinds of beech forest (with wood anemone, boxwood, fescue and Pyrenean squill), Common Oak woods and alder woods, which account for most of the riverside woodland in the area. In the Puigsacalm-Santa Magdalena mountain range the situation is similar. There is Atlantic vegetation on the north-facing slopes and in the shady valley bottoms, ilex woodland on the lower and south-facing slopes and oak woods in the intermediate areas.

Scrub (Catalan: "bosquines") is the name given to all those areas with vegetation (mainly bushes), but lacking trees. The scrub areas you will encounter on the itineraries mainly consist of broom and fern scrub. There are also zones with higher box-wood and juniper scrub; bramble bushes are also very widespread. In places, there are large almost impenetrable masses of bramble, hawthorn, sloe-bush, wild rose, etc..

Meadows or areas of vegetation predominantly grass-covered (these areas are on the decrease due to the decline in extensive livestock farming) are still to be seen in certain zones of the Natural Park and more so in the Puigsacalm-Santa Magdalena range. Two kinds of meadow can be encountered: firstly those with high grass, where gramineae and seed-producing plants predominate, and secondly, meadows with mixed plantlife, where small weeds are predominant. Another rather more uncommon possibility are the waste lands (Catalan: "erms"), a name given to sparsely vegetated meadows with patches entirely devoid of vegetation.

Ruderal plant communities appear in regions where nitrification of the soil and the compact nature of the ground prevent the normal appearance of characteristic plant life, thus modifying the area's normal structures:

roadsides, barren land affected by human activity, etc. These areas are much degraded and it is not surprising that many of the plant species here should be prickly plants   with permanent subterranean organs, capable of rapidly producing large quantities of seeds which are the staple diet of many seed-loving birds. The numbers of these species of birds increase in harmony with the spread of this kind of vegetation.

The **cultivated areas** are a very important part of the present make-up of the volcanic zone, but there are none in the Puigsacalm-Santa Magdalena area, which is of a craggy nature. The lay-out of the cultivated areas in the form of a mosaic is well-adapted to the physiographical conditions of the land. Development of the area by man has been conducted in harmony with the environment. Cultivation of animal fodder crops (such as maize, turnips, alfalfa, etc.) and winter grains predominates; poultry-feed crops such as buck wheat are still grown in the region, though they are on the decline. Family market gardening is quite widespread though, and rounds off the agricultural activity of the area.

How to visit the area

To visit these areas, the best idea would be to establish your base in Olot, the capital of the *comarca* and a town of about 30,000 inhabitants. From Ripoll you can reach Olot (if you are coming from Núria, the previous itinerary area) along the C-150 road. Olot is 31 kms from Ripoll on a winding but beautiful

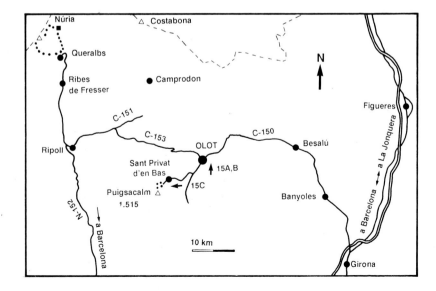

road. If you are coming from Barcelona, the best idea is to head for the C-150 road at Girona. You will have to drive 51 kms before you reach Olot, passing en route through Banyoles, with its fine lake of karstic origin, and Besalú, with its magnificent Roman bridge and Romanesque churches.

When you reach Olot, the best thing is to head for the information centre, the Casal dels Volcans (Volcano House), where you will be supplied with maps and information brochures for the whole area. The Casal dels Volcans is in Avinguda de Santa Coloma, at the beginning of the C-152 road that leads to Santa Coloma. It should not be difficult for you to find because there are plenty of signposts in the city centre. It is open all the year round from 10 am to 2 pm in the morning, and from 4 pm to 6 pm in the afternoon.

You are recommended to spend at least a day and a half in this area, which has three itineraries that will enable you to know the region. The 3 itineraries (15A in the urban area, 15B in the volcanic zone and 15C at Santa Magdalena) may be visited in the following way: one whole morning for 15A, the afternoon for 15B and the following morning for 15C. If you have more time available, the birdwatching will obviously be more productive.

The lack of large-scale migration feeding areas, wintering grounds or breeding colonies makes it possible to recommend a visit at any time of the year. Apart from the interesting resident species, the different seasons all bring in species that will make your visit worthwhile.

Birdwatching

15A. City itinerary in the botanical gardens of the Casal dels Volcans and on the Montsacopa volcano

Starting point and end of the itinerary: Olot **Time needed**: half a day **Means of transport**: on foot

The first itinerary enables you to take advantage of your visit to the information centre (Casal dels Volcans) by having a look round the **botanical garden** that surrounds the house. It is good for plants and birds. The park is quite small (3 hectares) and may be visited in an hour or so. It conserves an interesting area of the old Common Oak wood that used to cover the Olot plain, as well as a large variety of plants that show the botanical wealth of the area. The birdlife includes a good range of small birds that are also present in the oak woods of the region (the larger species cannot adapt to such a small garden within the city). The presence of old, 25 metre high trees (some of which are over 250 years old) guarantees the availability of food and breeding sites. The relative scarcity of predators (due to the characteristics of the place) and the

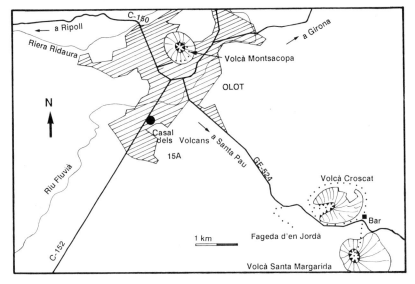

provision of feeding tables and nesting boxes make this garden a haven for
Great Tit, Blue Tit, Long-tailed Tit, Nuthatch, Short-toed Treecreeper and
Firecrest, which all breed here in good numbers. Blackbird and Blackcap are
also common (more so than Sardinian Warbler and Song Thrush), and feed on
the large amount of berries and other fruit growing on the ivy (that covers most
of the perimeter fence), holly, butcher's broom, cherry and apple trees. In
winter there are many finches here, mainly Chaffinch and Greenfinch, but also
Hawfinch, Serin and Bullfinch, as well as thrushes and Dunnock that also
winter in the garden. One must also mention the regular presence in the garden
of Wryneck, Little Owl and Tawny Owl, species that breed nearby. As it is a
small and well signposted park, and the birds are fairly evenly distributed about
its 3 hectares, no specific itinerary is necessary here.

The second part of this itinerary begins in the centre of Olot, in the
Passeig d'en Blay (Blay Avenue), popularly known as "El Firal" (lit. the
fairground). You will have to make your way round Sant Esteve church following Esglaiers street for a few metres as far as the first turning on the left
(Macarnau street), which slopes gently up to the Olot cemetery. You will pass
the nuns' school on your right. It has a courtyard with pine trees where in the
early morning you may well see Collared Dove cooing from some prominent
branch. When you come alongside the cemetery wall, you should follow the
signposts and take the path to the right which leads straight to the volcano. You
will pass through an area with houses and odd cabbage patches here and there
until the path turns north and leaves the built-up area behind, climbing steeply

now with birch and acacias on either side of the path. The habitat you will find now will be mixed orchards, uncultivated areas and grassy patches with trees and sparse bushes and ruderal vegetation that may be explained by the fact the area is subject to intensive human activity. This kind of vegetation favours the presence of seed-eating birds: finches (Serin, Greenfinch, Linnet, Goldfinch and in winter, Chaffinch), sparrows and buntings (Cirl Bunting in summer) that may be seen almost anywhere along the way. On the way up, in the colder months you will see Meadow Pipit darting about in the open areas (orchards and uncultivated ground). White Wagtail and Stonechat will also be about, but these species are present throughout the year. On orchard fences you will see Spotted Flycatcher waiting for some insect to fly past. Fifteen minutes after the beginning of the climb (half an hour since you left the car) you will arrive at the top of the **Montsacopa volcano**. It is Strombolian, having a round, central crater that may be skirted following along the rim. You will soon come to a look-out tower built during the French occupation in 1812. After the tower you will come to the north-facing side of the crater. It is covered in dense clumps of broom and sparser patches of brambles, which provide cover for several species such as Dartford Warbler (in winter you may also see Sardinian Warbler, and in summer, Nightingale, in the centre of the crater and on the sunny slopes). If you keep walking on along the path, you will pass another tower before coming to the Sant Francesc de Paula hermitage. It is a simple XVIIth century building, which had walls build around it by the French in 1812. From here, and from the towers, there is a marvellous view, with Olot below and the volcanoes around the city. The Puigsacalm-Santa Magdalena mountain looms up in the south-west. In summer, the starlings will be singing all about you, and you may catch a glimpse of a Wren or, if it is getting dark, you may hear the intriguing hisses of the Barn Owl. The return walk along the same path will take you back to the Passeig d'en Blay. You will have been walking for an hour and a half (at a birdwatcher's gait).

15B. Itinerary in the Jordà beech wood and the Santa Margarida and Croscat volcanoes

Starting point and end of the itinerary: Olot **Time needed**: 4 hours **Means of transport**: by car and on foot

To begin itinerary 15B, you should take the Ge-524 road which goes to Banyoles via Santa Pau. At km 4 you will come to the first stopping place. On the left-hand side of the road there is a car park in a small leisure area. On the right, there is the path that leads into the beech wood with a monolith in memory of Joan Maragall (Joan in Catalan is a man's name), the great Catalan poet who wrote a marvellous poem about the **Jordà beech** wood at this very spot. The birds you will be finding in this forest (they are more easily heard than seen due to the thick forest canopy!) are Jay, Wood Pigeon and above all tits. Great Tit, Blue Tit, Long-tailed Tit, Marsh Tit and Crested Tit (the latter species in winter alone) are all common here although the rather "tame" nature of the forest means that there are not too many old trees with holes to breed in. In the colder months of the year, the tits (not Marsh Tit however) gather together in mixed flights to which Firecrest and Treecreeper are added. As 75% of the Natural Park is forested, it is not surprising that these woodland species will be found on most of the itinerary. Goshawk is the principal raptor here, although its shyness and the lack of visibility in the area make it a difficult species to spot. The path is clearly marked out and in ten minutes you will come to a kind of hump, a small protuberance produced by lava flow. There is another path leading off from here. It will take you back to the steps at the entrance in a quarter of an hour. Take the car again and follow the road until you come to a straight stretch of road just after km 6. Leave the car at the bar (Santa Margarida) on the left. To go to **Santa Margarida volcano** (it is well signposted), you must cross the road and climb a track that runs parallel with the road for a short while before passing behind a plantation pine wood and turning off to the right. You will come to another junction where you should keep going straight on to a dark farmhouse, with its accompaniment of Swallow nests in the hay-lofts; before arriving there, though, it is worth scanning the pastures and the surrounding ilex trees beneath you, where with your binoculars you may well spot various species of birds: Green Woodpecker (which can also be pinpointed along the way thanks to its strident "horse-neighing" call), Song Thrush, and, in winter, flocks of Common Starling and other species such as Blackbird and Robin, which will be regular species along the way because of the large amount of plant cover in the area. After passing the house, you will come to a small pass where there are three old chestnut trees followed by a steep climb that will lead you to the top of the volcano. Despite the first impression, it is really a horse-shoe crater; being adjacent to a concave calcareous mountain contour makes the volcano seem to have a circular crater, though. Before descending along the path you have come up on, you might try and spot Bonelli's Warbler, which inhabits the ilex woodland on the crater perimeter in the breeding season. You can also look out for the pair of Raven that often fly over the area. It is also a good place to listen out for the loud hooting of various Tawny Owls marking out their territories as from the month of December. You will reach the car after about an hour and a quarter's walk, but do not take it yet because you can now have a walk about the **Croscat volcano**. Take the path that heads off to the north, passing beside the Santa Margarida restaurant and a farm house, where Hoopoes are often to be seen in all but the coldest months.

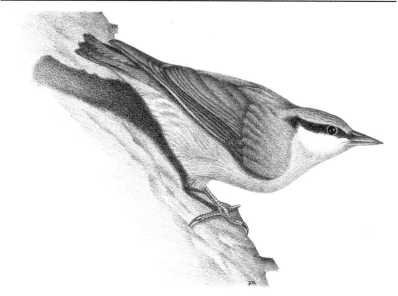

Nuthatch

The predominant terrain near you is basically cultivated land, and the birdlife you have been seeing up to now will start to change. In winter, Chaffinch will be by far and away the commonest species, and if you look carefully at the flights, you may well spot the odd Brambling in among them. There are also large flights of Tree Sparrow and Rock Bunting, although the buntings are by no means regular, being rather erratic in their movements. Cirl Bunting, which breeds in good numbers in summer, should also be seen on this stretch of track that runs beside a pyroplastic embankment. The track heads towards the north-facing slope of the volcano, leaving aside two other tracks, one to the left and another to the right. When the Croscat volcanic cinder extraction works come into view, in winter you will begin to see Meadow Pipit and Skylark in the fields on the other side of the road. Quail will also be seen there in summer, as well as Magpie, Carrion Crow and White Wagtail at all times of year. Any one of these species may at any moment be attacked by Sparrowhawk. The pair of Short-toed Eagle that breed in a local oak tree may often be seen in the sky above the Batet plateau (where there are fields on the slopes). On the terraced embankments on the other side, you may well see the plump figure of the Red-legged Partridge. Turtle Dove may also be seen on the electric wires which are at the spot that you pass a path at right angles to the one you are on. Here the cultivated fields give way to densely vegetated bushy areas with odd trees here and there. You should see plenty of Blackcap along this path in winter, a time of year when Dunnock and Bullfinch are also to be seen. In spring you will also be able to hear the characteristic call of the Cuckoo, as well as that of Nuthatches in among the thick undergrowth of the area. You will now pass by two abandoned farm houses. Keep on until you come to Can Pagès (Catalan: the house of Pagès). It is an inhabited *masia* (farm) where you should now take a small path that in 5 minutes will lead you through an area of low vegetation, bushes (hawthorn, broom and ferns) and odd trees to the base of the volcano. You may come across the intriguing Red-backed Shrike here, as well as Mistle Thrush singing from the top of a tree. If you look up at the sky about the Croscat, it is not uncommon to see the silhouette of a Buzzard hunting for its prey. Once you have seen the crater, return to Can Pagès to continue along the track as far as the road, which you will have to follow for about 200 metres. Once you have passed the can Bastans restaurant, take the small path on the left that runs parallel with a fence. You will come to a crossroads where you should turn right following along the Can Xel restaurant swimming-pool wall. After a short climb, the path begins to descend and the road which you must take to cover the short distance to the Santa Margarida restaurant, will soon come into view. You will reach the restaurant (where you left the car) after about 2 hours' walking. This marks the final stage of the itinerary, which will have taken about 4 hours if you have not walked too slowly!

15C. Puigsacalm itinerary

Starting point and end of the itinerary: Olot **Time needed**: 6 hours **Means of transport**: by car and on foot

The last itinerary consists of a fine excursion in very picturesque areas. The walk will take about 5 or 6 hours , and you will have to climb 750 metres. You will have to drive out of Olot on the Santa Coloma road as far as Les Preses at km 4. There you must turn right after passing the Vertisol hotel. You should take a small road that leads to Sant Privat, which is about 6 kms away. When you get to Sant Privat, drive through the village until you come to the last bend before coming to the old village centre with its church. Here you must take a track to the left. After crossing a stream, where Dipper are to be seen, drive past a children's summer home (on your right), and on to a picnic area in a pine grove. Leave the car at the end of this leisure area immediately after crossing a path running at right angles to the one you are on. Here you start walking. You should follow the track up the stream for about 10 minutes through an area of thick fern, bramble and hazel scrub with sparse deciduous trees and small patches of grass here and there. When you come to some small crags that appear through the oak wood on the other side of the stream, there is a path that

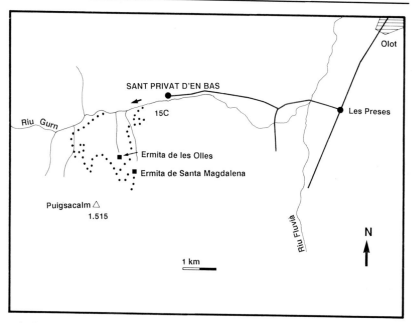

winds its way up to the southern slope. Before climbing up this path, though, it is worth having a look at the cliffs to the west because you can often see a pair of Hobbies there in summer. To the north, above the south-facing slopes, Buzzard are also commonly seen. The path up the mountain has a long series of winding curves with three hairpin bends to the west, and two to the southeast. On the first and second bend to the west you will have to ignore two paths that lead off to the left of the path. The path will start to get narrower at a place beside some enormous boulders that have come away from the cliff face. Soon it will become little more than a footpath that leaves the scrub as it enters a beautiful beech wood. In the preceding habitat, the principal birds that may be seen are Bullfinch, which are to be seen both in summer (normally in pairs) and in winter. At this time of year it is more common to see small flocks of 3 or 5 birds of the same sex, especially males. In summer you will also see Red-backed Shrike (on their perches at the top of hawthorn bushes), Golden Orioles in one of the trees in the copses, as well as the odd Green Woodpecker, which may be identified by its strident alarm call. The birdlife in the beech wood you are now entering is very similar to that which you have already observed on your walk in the Fageda d'en Jordà (cf. itinerary 15B). Great Spotted Woodpecker is the only outstanding species to be added in this area, where there are plenty. They are easy to identify both visually and by listening out for its drumming on tree trunks. The path is now very beautiful, and has a little paving along the way. It takes us up the mountain, and skirts a large crag. When you come to a small stream, the path will begin to wind its way steeply upwards for a short while. You will have to pass along a ledge beneath the crag and you will soon come to a small pass. After passing a sheep pen, you take a small path to the left that passes first through an area of box-wood. There follows a meadow with patches of broom which leads down to the track you should not leave until you reach Santa Magdalena. The landscape varies, as does the birdlife. You now come to a zone with wide pasture meadows, with patches of juniper and the odd tree, a habitat that is very suitable for Song Thrush, which are very numerous here, Yellowhammer (visible singing from the tops of the juniper bushes in the breeding season), and two species that you will have seen on the other two itineraries in winter, but which here are resident species breeding in the area: Goldcrest and Dunnock.

The path then leads down into two cool hollows covered in beech trees. You will cross two streams before coming to the **Santa Magdalena del Mont esplanade**. The hermitage is situated in pasture meadows, and has the odd large oak tree and ash tree growing nearby. A little further up there is a small green summit. You are recommended to set aside a few minutes for gazing at the magnificent view from the top. The open space about you enables you to identify different species on the wing: Raven (that breed on the Puigsacalm ledges), Chough, and Alpine Chough on cold winter days; Alpine Swift flashing over you and Crag Martins fluttering about the radio transmitting aerial at this spot. These two latter species are only to be seen in summer. Sometimes it is also possible to identify Peregrine Falcon on the crags that descend beneath you on the southern side of the mountain. It may be perched on a tree waiting for prey to fly within striking distance or else flying about on the cliff face. The majestic Golden Eagle, flying across from its distant breeding areas, is also to be seen occasionally. In winter, Alpine Accentor are quite common here, whereas in summer it is the Tree Pipit and Black Redstart that may be seen here. The pipit carries out its spectacular parachute descent as it sings its way down from the sky to the tree-tops. The Black Redstart, on the other hand, makes use of the old *masia* (farm) and the church to breed in.

To climb down the mountain, to begin with you must take the same path. But as soon as you begin to enter the area where the beech and box-wood are predominant, there is a path off to the right that leads straight down to Les Olletes, the famous hermitage which is built into the cliff itself. The path continues to descend through the beech wood until the woodland begins to turn into thick scrub and dense woodland. You will come to a path that you must take briefly. After a bend you should once again take the small path that will take you to the Can Turon hostal, from where the track will lead you back to the car in 10 minutes. On the way down you will find two habitats: beech wood and wooded scrub. The same birds will be encountered as on the way up, although there is also a chance of seeing Coal Tit among the sparce pines you find along the way.

Board and lodging

Olot is the best place from which to carry out the itineraries. You can stay, among other hotels, at the Hotel Motsacopa, in the city centre, at the Hostal de la Perla, in Avinguda Santa Coloma (a little beyond the Casal dels Volcans) or at the Narmar boarding house, in the Plaça Major, which is also in the city centre. At the Torre Malagrida in the Passeig de Barcelona, there is also a Youth Hostal where you may put up for a very reasonable price. For those who prefer camping, there is a camping site (Les Tries) on the left on the way into Olot from Girona on the C-150 road.

The local cuisine may be sampled, for example, at Ca la Nàsia restaurant, on the C-113 road that leads to Camprodon. The La Deu and La Moixina restaurants are on a turning off to the left on the Avinguda Santa Coloma, before leaving Olot. Apart from getting a good meal here, you can also enjoy the marvellous scenery and the fountains (Font Moixina) with their coll and clear waters. Between Olot and Santa Pau (near one of the areas visited on itinerary 15B), you will come to the Restaurant dels Ossos and the Can Bastans restaurant. The day you visit Santa Magdalena, it may be useful for you to know that there are two good restaurants in Sant Privat right beside the main road: Ca la Carmelita and Can Mulleras.

Other places of interest

- The medieval town of Santa Pau. Church, castle, square and walls make up a fine architectural setting. It is 9.5 kms from Olot on the Ge-524 road.

- Castellfollit de la Roca. A small village perched on top of a spectacular basalt cliff, with the church of Sant Salvador on the very edge of the abyss. It is 6 kms from Olot on the C-150 road (which goes to Girona).

- The image of the Mare de Déu del Tura (Our Lady of Tura). A XIIth century Romanesque statue of the black Virgin and Child. It is one of the most beautiful works of art of the Catalan Romanesque period and is in the Tura church in the centre of Olot. Visiting hours are not regular.

- Sant Esteve church, Olot. A neoclassical building with interesting works of art. In the centre of Olot. Visiting hours are not regular.

- The Garrotxa museum (Museu Comarcal de la Garrotxa). A collection of the most representative works illustrative of the activities of the *comarca* over the late XVIIIth century - early XXth century period. In the old part of Olot. Open from 10 am to 1 pm, and from 4 pm to 7 pm.

SPECIALITIES

urple Heron (Agró roig) *Ardea purpurea.*
The Delta of the river Ebre is the principal breeding site in Catalonia for is species, although it also breeds at other sites. On the itineraries covered in is book, it can also be seen at the Aiguamolls de l'Empordà (especially on nerary 2B), southern Costa Brava (itinerary 3C) and Sant Llorenç de ontgai (itinerary 10B). It is basically associated with well-vegetated fresh- iter wetlands. In the Delta of the river Ebre, a good many birds can be seen the mixed colony at La Nòria (itinerary 7C). This species is to be seen in italonia from the end of March until September. When seen flying in bad ht, a good field mark (that will help you to distinguish it from Grey Heron) he length of the hind toe. Purple Heron have longer toes than Grey Heron :ause of the different habitats they are associated with. Purple Heron fly with ir hind toe sticking upwards. This makes their feet look larger. Grey Heron ve a shorter hind toe and can close their feet in flight.

quacco Heron (Martinet ros) *Ardeola ralloides*
You are likely to see this species in the Delta of the river Ebre, which he species' most important breeding site in the Iberian Peninsula, and the y one in Catalonia. The egretry at La Nòria (itinerary 7C), where you will : Squacco Herons coming and going from the nest from the beginning of ie until the end of August, is the best site for this species. The species is sent in the Delta from mid-April until the beginning of October, and can be n throughout this period, especially in the paddy fields and on all the coastal oons. When sitting, the species has a buffish colour, but on the wing it looks reat deal whiter. If visibility is not good, it can even be confused with a Cattle ret in breeding plumage.

hite Stork (Cigonya) *Ciconia ciconia*
The only wild population left in Catalonia is in the Segre river valley he Central Depression. This river valley, known as the "route of the Storks", :s up Lleida with itinerary 9C (cf. page 154). Of all the nests on this route, most visible one is at Menàrguens. On the second half of itinerary 9B (in gon), you will also be passing by several Storks' nests. The one at Ballobar

is particularly interesting because it can be observed from its own level. The nests are occupied from March to June, but several birds winter in the area. In the Aiguamolls de l'Empordà, there is a White Stork reintroduction project under way. Several birds can be seen all the year round, especially feeding on the El Matà paddy fields (itinerary 2A).

Flamingo (Flamenc) *Phoenicopterus ruber*

There are large flocks of Flamingo on the Delta of the river Ebre throughout the year, especially in summer. You are sure to see them from the Punta de la Banya observatory (itinerary 7C). There are sometimes flocks of over a thousand birds. Small flocks of Flamingo are often seen on La Rogera lagoon in the Aiguamolls de l'Empordà (itinerary 2A), especially during migration and in winter.

Red-crested Pochard (Xibec) *Netta rufina*

This species of duck can be seen in good numbers throughout the year on the Delta of the river Ebre, its only breeding site in Catalonia. The species can also be seen at other Catalan sites (Aiguamolls de l'Empordà etc.) during its post-breeding season movements and in winter. One particularly charming sight is the flotilla of females, accompanied by swarms of young ducklings that invade the rice paddies to feed on small invertebrates. In the breeding season this species prefers shallow lagoons, but in winter it is to be found on the large lagoons.

Bearded Vulture (Trencalós) *Gypaetus barbatus*

It either frequents or breeds in the areas covered in chapters 10, 11, 12, 13 and 14. Its most regular sites are at the Montrebei gorge (itnerary 10A) and from the Camp del Teixó, on the south side of the Moixeró range (itinerary 13A). You must sometimes be very patient and wait at a good vantage spot, scanning the mountain ridges they love to skirt. You must also keep an eye on the sky, for this species often flies at a tremendous height. Bearded Vulture tend to wander away from their habitual territories once the breeding season is over, in late summer and early autumn. It is during this period (when the livestock is out pasturing on the mountains) that you are most likely to see it in Pyrenean areas where it does not breed (eg. Núria and Andorra). The species is unmistakable when seen from nearby. When seen from afar, you must observe its flight silhouette (long narrow wings and diamond-shaped tail).

Egyptian Vulture (Aufrany) *Neophron percnopterus*

At present, this species can only be found in western Catalonia. The best sites for Egyptian Vulture are the Montsec d'Ares (itinerary 10A) and the cliffs on the river on the way out of Alcolea de Cinca in Aragon (itinerary 9B). It comes to the area at the beginning of March and leaves in mid-September. When seen from afar, it is possible to mistake it for a light phase Booted Eagle, or even for a White Stork. Its flight silhouette, however, is quite distinct.

Griffon Vulture (Voltor comú) *Gyps fulvus*

Of the areas covered in this book, there are only breeding colonies in the Montsec and in the Ports de Tortosa i Beseit. You are almost certain to see this species if you follow the itineraries in the Montsec d'Ares (itinerary 10A) or along he La Galera gorge (itinerary 8A). In summer they are less common in their breeding areas, but they are more commonly seen in the western Catalan Pyrenees (at Aigüestortes-Sant Maurici and Andorra). It can easily be identified by its large size and flight silhouette, as well as by its habit of flying in groups.

Booted Eagle (Àguila calçada) *Hieraetus pennatus*

It is a rare and local breeding species in Catalonia, being slightly commoner in the western part of the country. Of the areas covered in this handbook, you are most likely to see this species (from April to September) in the Montsec and, above all, in the area about the Noguera Ribagorçana river, just north of the Montrebei gorge (itinerary 10A). Although it is basically a summer visitor to Europe, this species has been recorded wintering in small numbers (up to eight) in the Aiguamolls de l'Empordà since 1980. It can be seen in this area from November to February, especially hunting on the El Matà paddy fields (itinerary 2A), in the Tres Ponts area (itinerary 2B) and at Caramany Island (itinerary 2C). Both plumage phases are present.

Bonelli's Eagle (Àguila cuabarrada) *Hieraetus fasciatus*

Several pairs are to be found breeding in or around the areas visited in chapters 1, 3, 4, 5, 6, 8 and 10. Two of the sites they can most regularly be seen are the valley of the river Siurana (itinerary 6B) and in front of the Sant Llorenç de Montgai reservoir (itinerary 10B). The best time of year to see Bonelli's Eagle is from the period the eaglets begin to fly (in mid-June) to December or January, when they start their spectacular courtship display. When there are eggs or chicks in the nest (from mid-February until early June), they are much less visible. The best field mark (to avoid confusion with other birds of prey such as Short-toed Eagle) is the contrast between the white of the under part of the body and the darker wings. Immature birds of reddish brown plumage are not rare on the Lleida steppes, especially on itinerary 9A.

Lesser Kestrel (Xoriguer petit) *Falco naumanni*

This is the species that has most recently become extinct in Catalonia. In the mid-eighties there were still several pairs breeding at Alcarràs, 9 kms from Lleida, and at Cap Norfeu (itinerary 1B). The reasons for its disappearance, however, would apparently have more to do with the situation in their African wintering grounds. It seems that the anthropophilous habits of this species bring it into close contact with the more developed areas of Africa where pesticides produced by industrialized countries are used in an uncontrolled fashion. On itinerary 9B, however, the odd bird can still be seen in the Aragonese Monegros area and in the Cinca valley (from March to September). The best site is the riverside cliff on the way out of Alcolea de Cinca. The species may be distinguished from Common Kestrel by the fact they never hover and by the difference in colours. The Generalitat's Nature Protection Service is currently running a programme to breed Lesser Kestrel in captivity, with a view to reintroducing the species by means of the technique known as "hacking".

Purple Gallinule (Polla blava) *Porphyrio porphyrio*

Although there have recently been records of this species in the deltas of the rivers Ebre and Llobregat (probably vagrant birds from the Sardinian or Andalusian populations), Purple Gallinule has been considered to be extinct in Catalonia since the turn of the century. A project to reintroduce the species was initiated by DE.PA.NA. (Defensa del Patrimoni Natural, a Catalan nature conservation society) in the summer of 1989. The project is being carried out in association with the General Directorate for the Environment. The first phase of the project has so far introduced 38 birds from the Doñana national Park and the Guadalquivir marshes (Andalusia) into the Aiguamolls de l'Empordà. The ideal habitat for this species is freshwater marsh with plenty of bullrush such as there is at the Gall Marí hide (Itin. 2A). They can be seen sunning themselves in prominent places or rooting out the bullrush stalks they feed on. A close watch will have to be kept on their progress over the next few years. All birdwatchers are kindly asked to record all sightings of the bird in Catalonia (giving details of the number on the ring -if visible- they bear on their leg). If the first phase succeeds, the possibility of introducing the species in the Delta of the river Ebre will be studied.

Little Bustard (Sisó) *Tetrax tetrax*

A bird associated with the steppe areas to be found on all itineraries in chapter 9. You are likely to see it at dawn and dusk on the cereal plain north of Bellcaire (itinerary 9D) from the beginning of April until mid-June. You will be able to admire the male's two forms of courtship display: flying above the crops (you will see the flashing white of its wings) or else perched in the fields and in vegetation-free areas. The croaking sound it utters during the static display will help you to spot it. Outside the breeding season, groups of eight or twelve birds can be seen, especially in areas such as the fields between Aspa and Artesa de Lleida (itinerary 9A).

Black-winged Stilt (Cames llargues) *Himantopus himantopus*

This wader is found on shallow water (freshwater or saline), including paddy fields, and you are almost certain to see it in the Aiguamolls de l'Empordà (chapter 2) and in the Delta of the river Ebre (chapter 7), where the largest breeding populations in Catalonia are to be found. It also breeds on the Pals marshes (itinerary 3C), on the Delta of the river Llobregat and on the inland paddy fields at Lleida. This migratory species can be observed from mid-March to late September and early October. On passage, it can be seen almost anywhere there is water.

Stone Curlew (Torlit) *Burhinus oedicnemus*

Apart from occasional records from other areas, the two principal sites for this open country species are the Lleida Steppes and the Aiguamolls de l'Empordà. You are almost sure to see this species on the four itineraries in chapter 9, especially on gently sloping wasteland and in uncultivated areas near or between cultivated fields. Sites that are nearly infallible are the small hillocks and the barren areas at the end of itinerary 9D, once you have crossed the cereal area. The Stone Curlew's call is to be heard just before nightfall, and will help you to identify its whereabouts. It is not so common in the Aiguamolls de l'Empordà, but it is often seen on itinerary 2A, especially on the stretch behind the dune between the Massona and Rogera lagoons. It is present both in Lleida and on the Aiguamolls from February to October. In winter it is much rarer and more difficult to spot, although on occasions, flocks of up to a hundred birds have been seen. The shape and flight silhouette of this species is quite unmistakable, but its call can be confused with that of the Curlew (in areas where the two species coincide, as they do in the Aiguamolls).

Pratincole (Perdiu de Mar) *Glareola pratincola*

This species' only regular breeding site is the Delta of the river Ebre. Its most important breeding colony is on the barren areas about the Tancada lagoon (itinerary 7C), between the Baladres road and the sea. It is easy to see Pratincole on the wing or sitting on either side of the road here. Other interesting species also breed at this spot, which has incomprehensibly been left out of the Natural Park area. There are several housing estate projects threatening the area, one of which plans to build a huge holiday residential area. In the Garxal area (itinerary 7B) there is another Pratincole colony. The birds can be seen flying about on the stretch between the Riomar housing estate and the beach. Pratincole have bred irregularly in the Aiguamolls de l'Empordà and in the Delta of the river Llobregat, where the species can also be seen on migration. It is a summer visitor to Catalonia, and is present from March to September (exceptionally in October). It is very easy to identify on the wing and looks like a very large Swallow. When sitting on the ground, however, its sandy colour often makes it difficult to spot.

Slender Billed Gull (Gavina capblanca) *Larus genei*

It is a rather maritime gull and is associated primarily with salt water areas. The Delta of the river Ebre is its only Catalan breeding site. It has become increasingly common in the last few years. It has increased from 12 pairs in 1975 (first year breeding was effectively recorded) to 429 pairs in 1988. In the Delta it can be seen at the Garxal area (itinerary 7B), on the Sant Antoni salt pans, on the Trabucador spit (especially on the bay side), and at the Punta de la Banya (itinerary 7C). You will often see it swimming with its head raised up and bent forward, submerging the front half of its body in the water in its search for fish (in the same sort of fashion as dabbling ducks). Another of this species' fishing techniques is to skim over the water picking up the small fish on which it feeds. Its wing pattern is similar to that of Black-headed Gull; but it is larger, its neck is longer and its head is completely white. The majority of birds are to be found in the Delta in spring and summer, although more and more individuals are staying on in winter.

Audouin's Gull (Gavina corsa) *Larus audouinii*

It is one of the most interesting breeding species in Catalonia, and is furthermore on the increase. Audouin's Gull was originally a species on the Red Book list of endangered species and quite rare in Catalonia. It has now become relatively common. Thirty-six pairs began breeding in the Delta of the river Ebre in 1981. In 1982 the number of pairs rose to 200, 546 in 1983, about

1,200 in 1985 and 2,861 in 1988. Our country has a very real part to play in the conservation of this species. Over thirty per cent of the total world population breed here. It is a species that you must go to the Delta to see. Two good sites to spot it are the Garxal (itinerary 7B), and the Punta de la Banya (itinerary 7C), where it may be observed sitting on the salt pans or flying about on the beach. The species is basically a summer visitor to Catalonia, where it begins to arrive in March and April. Soon after the breeding period, in August, most adults and almost all young birds leave the area and probably head for the African coast where they winter. Although the colouring of the bird is similar to that of Herring Gull, its bright red beak (which from afar may appear to be black) makes the species unmistakable.

Whiskered Tern (Fumarell carablanc) *Chlidonias hybrida*

The Delta of the river Ebre is the only breeding site in Catalonia, although this species has undergone strong fluctuations in the last few years because of the use of insecticides and habitat destruction. In the Aiguamolls de l'Empordà Whiskered Tern are very frequent on passage, and some birds summer in the paddy fields. This species arrives in Catalonia in mid-March, although there have been odd records of birds wintering here. In spring migration, the species is commoner than in autumn. In spring birds have their spectacular summer plumage, but in autumn they have eclipse plumage and are less striking.

Black-bellied Sandgrouse (Xurra) *Pterocles orientalis*

Of the two species of sandgrouse in Catalonia, this is the rarer of the two. It is thus quite difficult to see. The Mormur hillock neighbourhood (itinerary 9C) is the area (covered in an itinerary in Catalonia) where you have the best chances of seeing this species. However, your chances of seeing it will increase considerably if you visit the nearby Monegros (in Aragon), as described in itinerary 9B. The best section of itinerary is the dust track that begins at Km 15, including the saline steppes it crosses and, above all, the plains that rise up on the left. One strategy for spotting this species is to take long walks through the barren and uncultivated lands, with the hope of putting them up. However, it is possible that they are more often seen by chance, when the "churrrr" of their call, quite different to the Pin-tailed Sandgrouse's, gives away the presence of the bird flying over. Other than the call, the black belly (but not the similar flight silhouette and straight flight) will help us to tell it apart from Pin-tailed Sandgrouse. The species is present all the year round in the area, although in winter they are more difficult to come across because they group together.

Pin-tailed Sandgrouse (Ganga) *Pterocles alchata*

This species is more common in Catalonia than the Black-bellied Sandgrouse. It is not rare to see it on the large plains before you reach Artesa de Lleida (itinerary 9A), especially from April to July. It can also be seen on itinerary 9B (in the Aragonese Monegros area) at the same sites that are given for the Black-bellied Sandgrouse. Its habits are also similar to those of the former species, and the advice given for the observation of Black-bellied Sandgrouse does apply to to Pin-tailed Sandgrouse. Its white belly, its long tail feathers and its call, a loud "gang-gang" are its distinguishing features.

Great Spotted Cuckoo (Cucut reial) *Clamator glandarius*

This species is not difficult to see at the right spots although it does not stay put in any fixed territory because it is a parasitical species. The best areas to see it are the Lleida steppes and the Aiguamolls de l'Empordà. It can be seen at this latter site in the olive groves there are before coming to Palau (itinerary 2B) or in the pine woods in the vicinity of the Empúries ruins (itinerary 2C). The best areas in Lleida are on the latter half of itinerary 9A, between Aspa and Artesa, and the area before crossing the cereal plains on itinerary 9D. Adults arrive in February and leave in June, as soon as they have laid their eggs. Young birds of the year may stay on for the whole month of July, and occasionally a little longer. The best period to see Great Spotted Cuckoo is from the end of February to April, when it is given away by its strident "ke-ke-ke" call, often made on the wing. The abundance of Magpies (virtually the only species it parasitizes on) is a clue to the likely areas for this species. The excited flight of magpies (in pursuit of Great Spotted Cuckoos) may well be the sign that gives this species away!

Red-necked Nightjar (Siboc) *Caprimulgus ruficollis*

This species, which is very similar to the Common Nightjar, is also a summer visitor and a migrant in Catalonia. It arrives in late April or early May and leaves in September or early October. Breeding pairs have their territories in areas of sparse woodland, in recently planted woods, and in cultivated areas. They are especially common in vineyards and almond groves. Red-necked Nightjar love dry and sunny slopes, and, unlike Common Nightjar, they avoid shady places and areas above the altitude of 600 m. The two best areas for observing this species (on the itineraries described in this book) are the Lleida steppes (chapter 9) and the Montsec range (chapter 10), where you must look for it in suitable habitats. Its crepuscular habits, though, make it difficult to observe. Listen for its call, and keep your eyes open during night drives. It can often be seen sitting on the road.

Pallid Swift (Falciot pàl·lid) *Apus pallidus*

Pallid Swift is a summer visitor to Catalonia, where it arrives earlier and leaves later than Common Swift. The first sightings are in March, and it can be seen until the October-November period. Its distribution in Catalonia is basically limited to the coast. The best itineraries for this species are the Cap de Creus (chapter 1), southern Costa Brava (chapter 3) and Garraf (itinerary 5C). In good light, the colouring, and, above all, the white mark on the throat enable you to tell it apart from Common Swift, although it is often difficult to identify the species. Common Swift breed at most Pallid Swift breeding sites. Seeing the two species side by side will enable you to observe and identify them with greater ease.

Alpine Swift (Ballester) *Apus melba*

This is a summer visitor to Catalonia.It can be observed almost anywhere on migration, and in the breeding season it is very common in the Montgrí and Medes islands area (itinerary 3A and 3B), on itineraries in and around Barcelona (chapter 5), Montsant-Siurana (chapter 6) and Cadí-Moixeró (chapter 13). It breeds on great cliff faces or on high buildings in the cities. Alpine Swift arrive in Catalonia in late March and leave in the September-October period. Its large size, the white patch on the chest and belly and its typical screaming call make it unmistakable.

Bee-eater (Abellerol) *Merops apiaster*

A very typical and widespread species in Catalan Mediterranean areas. It needs earth or sand-banks to breed, and bores tunnels into the ground to make its nest. It is often found near rivers because bank erosion often makes ideal sites for their colonies. Although it can be seen almost everywhere, especially during migration, the best itineraries for the observation of this species are: Aiguamolls de l'Empordà (chapter 2), Montsant (chapter 6), Ports de Tortosa-Beceit (chapter 8), Lleida steppes (chapter 9) and Montsec (chapter 10). The species is present in Catalonia from mid-April until late September. Its typical fluted call helps you to spot the bird when flying high in the sky, and when it is flying above its concealed breeding colony.

Roller (Gaig blau) *Coracias garrulus*

This is one of the species (along with Stone Curlew and Lesser Grey Shrike) that is mainly to be seen on the Lleida and Empordà plains. In both areas it can be seen from late April to late August. The best place to see this species is probably at La Figuera, on itinerary 9C, after having crossed the

Balaguer-Alfarràs road and before arriving in the holm oak (*Quercus rotundifolia*) area in the higher part of the Serra Llarga mountains. Sparse almond groves and the edges of large fields are its favourite habitat. Similar areas can be found at the end of itninerary 9A. This species can also be seen in the Cortalet meadows (itinerary 2A) or from the footpath leading to the Vilahut bird observatory (hide). The species stands out for its colours and for its habit of sitting on prominent perches. Two excellent periods for the observation of this species are the month of May, when it carries out its spectacular display flight, and in July, when its favourite perches are the straw bales situated in harvested fields.

Hoopoe (Puput) *Upupa epops*

A very typical species that can be seen in sunny and open habitats from the coast up to the altitude of about 1600m. Most of the areas described in the book (other than Pyrenean ones) are ideal for the observation of this species. It is mainly a summer visitor to Catalonia, arriving very early on (in the second half of January). It returns to Africa from mid-July to October. In some coastal areas, such as the Empordà plain (chapter 2), Hoopoe can be seen in winter too. Be careful not to confuse its call (which normally has three similar notes) with that of the Cuckoo, which has two different and somewhat louder notes.

Dupont's Lark (Alosa becuda) *Chersophilus duponti*

Itinerary 9B is the only itinerary in the book offering the chance of seeing this species which has only recently been discovered as a European species. This very specialized lark needs large plains (at least 5 hectares) which are not too stony and have low sparse vegetation. Some of the esparto-grass zones on the first part of itinerary 9B (in the Aragonese Monegros area) have a combination of these characteristics and have small numbers of this species. In Catalonia there is only one zone of this kind, but it is very vulnerable, and the visits of too many birdwatchers would be harmful before special protection measures are brought in.

Because of the special interest of this species, we also supply a further protected site in Aragon. It is not included in the itineraries, and the high density of breeding pairs improves your chances of seeing Dupont's Larks. The site is called the Lomazas Steppe Birds Reserve. It is situated at Belchite, and was created by the Spanish Ornithological Society. The area is also good for other steppe species, and the ruins of the old derelict town of Belchite are an impressive exponent of the destruction caused by the Spanish Civil War. Belchite is 49 kms south-east of Zaragoza, and you can reach the area in 3 hours from Barcelona on the A-2 motorway. From Blechite you must take the road to Mediana; the Lomazas zone is on the right-hand side of the road. The plateaux on the top of the hillocks (Spanish: Lomazas = hillocks) are good sites for Dupont's Lark. Groups visiting the area should not split up because the ground is fragile and may be damaged. For further information, you are advised to get in touch with the Autonomous Administration (Equipo de Caza y Pesca/ Departamento de Agricultura, Ganadería y Montes/ Diputación General de Aragón/ Zaragoza) that is responsible for the area.

The song of the Dupont's Lark is very distinctive and easy to recognize. But it sings at great height and dives down so fast that it is practically impossible to spot on the wing. The best strategy is to walk through an area of steppe, where you may well see it darting along the ground, stopping now and again. If you can see it on the ground, the upright stance, its striped eyebrow, and, above all, its curved beak will help you to avoid any possible confusion, especially with young Tawny Pipit, that also have a spotted chest.

Calandra Lark (Calàndria) *Melanocorypha calandra*

This species can be seen without too much trouble on any of the itineraries in chapter 9. It is plentiful on itineraries 9C and 9D, especially in barley fields, above which it can often be seen hovering. It can also be seen on the ground, especially on the edges of paths. In winter, however, it is more abundant on the barren and uncultivated land on the second half of itinerary 9A, where it can often be seen in large flocks of up to several hundred birds. If you see the bird on the ground, the thick bill and the two large black patches on either side of the neck make the species unmistakable. In flight, the white trailing edge of the wing can be easily seen. This same field mark, though less clear, is also shared with Skylark; but the underside of the wings, which are cream-coloured in Skylark and black in Calandra Lark, dispel all confusion. Its song is also quite distinctive although it often imitates other species such as Goldfinch, Green Woodpecker, Common Swift and Kestrel.

Lesser Short-toed Lark (Terrerola rogenca) *Calandrella rufescens*

There are two zones where this species can be seen: the Delta of the river Ebre, where it is relatively easy to spot (for example on the saltings on the right-hand side of the Baladres road (itinerary 7C), or at several sites on the Lleida and Aragon steppes, where it is even more common. The best spot for this species in the Aragonese steppes is the large saline steppe that you cross 16km after the beginning of itinerary 9B, where it can be seen alongside Short-toed Lark and Calandra Lark. There are no grounds for confusion with Calandra Lark, and its spotted chest and the lack of the two darker patches on the flanks distinguish it from Short-toed Lark. Its very distinctive call, a brief "prrrt" similar to the House Martin's call, is uttered when it flies and on taking to the wing. If you visit its breeding areas from March to May, you will be able to identify it by the way it flies when singing (it goes round in circles, and does not rise gradually higher like Short-toed Lark). In winter, they gather together in flocks of varying size.

Thekla Lark (Cogullada fosca) *Galerida theklae*

It is a sedentary species in Catalonia, living in hilly and low mountain areas, usually under the altitude of 500 metres. It prefers stony and sloping ground with sparse bushes, and steppe areas too. It is generally absent from cultivated land in the plains and lowland areas in general, where it is substituted by Crested Lark. Both species coexist in some areas, but Thekla Lark tend to be the only *Galerida* lark on low Mediterranean mountainsides; this is the situation, for example, at the Cap de Creus (chapter 1) and in the Garraf massif (itinerary 5C), where you are almost sure to see it. It is also very common on the Lleida steppes, but at many sites it also coexists with Crested Lark. Other than the differences in colouring, which are often very difficult to see, the song is quite different and may well help to identify it.

Red-rumped Swallow (Oreneta cua-rogenca) *Hirundo daurica*

This species has been detected as a breeder as recently as the fifties (it may have been overlooked), and has two main breeding areas: the Cap de Creus-Albera mountains and the southern Costa Brava, although it has also been spotted in the Montsant and Siurana area. The best itinerary for this species is 3C, on the stretch between Sant Feliu de Guíxols and Tossa de Mar, from April to August. It can also be seen on the Cap de Creus (itinerary 1A) and at Siurana (itinerary 6B). In the village of Siurana you should be able to spot it without too much difficulty among Swallow, House Martin and Crag Martin, and this makes it the ideal place to check up on its distinguishing features. Its flight silhouette is similar to that of the Swallow, but it has a reddish white rump and its tail has a more "tubular" and elongated form. A check on the few places it can build its characteristic nest (that needs a fairly flat undersurface such as those to be found under bridges, tunnels and on old buildings) will provide further evidence of its breeding activity.

Alpine Accentor (Cercavores) *Prunella collaris*

It is present all the year round in Catalonia, although it inhabits different areas in summer and winter. In the breeding season it is to be found in Alpine and Subalpine areas, usually above 2,000 metres on altitude (the Montseny breeding population at 1,700 m is an outstanding exception). In winter, however, it comes down to lower mountain and coastal areas, though it is to be found at all times in rocky areas. You are sure to see the species on the climb up the Puigmal peak (itinerary 14C) where you will be able to see how tame this species is. If you do not want to work so hard for this species, you will be able to see it feeding tamely on the ski station bar terraces (eg. Núria, on itinerary 14A) outside the breeding season (but before the harshest snow storms force them out of the area). In mid-winter the species moves about in small flocks and is easy to see on the higher parts of the Monstant massif (itinerary 6A).

Black-eared Wheatear (Còlit ros) *Oenanthe hispanica*

A summer visitor to the Mediterranean area, where it is to be found on open ground in the warmer and dryer regions of Catalonia. It is very common on the Cap de Creus (chapter 1), and in the southern Costa Brava (chapter 3), Garraf (itinerary 5C), Montsant-Siurana (chapter 6), Ports de Tortosa i Beseit (chapter 8), Lleida steppes (chapter 9) and Montsec (chapter 10) areas. Spring passage begins at the end of March and autumn migration starts up in the first week in August. After mid-September it is most rare to see any birds lingering on. Males are most distinctive, but females of this species can sometimes be confused with those of Common Wheatear, although close observation of cheek, wing and tail colouring will help you to tell them apart.

Black Wheatear (Còlit negre) *Oenanthe leucura*

A very typical Mediterranean species associated with dry and stony areas without too much vegetation. It can be seen all the year round in Catalonia, although in winter it may move around a little. Cap de Creus and Montsant are the two best areas for Black Wheatear. Although it is a species with a low population density, the abundance of suitable breeding sites will enable you to see it at several spots. The following are places where you are almost certain to see the species, as long as you are patient: the castle of Sant Salvador and the tip of Cap de Creus (itinerary 1A), Cap Norfeu (itinerary 1B) and the beginning (and end) of itinerary 6A, beside the village of La Morera.

Rock Thrush (Merla roquera) *Monticola saxatilis*

A summer visitor to Catalonia. It breeds in both high mountain and several Mediterranean mountain areas, where it is at present spreading its range, almost certainly because of the increase in the amount of rocky and vegetation-free areas caused by forest fires. Good areas for watching Rock Thrush are the Garraf massif (itinerary 5C) and the itinerary along the southern side of the Moixeró range (itinerary 13A). One of the most regular observation sites, however, is the Perves pass, which is on one of the link routes between the two Aigüestortes National Park itineraries (cf. page 196). If you decide to take the northern road between the two itineraries (over the Bonaigua pass), the area beneath the Mare de Déu de les Ares sanctuary also offers good chances of seeing this species (cf. page 197). Rock Thrush are present in our country from April to September, but the best time to see the species is when it sings (April and May), for it often sits on telephone wires or on prominent perches. Its plumage, which would at first appear to be very striking, may in fact be an effective camouflage in rocky areas where there is reddish lichen of the same colour as its chest.

Blue Rock Thrush (Merla blava) *Monticola solitarius*

This rupicoline species is associated with dry and rocky habitats both in average height mountain areas and on the coast. It has recently begun to colonize villages and towns. The best observation areas for this species are the Cap de Creus (chapter 1), the Montgrí (itinerary 3A), Montserrat and Garraf (itineraries 5B and 5C), Montsant-Siurana (chapter 6) and Ports de Tortosa i Beseit (chapter 8). Blue Rock Thrush are sedentary in Catalonia, although in winter they tend to move about a little (especially young birds). The male sings from prominent rocks and buildings, its wings drooping and its tail opened out in a fan. In flight, the blue tint of its wings distinguishes it from Blackbird, although females of these two species could well be confused if it were not for their different habitats and behaviour.

Moustached Warbler (Boscarla mostaxuda) *Acrocephalus melanopogon*

The only *Acrocephalus* warbler of Mediterranean distribution that winters in Catalonia. Its breeding population is sedentary, although birds from the north winter here too. It breeds in the reedbeds with deepest water, and often makes its nest on the limit between the vegetation and the open water, preferably in bulrush. The best areas for observing this species are the Aiguamolls de l'Empordà (chapter 2) and the Delta of the river Ebre (chapter 7). In the breeding season its song is similar to that of Reed Warbler, but it is more varied and has a "crescendo" of clear notes which is similar to the song of the Nightingale. In migration, this species can be confused with Sedge Warbler (*Acrocephalus schoenobaenus*), but in winter it is the only wintering

---

Acrocephalus warbler, and can be identified without any difficulty. Its alarm call is useful for detecting its presence in all seasons.

Spectacled Warbler (Tallarol trencamates) *Sylvia conspicillata*

This warbler is rare and shy, and is therefore quite difficult to see. In the areas covered in this book, the site it can most easily be seen is in the Montgrí scrub (itinerary 3A). It can also be seen on other coastal ranges such as Garraf (itinerary 5C), in the Cap de Creus (itinerary 1A) and on the edges of some crop areas, in barren and uncultivated areas with sparse bushes on the Ebre plain (itineraries 9A and 9B). One of its distinguishing features is the habitat it is to be found in (it is the warbler that prefers the areas with the lowest and sparsest vegetation). It is typical to see Spectacled Warbler (either alone or in groups) flitting from bush to bush. Its white neck and the reddish brown patch on the wings (which is also visible on female and young birds) are excellent field marks to distinguish it from Subalpine Warbler, which also lives in the Montgrí and in the majority of the areas that are mentioned for Spectacled Warbler. Subalpine Warbler, however, prefer areas with higher scrub. They breed from April to June, but migrating birds make the species visible in Catalonia from the end of March until mid-October.

Subalpine Warbler (Tallarol de garriga) *Sylvia cantillans*

This warbler is a summer visitor to Catalonia, and inhabits mountain areas of average height as well as bushy and wooded Mediterranean habitats. It can be spotted on most of the itineraries, except for those in Pyrenean and coastal wetland areas, where it can only be spotted on migration. Subalpine Warbler begin to arrive on their breeding grounds in the second half of April, but migration starts at the end of March in Catalonia. It stays on there until mid-October. It breeds in the scrub, thickets and in ilex, pine and cork oak woodland undergrowth. Females and especially the young can be mistaken for Spectacled Warbler (*Sylvia conspicillata*), but the difference in the colouring of the wings aids correct identification.

Sardinian Warbler (Tallarol de capnegre) *Sylvia melanocephala*

This warbler's distribution is typically Mediterranean. In Catalonia it is only missing from Pyrenean areas above the altitude of 700 metres, although isolated nesting sites have indeed been recorded in different Mediterranean highland areas. It is one of the easiest warblers to spot on most of the itineraries. Its sedentary nature makes it easy to locate throughout the year.

Wallcreeper (Pela-roques) *Tichodroma muraria*

This species is present in Catalonia all the year round, although it is to be seen in different areas at different times of year. From May to October it occupies its breeding areas (on cliffs and in high mountain scree areas) and is especially attracted to shady rock faces and rocky gorges on rivers. In this season Wallcreeper are more easily located (it never wanders far from its territory), but the hostile nature of the habitat and its small size make it a difficult species to observe. Itineraries 13A, 13B, 14A and 14C pass through areas where there are breeding territories. It should not be too difficult to spot if you wait long enough at the specific points on the itineraries, listening out for its typical whistle. In winter, a large proportion of this species' population spreads throughout the country, and can be seen in any area with rocky cliff faces and even on sea cliffs (chapters 1, 3, 4, 5, 6, 8, and 10). In this season it is harder to locate the exact sites where it may be seen, for its movements are quite erratic. However, you tend to get better views of the species because it frequents much more accessible areas. The Montrebei cliffs (itinerary 10A), those at Siurana (itinerary 6B) and the ones in the Ports de Beseit (itinerary 8A) are a few of this species' most regular wintering areas. Its call, a strange warbling song uttered when climbing rock faces and a typical whistle made when on the wing, are distinctive sounds to listen for when tracking down this species out of the breeding season.

Penduline Tit (Teixidor) *Remiz pendulinus*

Penduline Tit (in Catalan it is called "Teixidor" (weaver) because of the bag-like nest it makes) is a species which is associated with two different kinds of habitats. In the breeding season, from April to late July, it is to be found in riverside woodland areas. In winter, its favourite habitat is reedbeds. The species' distribution in Catalonia is basically limited to the Empordà, the Ebre area (including the Delta) and the Lleida plains. It can be observed on its breeding territories on several of the itineraries: the river Set and the canal you come to when you drive into Artesa de Lleida (itinerary 9A); the river Cinca (in the wood which lies behind you when observing the riverside cliffs on the way out of Alcolea on itinerary 9B); the edges of Montgai reservoir (itinerary 10B); the "Basses d'en Coll" at Pals (itinerary 3C); and the Mugueta, in the Aiguamolls de l'Empordà (itinerary 2B). In winter, on the other hand, it is to be found in good numbers in the Tres Ponts reedbeds (itinerary 2B), at La Massona lagoon (itinerary 2A) and at the Encanyissada lagoon (itinerary 7C). Its soft call, a long and plaintive "siiou", can be heard in the top of poplar trees or in the reedbeds, enabling you to locate the species.

Lesser Grey Shrike (Trenca) *Lanius minor*

There are only three known breeding sites for this species in the whole Iberian Peninsula. Two of these sites are in Catalonia, and are on itineraries described in this book. The first site is the almond groves and fields between Aspa and Artesa de Lleida on the second half of itinerary 9A; the second is on the Empordà plain. In this latter zone it can be spotted on the final part of itinerary 2A, between the Can Comes meadow area and the Cortalet Information Centre. It can also be seen on itinerary 2B, both on the path leading to the Vilahut hide (in some years it breeds in the cork oaks to the right of the lagoon) and in the olive groves between Pau and Torre Mornau, where it can often be seen on the electric wires. At both sites (LLeida plains and Empordà), the number of birds varies greatly from year to year, as do the precise breeding locations. However, their habit of sitting on prominent perches makes it quite an easy species to spot if you are patient. Although Great Grey Shrike like a slightly different habitat and are almost totally absent from the Empordà in summer, you must check on this species whenever you see it. Many field guides can be a little confusing on the subject. They tend to feature the central and north European subspecies of Great Grey Shrike which has longer wing bars than Lesser Grey Shrike. The Iberian Great Grey Shrike, on the other hand, has much shorter ones. It also has a pinkish chest, as does the Lesser Grey. If you spot the black forehead, you can be sure that it is a Lesser Grey; but if you do not, you cannot be sure it is a Great Grey for this field mark is not very clear (and may be absent) in young and female birds. One key field mark in birds of any age or sex is the different proportion there is between wing and tail. Great Greys have a long tail and short wings and the tip of the wing only reaches as far as the base of the tail when the bird is sitting. The Lesser Grey, however, has a shorter tail and a proportionally longer wing which reaches almost as far as a point half-way down the tail. Lesser Greys do not arrive in Catalonia until early May. They leave in late August or early September. They do not migrate by way of the Iberian Peninsula, but across Europe and the Middle East to their winter quarters in East Africa.

Alpine Chough (Gralla de bec groc) *Pyrrhocorax graculus*

This typical high mountain member of the crow family is sedentary in the Pyrenees and only moves into the foothill area (where it mixes with Chough) in the coldest winters. You are likely to see it on the following Pyrenean itineraries: Aigüestsortes (chapter 11), Andorra (chapter 12), Cadí-Moixeró (chapter 13) and Núria (chapter 14). Alpine Chough are sometimes very tame, and approach hikers in search of left-overs. Other than the difference in beak colour and habitat, the calls of the two species are quite different. Beware of young Chough, that also have a yellow beak, although it is longer and curved.

Spotless Starling (Estornell negre) *Sturnus unicolor*

This sedentary species was considered to be an accidental in Catalonia until a short time ago. It has recently colonized this area and continues to extend its range. It now inhabits the southern and south-western *comarques* of Catalonia, where it coincides with the Common Starling, which also began breeding in Catalonia in 1960. The best areas for the observation of Spotless Starling are the Montsant (chapter 6), the Ports de Tortosa (chapter 8) and the Lleida steppes (chapter 9). At Menàrguens church (on the road linking itineraries 9B and 9C; cf. page 154), both species breed and it is a very good spot for observing the differences between them. Spotless Starling are very gregarious, and generally breed in colonies. They winter in huge flocks. The breeding period of Spotless Starling begins about 15 days after that of Common Starling. The eggs are laid in the first two weeks of April. In winter there are no difficulties telling the two species apart. In the breeding season, however, it has a blacker, more uniform and shiny plumage than Common Starling, which always retains a certain amount of white spots, especially on the back.

Rock Sparrow (Pardal roquer) *Petronia petronia*

Rock Sparrow is a sedentary species in Catalonia, and only moves about a little in winter. It breeds in rocky areas, on cliffs, in dry agricultural areas and small villages in dry and sunny areas. Its distribution is very local and erratic, and this factor makes it difficult to locate any regular breeding sites. You should be able to find the odd colony in the vicinity of the village of Ogassa (cf. page 236). On itinerary 6A you will also have a good chance of seeing Rock Sparrow. The best field mark to be looking out for is the long and bold supercilliary stripe, as well as lighter colouring and a shriller call than other sparrows.

Snow Finch (Pardal d'ala blanca) *Montifringilla nivalis*

It is present all the year round in Catalonia, but only breeds in Alpine meadows (with rocky outcrops) above the altitude of 2,200 metres. In winter it descends to lower areas in cold winters. Flocks are sometimes quite numerous (as many as 200 birds recorded in September). The best areas to see this species are Andorra (chapter 12), the Cadí-Moixeró mountains, and at

Coma Floriu (itinerary 13A), especially in winter. In autumn and winter, it can also be seen beside the Núria Sanctuary and at the Cremal bridge (itinerary 14A). In the breeding season, it can be seen at Coma de l'Embut (itinerary 14C). When it is in the vicinity of buildings (eg. ski resort bars) it is normally accompanied by Alpine Accentor and House Sparow. The breeding period for Snow Finch depends on the weather in high mountain areas, and on the onset of the spring thaw. Snow Finch are very spectacular on the wing, and can only be confused with Snow Bunting, with which they may coincide in habitat in winter and on migration. This circumstance, however, will be quite accidental.

Citril Bunting (Llucareta) *Serinus citrinella*

This finch breeds in the Pyrenees in Subalpine areas and in coniferous woods between the altitude of 1,200 metres and the tree line. In winter it descends to lower areas. In winter it moves about mixing in with flocks of Serin and other finches. They are often overlooked for this reason. It can be quite easily seen on almost all the Pyrenean itineraries (chapters 11, 12, 13, and 14). The yellow rump and the greyish green back are the most important field marks to look out for.

LIST OF BIRDS

	Status	Frequency
	P: present all the year round	V: very common
	S: summer visitor	Q: quite common
	W: winter visitor	u: uncommon
	m: on migration only	o: occasional

Red-throated Diver *Gavia stellata*	W	
Black-throated Diver *Gavia arctica*	W	
Great Northern Diver *Gavia immer*	W	
Little Grebe *Tachybaptus ruficollis*	P	
Great Crested Grebe *Podiceps cristatus*	P	
Black-necked Grebe *Podiceps nigricollis*	W	
Cory's Shearwater *Calonectris diomedea*	P	
Manx Shearwater *Puffinus puffinus*	P	
British Storm Petrel *Hydrobates pelagicus*	P	
Northern Gannet *Sula bassana*	W	
Common Cormorant *Phalacrocorax carbo*	W	Sporadic breeding on the Medes Islan
Shag *Phalacrocorax aristotelis*	P	
Eurasian Bittern *Botaurus stellaris*	P	
Little Bittern *Ixobrychus minutus*	S	
Night Heron *Nycticorax nycticorax*	S	Exceptional in winter
Squacco Heron *Ardeola ralloides*	S	
Cattle Egret *Bubulcus ibis*	P	
Little Egret *Egretta garzetta*	P	
Great Egret *Egretta alba*	W	
Grey Heron *Ardea cinerea*	P	
Purple Heron *Ardea purpurea*	S	
Black Stork *Ciconia nigra*	m	Exceptional in winter
White Stork *Ciconia ciconia*	P	
Glossy Ibis *Plegadis falcinellus*	m	Exceptional in winter
White Spoonbill *Platalea leucorodia*	m	
Greater Flamingo *Phoenicopterus ruber*	P	
Mute Swan *Cygnus olor*	P	
Bean Goose *Anser fabalis*	W	Irregular and rare
Greylag Goose *Anser anser*	W	
Shelduck *Tadorna tadorna*	P	
European Wigeon *Anas penelope*	W	
Gadwall *Anas strepera*	P	

Cap de Creus	Aiguamolls	C.Brava Sud	Montseny	Barcelona	Montsant	Delta Ebre	Ports	Lleida	Montsec	Aigüestortes	Andorra	Cadí	Núria	Garrotxa
1	**2**	**3**	**4**	**5**	**6**	**7**	**8**	**9**	**10**	**11**	**12**	**13**	**14**	**15**
o	u	u		o		o								
u	Q	u		o		u								
	o	o				o								
	Q	Q	o		o	V			Q		o			o
o	u	u		u	o	V			V					
	Q	u				V			o					
Q	o	u		u		u								
Q	o	u		u		u								
o	o	o		o		o								
V	o	Q		u		Q								
V	V	V	Q			V			o					
u	o	V		u		o								
	u	o				u			o					
	Q	u				V			o					
	u	Q		o		V			o					
	u	u				V								
	V	V		u		V								
	V	Q		o		V			o					o
	o					u								
o	V	Q	o	V		V		u	V		o	o		u
	V	u				V			V					
	o	o				o			o					
	V	o	o			u		V	o		o			o
	o					u								
	o					u								
	Q	o		o		V								
	V					o								
	o					o								
	u	o				Q			o					
	Q	o				V								
	Q	o		o		V			Q					
	Q	u				V			Q					

List 2

	Status	Frequency
	P: present all the year round	**V**: very common
	S: summer visitor	Q: quite common
	W: winter visitor	u: uncommon
	m: on migration only	o: occasional

Species	Status	Notes
Green-winged Teal *Anas crecca*	W	Exceptional breeding
Mallard *Anas platyrhynchos*	P	
Pintail *Anas acuta*	W	
Garganey *Anas querquedula*	m	Regular breeding in the Empordà
Common Shoveller *Anas clypeata*	W	Regular breeding in the Ebre's Delta
Marbled Teal *Marmaronetta angustirostris*	m	Exceptional breeding
Red-crsted Pochard *Netta rufina*	P	
European Pochard *Aythya ferina*	W	Regular breeding in the Ebre's Delta
Ferruginous Duck *Aythya nyroca*	W	
Tufted Duck *Aythya fuligula*	W	
Greater Sacup *Aythya marila*	W	
Eider *Somateria mollissima*	W	
Common Scoter *Melanitta nigra*	W	
Velvet Scoter *Melanitta fusca*	W	
Goldeneye *Bucephala clangula*	W	
Smew *Mergus albellus*	W	
Red-breasted Merganser *Mergus serrator*	W	
Goosander *Mergus merganser*	W	
Honey Buzzard *Pernis apivorus*	S	Abundant on migration
Black Kite *Milvus migrans*	S	Abundant on migration
Red Kite *Milvus milvus*	P	
Lammergeier *Gypaetus barbatus*	P	
Egyptian Vulture *Neophron percnopterus*	S	
Griffon Vulture *Gyps fulvus*	P	
Short-toed Eagle *Circaetus gallicus*	S	
Marsh Harrier *Circus aeruginosus*	P	
Hen Harrier *Circus cyaneus*	P	Only in summer in the Pyrenees ar
Montagu's Harrier *Circus pygargus*	S	
Northern Goshawk *Accipiter gentilis*	P	
European Sparrow Hawk *Accipiter nisus*	P	
Common Buzzard *Buteo buteo*	P	
Golden Eagle *Aquila chrysaetos*	P	

	Cap de Creus	Aiguamolls	C.Brava Sud	Montseny	Barcelona	Montsant	Delta Ebre	Ports	Lleida	Montsec	Aigüestortes	Andorra	Cadí	Núria	Garrotxa
	1	2	3	4	5	6	7	8	9	10	11	12	13	14	15
		V	Q	o	o	o	V			V		o			
	o	V	Q	u	V	o	V		o	V	o	o	o		u
		u	o		o		V			o					
		Q	o				Q			o					
		Q	u				V			Q					
							o								
		u	o				V								
		Q	u				V			Q					
		o					u			o					
		u	o				Q			u					
		o					u			o					
	o	u	o		o		u								
	o	u	o		o		Q								
		u	o		o		u								
		o					o								
		o					o								
		u	o				Q								
		o					o			o					
	u	u	u	u	u	u	u	u	u	u	u	u	u	u	u
	u	u	u	o	u	u	u	u	u	u	u	u	u	u	u
	o	o	o	o	o	o	o	o	u	Q	u	u	o	o	o
										Q	Q	u	Q	u	
				o	o	o	o	o	Q	Q	o	o	o		
					o	u	o	V	u	V	V	Q	u	o	
	u	Q	u	Q	u	Q	u	Q	Q	V	u	u	Q	Q	Q
	u	V	Q	o	Q	u	V	u	u	o		o			o
	o	Q	Q	o	u	o	Q	o	Q	o	o	u	o	Q	o
	o	u	o	o	o	o	u	o	Q	o	o	o	o	o	o
	o		u	Q	u	u		u		Q	u	u	Q	u	Q
	o	o	o	Q	Q	Q	o	Q	u	Q	Q	Q	Q	u	Q
	u	Q	Q	Q	u	u	Q	u	V	V	u	u	V	V	Q
	o			o	o	u		Q	u	Q	Q	Q	Q	Q	o

	Status		Frequency
	P: present all the year round		**V**: very common
	S: summer visitor		Q: quite common
	W: winter visitor		u: uncommon
	m: on migration only		o: occasional

Booted Eagle *Hieraaetus pennatus*	S	Regular winter visitor to the Emporc
Bonelli's Eagle *Hieraaetus fasciatus*	P	
Osprey *Pandion haliaetus*	m	Rare winter visitor
Lesser Kestrel *Falco naumanni*	S	Currently extinct in Catalonia
Common Kestrel *Falco tinnunculus*	P	
Red-footed Falcon *Falco vespertinus*	m	
Merlin *Falco columbarius*	W	
European Hobby *Falco subbuteo*	S	
Eleonora's Falcon *Falco eleonorae*	S	Late summer visitor (June-October)
Peregrine Falcon *Falco peregrinus*	P	
Rock Ptarmigan *Lagopus mutus*	P	
Capercaillie *Tetrao urogallus*	P	
Red-legged Partridge *Alectoris rufa*	P	
Grey Partridge *Perdix perdix*	P	
Common Quail *Coturnix coturnix*	S	Regular winter visitor
Ring-necked Pheasant *Phasianus colchicus*	P	Introduced species
Water Rail *Rallus aquaticus*	P	
Spotted Crake *Porzana porzana*	m	Rare winter visitor
Little Crake *Porzana parva*	m	
Baillon's Crake *Porzana pusilla*	S	
Corncrake *Crex crex*	m	Recently discovered as a breeder
Moorhen *Gallinula chloropus*	P	
Purple Gallinule *Porphyrio porphyrio*	P	Re-introduced species
Common Coot *Fulica atra*	P	
Common Crane *Grus grus*	m	Exceptional in winter
Little Bustard *Tetrax tetrax*	P	
Oystercatcher *Haematopus ostralegus*	P	Rare and irregular winter visitor
Black-winged Stilt *Himantopus himantopus*	S	Exceptional in winter
Avocet *Recurvirostra avosetta*	P	
Stone-Curlew *Burhinus oedicnemus*	P	
Pratincole *Glareola pratincola*	S	
Little Ringed Plover *Charadrius dubius*	S	

	Cap de Creus	Aiguamolls	C.Brava Sud	Montseny	Barcelona	Montsant	Delta Ebre	Ports	Lleida	Montsec	Aigüestortes	Andorra	Cadí	Núria	Garrotxa
	1	2	3	4	5	6	7	8	9	10	11	12	13	14	15
	o	u	o	o	o		o	o	o	u		o	o		
	u	o	u	Q	u	Q	o	Q	u	Q					
	o	u	o	o	u	o	Q	o	o	o		o			
				o					u						
	V	V	V	Q	V	V	Q	V	V	V	Q	V	V	V	Q
		o													
		u	o		o		u	o	Q	o					
	o	u	u	u	u	o	u	u	Q	u			u	u	u
		o	o		o		o								
	u	u	u	u	u	V	u	V	Q	Q	u	u	u	u	u
											u	u		Q	
											u	u	u	o	
	V	V	Q	Q	Q	Q		Q	V	V		u	Q		Q
												u	u	Q	Q
	u	Q	u	u	u	u	Q	u	V	V	o	u	Q	o	o
		u		u						o					
		Q	u	o			o		V		u	Q			
		u	o				u			o					
		o	o				o								
		o					u								
		o		o			o			o					
	u	V	V	u	o	u	V		u	V		o			V
		Q													
		V	Q		o		V			V					o
		o	o	o	o	o	u	o	o	o		o			
		o							V	o					
		u	o				Q								
	o	V	Q				V			o					
		u	o				V			o					
		Q	u	o	o		o		V	o			o		
		u	o				V								
		Q	u	u	o		Q			o			u		

	Status		Frequency
	P: present all the year round		**V**: very common
	S: summer visitor		Q: quite common
	W: winter visitor		u: uncommon
	m: on migration only		o: occasional

Ringed Plover *Charadrius hiaticula*	m	Rare winter visitor
Kentish Plover *Charadrius alexandrinus*	P	Rare in winter
Dotterel *Charadrius morinellus*	S	Small breeding population
Golden Plover *Pluvialis apricaria*	W	
Grey Plover *Pluvialis squatarola*	W	
Lapwing *Vanellus vanellus*	W	Rare breeder in the Delta of the river
Knot *Calidris canutus*	m	
Sanderling *Calidris alba*	m	Rare winter visitor
Little Stint *Calidris minuta*	W	
Temmink's Stint *Calidris temminckii*	m	
Curlew Sandpiper *Calidris ferruginea*	m	
Dunlin *Calidris alpina*	W	
Ruff *Philomachus pugnax*	m	Rare winter visitor
Jack Snipe *Lymnocryptes minimus*	W	
Common Snipe *Gallinago gallinago*	W	
Woodcock *Scolopax rusticola*	P	
Black-tailed Godwit *Limosa limosa*	W	
Bar-tailed Godwit *Limosa lapponica*	m	Exceptional in winter
Whimbrel *Numenius phaeopus*	m	
Curlew *Numenius arquata*	W	
Spotted Redshank *Tringa erythropus*	m	Rare winter visitor
Redshank *Tringa totanus*	P	
Marsh Sandpiper *Tringa stagnatilis*	m	
Greenshank *Tringa nebularia*	m	Rare winter visitor
Green Sandpiper *Tringa ochropus*	m	Exceptional in winter
Wood Sandpiper *Tringa glareola*	m	
Common Sandpiper *Actitis hypoleucos*	P	
Turnstone *Arenaria interpres*	m	Rare winter visitor
Red-necked Phalarope *Phalaropus lobatus*	m	
Pomarine Skua *Stercorarius pomarinus*	m	
Arctic Skua *Stercorarius parasiticus*	m	
Great Skua *Stercorarius skua*	W	

Cap de Creus	Aiguamolls	C.Brava Sud	Montseny	Barcelona	Montsant	Delta Ebre	Ports	Lleida	Montsec	Aigüestortes	Andorra	Cadí	Núria	Garrotxa
1	**2**	**3**	**4**	**5**	**6**	**7**	**8**	**9**	**10**	**11**	**12**	**13**	**14**	**15**
	Q	u		o		V			o					
	V	Q		o		V								
	o							o				o	o	
	Q	u				Q		o						
	V	u		o		V								
	V	Q	u	o	o	V	o	Q	Q			o		Q
	u	o				Q								
	u	u		o		V								
	Q	u				V								
	o	o				u								
	u	u				u								
	V	u		o		V								
	V	Q		o		V			o					
	o	o	o			u			o					o
o	V	Q	u		o	V	.		u		o			u
o	o	o	Q	u	u	o	u	o	o	u	u	o	o	Q
	Q	u				V			o					
	u	o				Q								
	u	o				Q								
	V	u		o		V								
	Q	u				Q			o					
o	V	Q		o		V			u					
	o	o				u								
	Q	u				Q			o					
	Q	u	o			Q			o					o
	Q	u	o			V			o					
o	Q	u	u	o		Q				Q	u	u	u	o
	u	o				Q								
	o					o								
						o								
u	o	o		o		u								
u	o	o		o		u								

	Status P: present all the year round S: summer visitor W: winter visitor m: on migration only	Frequency **V**: very common Q: quite common u: uncommon o: occasional
Mediterranean Gull *Larus melanocephalus*	W	Exceptional breeding on the Ebre'
Little Gull *Larus minutus*	W	
Black-headed Gull *Larus ridibundus*	P	
Slender-billed Gull *Larus genei*	P	
Audouin's Gull *Larus audouinii*	S	
Common Gull *Larus canus*	W	
Lesser Black-backed Gull *Larus fuscus*	W	Small breeding population in the
Herring Gull *Larus cachinnans*	P	
Kittiwake *Rissa tridactyla*	W	
Gull-billed Tern *Gelochelidon nilotica*	S	
Caspian Tern *Sterna caspia*	m	Exceptional breeding in the Ebre
Lesser Crested Tern *Sterna bengalensis*	S	Exceptional breeding in the Ebre
Sandwich Tern *Sterna sandvicensis*	P	
Common Tern *Sterna hirundo*	S	
Little Tern *Sterna albifrons*	S	
Whiskered Tern *Chlidonias hybridus*	S	
Black Tern *Chlidonias niger*	m	Local and rare breeding
White-winged Black Tern *Chlidonias leucopterus*	m	
Razorbill *Alca torda*	W	
Atlantic Puffin *Fratercula arctica*	W	
Black-bellied Sandgrouse *Pterocles orientalis*	P	
Pintailed Sandgrouse *Pterocles alchata*	P	
Feral Rock Pigeon *Columba livia*	P	
Stock Dove *Columba oenas*	P	
Wood Pigeon *Columba palumbus*	P	
Collared Dove *Streptopelia decaocto*	P	Extending its range
Tórtora *Streptopelia turtur*	S	
Rose-ringed Parakeet *Psittacula krameri*	P	A regular population resulting
Monk Parakeet *Myiopsitta monachus*	P	A regular population resulting
Great Spotted Cuckoo *Clamator glandarius*	S	
European Cuckoo *Cuculus canorus*	S	
Barn Owl *Tyto alba*	P	

Cap de Creus	Aiguamolls	C.Brava Sud	Montseny	Barcelona	Montsant	Delta Ebre	Ports	Lleida	Montsec	Aigüestortes	Andorra	Cadí	Núria	Garrotxa
1	2	3	4	5	6	7	8	9	10	11	12	13	14	15
o	o	o		V		V			o					
o	u	o		u		Q								
V	V	V	u	V	o	V	o	u	Q			o		u
	o					V								
	o			o		V								
o	o			o		o								
o	u	o		V		V								
V	V	V	Q	V	o	V	o	o	u			Q	Q	V
u	o	o		o		u								
o	u	o		o		V								
o	o					Q								
						u								
Q	Q	Q		V		V								
u	Q	u		u		V								
o	u	o				V								
u	V	u		o		V			o					
u	Q	u		u		Q			o					
	o					o								
u	Q	Q		u		Q								
				o		o								
								u						
								Q						
		o							o					u
u	Q	u	u	Q	V	o	Q	V	u	u	u	u	u	o
u	V	Q	V	V	V	u	V	V	V	V	Q	V	Q	V
	Q			o		o			o					u
u	Q	Q	V	V	V	u	V	V	V	o	u	o	o	Q
				u										
				V										
o	Q	u	o	u	o	o		Q	Q					
Q	V	V	Q	V	V	V	Q	V	V	V	Q	V	Q	Q
u	Q	Q	Q	u	u	Q	u	Q	Q			u	o	Q

Status	Frequency
P: present all the year round	**V**: very common
S: summer visitor	**Q**: quite common
W: winter visitor	**u**: uncommon
m: on migration only	**o**: occasional

Scops Owl *Otus scops*	S	
Eagle Owl *Bubo bubo*	P	
Little Owl *Athene noctua*	P	
Tawny Owl *Strix aluco*	P	
Long-eared Owl *Asio otus*	P	
Short-eared Owl *Asio flammeus*	W	
Tengmalm's Owl *Aegolius funereus*	P	
European Nightjar *Caprimulgus europaeus*	S	
Red-necked Nightjar *Caprimulgus ruficollis*	S	
Common Swift *Apus apus*	S	
Pallid Swift *Apus pallidus*	S	
Alpine Swift *Apus melba*	S	
Common Kingfisher *Alcedo atthis*	P	
Bee-eater Merops *apiaster*	S	
Common Roller *Coracias garrulus*	S	
Hoopoe *Upupa epops*	S	Winters at a few sites
Wryneck *Jynx torquilla*	S	Rare in winter
Green Woodpecker *Picus viridis*	P	
Black Woodpecker *Dryocopus martius*	P	
Great Spotted Woodpecker *Picoides major*	P	
Lesser Spotted Woodpecker *Picoides minor*	P	
Dupont's Lark *Chersophilus duponti*	P	
Calandra Lark *Melanocorypha calandra*	P	
Short-toed Lark *Calandrella brachydactyla*	S	
Lesser Short-toed Lark *Calandrella rufescens*	P	
Crested Lark *Galerida cristata*	P	
Thekla Lark *Galerida theklae*	P	
Wood Lark *Lullula arborea*	P	
Sky Lark *Alauda arvensis*	P	
Sand Martin *Riparia riparia*	S	
Roquerol *Ptyonoprogne rupestris*	P	
Barn Swallow *Hirundo rustica*	S	Occasional winter visitor

	Cap de Creus	Aiguamolls	C.Brava Sud	Montseny	Barcelona	Montsant	Delta Ebre	Ports	Lleida	Montsec	Aigüestortes	Andorra	Cadí	Núria	Garrotxa
	1	**2**	**3**	**4**	**5**	**6**	**7**	**8**	**9**	**10**	**11**	**12**	**13**	**14**	**15**
	u	Q	Q	u	Q	Q	u	u	V	V	u	u	Q	u	Q
	u		u	u	u	u		u	o	Q	o	u	u	o	u
	u	Q	Q	Q	Q	V	o	Q	V	V	o	u	o	o	Q
	o	u	u	V	V	V		V		Q	u	V	V	V	Q
	o	o	o	u	u	u	o	u	u	Q	o	u	u	o	u
		u	o				u		o	o					
											u		u		
		o	u	u	Q	u	o	u	o	Q		u	Q		u
	u			o	o	o	o	u	Q	Q					
	V	V	V	V	V	V	V	V	V	V	V	V	V	V	V
	Q	u	Q	o	Q		o		o	o					
	Q	u	V	u	V	V	o	Q	Q	Q	u	u	V	u	Q
	o	Q	u	u	o	u	Q	u	o	Q	u	u	o	u	u
	u	V	Q	u	Q	V	u	V	V	V	o	o	o	o	Q
		Q	u	o			o		V	u					
	Q	V	V	Q	V	V	V	V	V	V	u	u	o	u	V
	o	o	o	u	Q	u	o	u	o	u	u	u	Q	u	Q
	u	V	V	V	Q	V	o	V	V	V	V	Q	V	V	V
											Q	Q	Q		
		u		u		u		u		V	V	V	V	V	Q
				o									o		
								o							
	o			o					V	Q					
	u	u	o			u	V		V		u	o			
		o	o				Q		V						
	o	V	V	Q	Q	u	V	V	V	V		o	V		Q
	V	o	Q		V	u		Q	V	Q					
	u	o	o	u	Q	V	o	Q	u	V	u	V	u	u	u
	Q	V	V	V	Q	u	Q	Q	V	V	u	V	V	V	u
	o	Q	u	o	o	o	Q	o	V	u					
	V	o	V	Q	V	V	o	V	u	V	V	V	V	V	V
	V	V	V	V	V	V	V	V	V	V	V	V	V	V	V

	Status	Frequency
	P: present all the year round	V: very common
	S: summer visitor	Q: quite common
	W: winter visitor	u: uncommon
	m: on migration only	o: occasional

Red-rumped Swallow *Hirundo daurica*	S	
House Martin *Delichon urbica*	S	
Tawny Pipit *Anthus campestris*	S	
Tree Pipit *Anthus trivialis*	S	
Meadow Pipit *Anthus pratensis*	W	
Red-throated Pipit *Anthus cervinus*	m	
Rock Pipit *Anthus spinoletta*	P	
Yellow Wagtail *Motacilla flava*	S	
Grey Wagtail *Motacilla cinerea*	P	
Pied Wagtail *Motacilla alba*	P	
Dipper *Cinclus cinclus*	P	
Wren *Troglodytes troglodytes*	P	
Dunnock *Prunella modularis*	P	
Alpine Accentor *Prunella collaris*	P	In high mountain areas in summer a
Rufous Bushchat *Cercotrichas galactotes*	m	Breeding not certain
European Robin *Erithacus rubecula*	P	
Nightingale *Luscinia megarhynchos*	S	
Bluethroat *Luscinia svecica*	W	
Black Redstart *Phoenicurus ochruros*	P	
Common Redstart *Phoenicurus phoenicurus*	S	Local and rare breeding
Whinchat *Saxicola rubetra*	S	
Stonechat *Saxicola torquata*	P	
Common Wheatear *Oenanthe oenanthe*	S	
Black-eared Wheatear *Oenanthe hispanica*	S	
Black Wheatear *Oenanthe leucura*	P	
Rock Thrush *Monticola saxatilis*	S	
Blue Rock Thrush *Monticola solitarius*	P	
Ring Ouzel *Turdus torquatus*	S	Exceptional in winter
Blackbird *Turdus merula*	P	
Fieldfare *Turdus pilaris*	W	
Song Thrush *Turdus philomelos*	P	
Redwing *Turdus iliacus*	W	

	Cap de Creus	Aiguamolls	C.Brava Sud	Montseny	Barcelona	Montsant	Delta Ebre	Ports	Lleida	Montsec	Aigüestortes	Andorra	Cadí	Núria	Garrotxa
	1	2	3	4	5	6	7	8	9	10	11	12	13	14	15
	o	o	Q		o	Q			o			o			
	V	V	V	V	V	V	V	V	V	V	V	V	V	V	V
	u	u	o	u	Q	u	u	Q	u	u	o	o	o	u	o
	u	u	u	Q	u	u	o	u	o	o	V	V	V	Q	Q
	u	Q	Q	u	V	Q	V	V	V	V	u	Q	Q	u	V
		u	o					o	o			o			
	u	Q	u	u	o	u	Q	u	o	u	V	V	V	V	Q
	u	V	Q		o	u	V		o	u		u	Q	o	o
	u	u	u	Q	V	V	u	V	u	Q	V	V	V	V	V
	Q	V	V	V	V	V	V	V	Q	V	V	V	V	Q	V
			u		u		u			u	Q	Q	V	V	Q
	u	u	Q	V	V	V	o	V	u	Q	V	V	V	V	V
	u	u	Q	Q	V	V	u	V	u	Q	V	V	V	Q	V
	Q			u	u	V		Q		Q	u	V	V	V	u
	o						o								
	V	V	V	V	V	V	Q	V	V	Q	V	V	V	V	V
	V	V	V	V	V	V	u	V	V	V	V	V	Q	V	V
		u	o					u			o				
	V	Q	V	V	V	V	Q	V	V	V	V	V	V	V	Q
	u	u	u	Q	Q	u	u	u	u	o	o	u	o	o	u
	u	u	u	u	u	u	u	o	o	u	u	Q	u	u	u
	V	V	V	V	V	V	u	Q	V	V	Q	u	Q	Q	V
	Q	Q	Q	Q	u	u	Q	u	V	Q	V	V	V	V	u
	V	o	V	u	V	V	u	V	V	Q		o			o
	Q		Q		u	V		u	Q	u					
	Q		o	u	Q	u	o	u		u	u	u	Q	Q	
	V		V	o	V	V		V	Q	Q			o		
	o	o	o	o	u	u	o	u	o	o	Q	V	V	Q	o
	Q	Q	V	V	V	V	u	V	Q	V	V	V	V	V	V
	o	o	o	o	o	u	o	o	o	o	o	u	u	u	o
	V	Q	Q	V	V	Q	u	V	V	Q	V	V	V	u	V
	u	o	u	u	o	u	u	u	u	o	o	u	o	o	u

	Status	Frequency
	P: present all the year round	**V**: very common
	S: summer visitor	Q: quite common
	W: winter visitor	u: uncommon
	m: on migration only	o: occasional

Mistle Thrush *Turdus viscivorus*	P
Cetti's Warbler *Cettia cetti*	P
Fan-tailed Warbler *Cisticola juncidis*	P
Grasshopper Warbler *Locustella naevia*	m
Savi's Warbler *Locustella luscinioides*	S
Moustached Warbler *Acrocephalus melanopogon*	P
Aquatic Warbler *Acrocephalus paludicola*	m
Sedge Warbler *Acrocephalus schoenobaenus*	m
Marsh Warbler *Acrocephalus palustris*	m
Reed Warbler *Acrocephalus scirpaceus*	S
Great Reed Warbler *Acrocephalus arundinaceus*	S
Olivaceous Warbler *Hippolais pallida*	m Nidificació dubtosa
Icterine Warbler *Hippolais icterina*	m
Melodious Warbler *Hippolais polyglotta*	S
Dartford Warbler *Sylvia undata*	P
Spectacled Warbler *Sylvia conspicillata*	S
Subalpine Warbler *Sylvia cantillans*	S
Sardinian Warbler *Sylvia melanocephala*	P
Orphean Warbler *Sylvia hortensis*	S
Whitethroat *Sylvia communis*	S
Garden Warbler *Sylvia borin*	S
Blackcap *Sylvia atricapilla*	P
Bonelli's Warbler *Phylloscopus bonelli*	S
Wood Warbler *Phylloscopus sibilatrix*	m
Chiff-chaff *Phylloscopus collybita*	P
Willow Warbler *Phylloscopus trochilus*	m
Goldcrest *Regulus regulus*	P
Firecrest *Regulus ignicapillus*	P
Spotted Flycatcher *Muscicapa striata*	S
Pied Flycatcher *Ficedula hypoleuca*	S Local and rare breeding
Bearded Tit *Panurus biarmicus*	P
Long-tailed Tit *Aegithalos caudatus*	P

Cap de Creus	Aiguamolls	C.Brava Sud	Montseny	Barcelona	Montsant	Delta Ebre	Ports	Lleida	Montsec	Aigüestortes	Andorra	Cadí	Núria	Garrotxa
1	**2**	**3**	**4**	**5**	**6**	**7**	**8**	**9**	**10**	**11**	**12**	**13**	**14**	**15**
u	o	u	Q	Q	Q	o	V	Q	V	V	V	V	V	V
Q	V	V	Q	u	V	V	Q	Q	V			o	u	Q
Q	V	V	Q	u	u	V		u	u			o		u
o	o	o		o	o	o			o					
	u	o			o	V			o					
	Q	u				Q			o					
	o					o			o					
	o	o				u			o					
	o	o				o								
o	V	V		u	u	V		u	Q					u
o	V	V	u	o	u	V		V	V					
									o					
	o	o												
Q	Q	Q	u	Q	Q	Q	Q	Q	Q	u	Q	u	Q	u
Q	u	Q	u	V	V	Q	V	V	Q	u	u	u	u	u
u	o	u		u		o	u	u	o					
u	u	u	u	u	Q	u	Q	Q	Q	o	u	o	o	Q
V	Q	V	Q	V	V	u	V	V	V	o	u	o	o	Q
u	o	u	o	u	u	o	u	u	u			o		
u	u	u	u	u	u	u	u	u	u	u	u	Q	u	u
u	u	u	u	Q	u	u	Q	u	Q	V	Q	Q	u	u
V	V	V	V	V	V	u	V	Q	V	Q	Q	V	V	V
u	o	u	u	V	V	o	V	Q	Q	u	Q	u	Q	Q
	o	o	o	o		o			o		o			o
V	V	V	Q	V	V	V	Q	V	V	V	Q	V	V	V
Q	Q	Q	u	Q	u	Q	u	Q	u	u	u	u	u	u
u	o	u	Q	u	Q	o	u		o	V	V	V	Q	Q
u	o	Q	Q	V	V	o	V	u	V	V	Q	Q	V	V
u	u	u	u	Q	u	u	Q	Q	Q	u	u	o	Q	Q
u	u	u	u	u	u	u	u	Q	u	u	u	u	u	u
	u	o				Q								
u	u	V	V	V	V	o	V	u	Q	V	V	Q	V	V

	Status	Frequency
	P: present all the year round	**V**: very common
	S: summer visitor	Q: quite common
	W: winter visitor	u: uncommon
	m: on migration only	o: occasional

Marsh Tit *Parus palustris*	P	
Crested Tit *Parus cristatus*	P	
Coal Tit *Parus ater*	P	
Blue Tit *Parus caeruleus*	P	
Great Tit *Parus major*	P	
Nuthatch *Sitta europaea*	P	
Wallcreeper *Tichodroma muraria*	P	In high mountain areas in summer
Treecreeper *Certhia familiaris*	P	
Short-toed Treecreeper *Certhia brachydactyla*	P	
Penduline Tit *Remiz pendulinus*	P	
Golden Oriole *Oriolus oriolus*	S	
Red-backed Shrike *Lanius collurio*	S	
Lesser Grey Shrike *Lanius minor*	S	
Great Grey Shrike *Lanius excubitor*	P	
Woodchat Shrike *Lanius senator*	S	
Jay *Garrulus glandarius*	P	
Magpie *Pica pica*	P	
Alpine Chough *Pyrrhocorax graculus*	P	
Chough *Pyrrhocorax pyrrhocorax*	P	
Jackdaw *Corvus monedula*	P	
Carrion Crow *Corvus corone*	P	
Raven *Corvus corax*	P	
Common Starling *Sturnus vulgaris*	P	
Spotless Starling *Sturnus unicolor*	P	
House Sparrow *Passer domesticus*	P	
Tree Sparrow *Passer montanus*	P	
Rock Sparrow *Petronia petronia*	P	
Snow Finch *Montifringilla nivalis*	P	
Chaffinch *Fringilla coelebs*	P	
Brambling *Fringilla montifrigilla*	W	
Serin *Serinus serinus*	P	
Citril Finch *Serinus citrinella*	P	

Cap de Creus	Aiguamolls	C.Brava Sud	Montseny	Barcelona	Montsant	Delta Ebre	Ports	Lleida	Montsec	Aigüestortes	Andorra	Cadí	Núria	Garrotxa
1	**2**	**3**	**4**	**5**	**6**	**7**	**8**	**9**	**10**	**11**	**12**	**13**	**14**	**15**
			Q							u	u	u	u	Q
Q		V	Q	V	V	o	V		Q	V	V	V	Q	Q
o		o	Q	V	Q	o	V		V	V	V	V	V	Q
Q	u	V	V	V	V	o	V	V	V	V	V	u	Q	V
V	Q	V	V	V	V	o	V	V	V	V	V	V	V	V
		o	Q				Q		u	Q	Q	V	V	Q
u		u	o	u	Q		u	o	u	u	u	Q	u	
										u	Q	o	u	
Q	u	V	Q	V	V	o	V	Q	Q	V	V	V	V	Q
	Q	Q	o				Q	V	V					
u	Q	Q	Q	Q	Q	o	Q	V	Q	u	u	o	o	Q
		u							o	Q	Q	V	Q	Q
	u	o					Q							
u	u	u	u	Q	Q	u	Q	Q	Q	u	u	Q	u	u
V	Q	Q	u	Q	V	Q	V	Q	Q	u	u	Q	o	u
u		V	V	V	V		V		V	V	V	V	V	V
V	V	V	V	V	V	o	V	V	V	V	o	V	V	V
										Q	V	V	V	V
			o				V	V	Q	V	V	V	V	o
Q	V	V	u	Q	o	o	u	Q	Q			o		o
	o	o	o				u	Q	V	V	Q	V	V	V
Q	o	Q	u	Q	V	o	V	Q	V	V	V	V	V	Q
V	V	V	V	V	V	V	u	V	V	o	o	V	o	V
				o	u	V	Q	V	V	Q				
V	V	V	V	V	V	V	V	V	V	V	V	V	V	V
u	Q	Q	u	u	u	V	u	V	V	u	u	u	Q	V
u	o	u	o	u	Q		u	u	Q	o	u	o	u	u
		o				o				o	u	u	u	
V	V	V	V	V	V	Q	V	V	V	V	V	V	V	V
o	o	o	u	o	o	o	o	o	o	o	u	o	o	u
Q	Q	V	Q	V	V	Q	V	Q	V	Q	V	V	Q	V
							u		o	V	V	V	V	o

Status	Frequency
P: present all the year round	V: very common
S: summer visitor	Q: quite common
W: winter visitor	u: uncommon
m: on migration only	o: occasional

Greenfinch *Carduelis chloris*	P	
Goldfinch *Carduelis carduelis*	P	
Siskin *Carduelis spinus*	P	Small breeding population
Linnet *Carduelis cannabina*	P	
Red Crossbill *Loxia curvirostra*	P	
Bullfinch *Pyrrhula pyrrhula*	P	
Hawfinch *Coccothraustes coccothraustes*	W	Local and rare breeding
Snow Bunting *Plectrophenax nivalis*	W	
Yellowhammer *Emberiza citrinella*	P	
Cirl Bunting *Emberiza cirlus*	P	
Rock Bunting *Emberiza cia*	P	
Ortolan Bunting *Emberiza hortulana*	S	
Reed Bunting *Emberiza schoeniclus*	P	
Corn Bunting *Miliaria calandra*	P	

	Cap de Creus	Aiguamolls	C.Brava Sud	Montseny	Barcelona	Montsant	Delta Ebre	Ports	Lleida	Montsec	Aigüestortes	Andorra	Cadí	Núria	Garrotxa
	1	2	3	4	5	6	7	8	9	10	11	12	13	14	15
	Q	Q	Q	Q	V	Q	Q	V	Q	V	u	u	Q	Q	V
	V	V	V	Q	V	V	Q	V	V	V	V	Q	Q	Q	V
	o	o	u	u	Q	u	o	u	o	o	u	Q	V	Q	u
	V	Q	V	Q	u	V	Q	V	V	V	u	Q	u	Q	Q
			u	u	u	u		V		u	V	V	V	V	
					Q	u	u		u	o	Q	Q	Q	Q	Q
		o		u	o	o	o	o	u	o	o	o	o	o	Q
	o	o		o			o								
	u	o	o	u	o	o	o	o	u	u	Q	V	V	Q	Q
	Q	u	Q	Q	V	V	u	V	Q	Q	u	u	u	u	V
	Q	o	u	V	Q	V	o	V	Q	V	Q	V	V	V	V
	Q	o	u	u	Q	u	o	u	Q	u	u	u	u	u	u
	o	V	Q	o	o	o	V		o	Q					u
	V	V	V	Q	u	Q	u	Q	V	Q		o	Q	o	u

APPENDICES

APPENDIX A

LIST OF ACCIDENTAL BIRDS IN CATALONIA

Great Grebe *Podiceps major*
Red-necked Grebe *Podiceps griseigena*
Slavonian Grebe *Podiceps auritus*
Bulwer's Petrel *Bulweria bulwerii*
Greater Shearwater *Puffinus gravis*
Sooty Shearwater *Puffinus griseus*
Leach's Storm Petrel *Oceanodroma leucorhoa*
Cape Gannet *Sula capensis*
Pigmy Cormorant *Phalacrocorax pygmeus*
Eastern White Pelican *Pelecanus onocrotalus*
American Bittern *Botaurus lentiginosus*
Western Reef Heron *Egretta gularis*
White-faced Whistling Duck *Dendrocygna viduata*
Whistling Swan *Cygnus columbianus*
Whooper Swan *Cygnus cygnus*
Pink-footed Goose *Anser brachyrhynchus*
White-fronted Goose *Anser albifrons*
Barnacle Goose *Branta leucopsis*
Brent Goose *Branta bernicla*
Ruddy Shelduck *Tadorna ferruginea*
Wood Duck *Aix sponsa*
Mandarin *Aix galericulata*
Blue-winged Teal *Anas discors*
King Eider *Somateria spectabilis*
Long-tailed Duck *Clangula hyemalis*
Ruddy Duck *Oxyura jamaicensis*
White-headed Duck *Oxyura leucocephala*
Black-shouldered Kite *Elanus caeruleus*
White-tailed Sea Eagle *Haliaeetus albicilla*
European Black Vulture *Aegypius monachus*
Pallid Harrier *Circus macrourus*
Rough-legged Buzzard *Buteo lagopus*
Greater Spotted Eagle *Aquila clanga*
Imperial Eagle *Aquila heliaca*
Lanner Falcon *Falco biarmicus*

Red-knobbed Coot *Fulica cristata*
Great Bustard *Otis tarda*
Cream-coloured Courser *Cursorius cursor*
Sociable Plover *Chettusia gregaria*
Great Knot *Calidris tenuirostris*
Pectoral Sandpiper *Calidris melanotos*
Purple Sandpiper *Calidris maritima*
Broad-billed Sandpiper *Limicola falcinellus*
Buff-breasted Sandpiper *Tryngites subruficollis*
Great Snipe *Gallinago media*
Lesser Yellowlegs *Tringa flavipes*
Terek Sandpiper *Xenus cinereus*
Spotted Sandpiper *Actitis macularia*
Grey Phalarope *Phalaropus fulicarius*
Laughing Gull *Larus atricilla*
Sabine's Gull *Larus sabini*
Ring-billed Gull *Larus delawarensis*
Great Black-backed Gull *Larus marinus*
Royal Tern *Sterna maxima*
Roseate Tern *Sterna dougallii*
Sooty Tern *Sterna fuscata*
Common Guillemot *Uria aalge*
Little Auk *Alle alle*
Blue-cheeked Bee-eater *Merops superciliosus*
White-winged Lark *Melanocorypha leucoptera*
Richard's Pipit *Anthus novaeseelandiae*
Petchora Pipit *Anthus gustavi*
Waxwing *Bombycilla garrulus*
River Warbler *Locustella fluviatilis*
Marmora's Warbler *Sylvia sarda*
Barred Warbler *Sylvia nisoria*
Lesser Whitethroat *Sylvia curruca*
Red-breasted Flycatcher *Ficedula parva*
Collared Flycatcher *Ficedula albicollis*
Azure-winged Magpie *Cyanopica cyana*

Nutcracker *Nucifraga caryocatactes*
Rook *Corvus frugilegus*
Rose-coloured Starling *Sturnus roseus*
Spanish Sparrow *Passer hispaniolensis*

Redpoll *Carduelis flammea*
Red-headed Bunting *Emberiza bruniceps*
Black-headed Bunting *Emberiza melanocephala*

APPENDIX B

LIST OF MAMMALS, REPTILES AND AMPHIBIANS IN CATALONIA

MAMMALS

Insectivores

- Western Hedgehog *Erinaceus europaeus*
- Algerian Hedehog *Erinaceus algirus*
- Pyrenean Desman *Galemys pyrenaicus*
- Northern Mole *Talpa europaea*
- Common Shrew *Sorex araneus*
- Millet's Shrew *Sorex coronatus*
- Pygmy Shrew *Sorex minutus*
- Water Shrew *Neomys fodiens*
- Miller's Water Shrew *Neomys anomalus*
- Common European White-toothed Shrew *Crocidura russula*
- Pygmy White-toothed Shrew *Suncus etruscus*

Bats

- Greater Horseshoe Bat *Rhinolophus ferrum-equinum*
- Mediterranean Horseshoe Bat *Rhinolophus euryale*
- Mehely's Horseshoe Bat *Rhinolophus mehelyi*
- Lesser Horseshoe Bat *Rhinolophus hipposideros*
- Schreiber's Bat *Miniopterus schreibersi*
- Greater Moused-eared Bat *Myotis myotis*
- Lesser Moused-eared Bat *Myotis blythi*
- Daubenton's Bat *Myotis daubentoni*
- Long-fingered Bat *Myotis capaccinii*
- Bechstein's Bat *Myotis bechsteini*
- Natterer's Bat *Myotis nattereri*
- Geoffroy's Bat *Myotis emarginatus*
- Common Pipistrelle *Pipistrellus pipistrellus*

- Kuhl's Pipistrelle *Pipistrellus kuhli*
- Savi's Pipistrelle *Pipistrellus savii*
- Nathusius's Pipistrelle *Pipistrellus nathusii*
- Serotine *Eptesicus serotinus*
- Grey Long-eared Bat *Plecotus austriacus*
- Common Long-eared Bat *Plecotus auritus*
- Barbastelle *Barbastella barbastellus*
- Noctule *Nyctalus noctula*
- Leisler's Bat *Nyctalus leisleri*
- Free-tailed Bat *Tadarida teniotis*

Lagomorphs

- Brown Hare *Lepus europaeus*
- Rabbit *Oryctolagus cuniculus*

Rodents

- Red Squirrel *Sciurus vulgaris*
- Alpine Marmot *Marmota marmota*
- Garden Dormouse *Eliomys quercinus*
- Fat Dormouse *Glis glis*
- Wood Mouse *Apodemus sylvaticus*
- Ship Rat *Rattus rattus*
- Common Rat *Rattus norvegicus*
- House Mouse *Mus musculus*
- Algerian Mouse *Mus spretus*
- Bank Vole *Clethrionomys glareolus*
- Sothwestern Water Vole *Arvicola sapidus*
- Northern Water Vole *Arvicola terrestris*
- Pyrenean Pine Vole *Microtus pyrenaicus*
- Mediterranean Pine Vole *Microtus duodecimcostatus*
- Snow Vole *Microtus nivalis*
- Common Vole *Microtus arvalis*
- Field Vole *Microtus agrestis*

Even-toed Ungulates

- Wild Boar *Sus scrofa*
- Chamois *Rupicapra rupicapra*
- Spanish Ibex *Capra pyrenaica*
- Mouflon *Ovis musimon*
- Red Deer *Cervus elaphus*
- Fallow Deer *Dama dama*
- Roe Deer *Capreolus capreolus*

Carnivores

- Red Fox *Vulpes vulpes*
- Brown Bear *Ursus arctos*
- Weasel *Mustela nivalis*
- Stoat *Mustela erminea*
- American Mink *Mustela vison*
- European Polecat *Mustela putorius*
- Pine Marten *Martes martes*
- Beech Marten *Martes foina*
- Badger *Meles meles*
- Otter *Lutra lutra*
- Genet *Genetta genetta*
- Wild Cat *Felis silvestris*
- Lynx *Lynx lynx*

Whales and dolphins

- Blue Whale *Balaenoptera musculus*
- Fin Whale *Balaenoptera physalus*
- Sei Whale *Balaenoptera borealis*
- Minke Whale *Balaenoptera acutorostrata*
- Humpback Whale *Megaptera novaeangliae*
- Sperm Whale *Physeter macrocephalus*
- Cuvier's Whale *Ziphius cavirostris*
- Common Dolphin *Delphinus delphis*
- Striped Dolphin *Stenella coeruleoalba*
- Bottle-nosed Dolphin *Tursiops truncatus*
- Killer Whale *Orcinus orca*
- Long-finned Pilot Whale *Globicephala melaena*
- Risso's Dolphin *Grampus griseus*

86 species in all

REPTILES

Turtles and Tortoises

- Hermann's Tortoise *Testudo hermanni*
- Stripe-necked Terrapin *Mauremys caspica*

- European Pond Terrapin *Emys orbicularis*
- Leathery Turtle *Dermochelys coriacea*
- Loggerhead Turtle *Caretta caretta*
- Green Turtle *Chelonia mydas*

Lizards

- Moorish Gecko *Tarentola mauritanica*
- Turkish Gecko *Hemidactylus turcicus*
- Spiny Footed Lizard *Acanthodactylus erythrurus*
- Ocellated Lizard *Lacerta lepida*
- Green Lizard *Lacerta viridis*
- Sand Lizard *Lacerta agilis*
- Viviparous Lizard *Lacerta vivipara*
- Iberian Rock Lizard *Lacerta monticola*
- Common Wall Lizard *Podarcis muralis*
- Spanish Wall Lizard *Podarcis hispanica*
- Large Psammodromus *Psammodromus algirus*
- Spanish Psammodromus *Psammodromus hispanicus*
- Slow Worm *Anguis fragilis*
- Bedriaga's Skink *Chalcides bedriagai*
- Three-toed Skink *Chalcides chalcides*
- Amphisbaenian *Blanus cinereus*

Snakes

- Western Whip Snake *Coluber viridiflavus*
- Horseshoe Whip Snake *Coluber hippocrepis*
- Smooth Snake *Coronella austriaca*
- Southern Smooth Snake *Coronella girondica*
- Aesculapian Snake *Elaphe longissima*
- Ladder Snake *Elaphe scalaris*
- Montpellier Snake *Malpolon monspessulanus*
- Grass Snake *Natrix natrix*
- Viperine Snake *Natrix maura*
- Asp Viper *Vipera aspis*
- Lataste's Viper *Vipera latasti*

33 species in all

AMPHIBIANS

Newts and salamanders

- Fire Salamander *Salamandra salamandra*

- Pyrenean Brook Salamander *Euproctus asper*
- Palmate Newt *Triturus helveticus*
- Marbled Newt *Triturus marmoratus*
- Sharp-ribbed Salamander *Pleurodeles waltl*

Frogs and toads

- Painted Frog *Discoglossus pictus*
- Midwife Toad *Alytes obstetricans*

- Western Spadefoot *Pelobates cultripes*
- Parsley Frog *Pelodytes punctatus*
- Common Toad *Bufo bufo*
- Natterjack *Bufo calamita*
- Common Tree Frog *Hyla arborea*
- Stripeless Tree Frog *Hyla meridionalis*
- Grass Frog *Rana temporaria*
- Marsh Frog *Rana perezi*

15 species in all

APPENDIX C

INSTRUCTIONS FOR ENTRANCE OR PHOTOGRAHPY IN NATURE RESERVES

The National Park, and some of the nature reserves and parks covered in this book, have limited access and prohibitions for some kinds of activities. To avoid breaking any of the rules, signs and itineraries must be respected in each of these areas. Access regulations and the rules to be followed in reserve areas are usually provided at the Information Centres. Under no circumstance must you enter areas that are out of bounds nor Integral Nature Reserves (Reserves Naturals Integrals), unless a particular itinerary so permits.

If you wish to carry out a specific biological or geological study that affects the whole or part of a nature reserve (including professional photographic, film or video work), you must ask for permission at the Department of Agriculture, Livestock-rearing and Fisheries (DARP). Institutions and individuals wishing to carry out these studies or activities must supply a report (giving reasons for your work) and an application on official forms which will be supplied by the local DARP branch offices or by the parks themselves.

The local DARP branch offices will take a decision, having considered the report supplied by the park's governing body. This permit will specify the conditions under which these activities may be carried out.

Once the report or the study has been carried out, it will be necessary to state in an explicit fashion (in the study, publication or film) that it was carried out in the reserve area in question, with the support of DARP.

If there is a clause on the permit that insists on an escort of official technicians or guards for those carrying out the activities, applicants will have to pay the official tariffs for consultation and surveillance.

An extract of the regulation of October 7th 1987, which sets the prices for consultation and surveillance work done by DARP officials in nature reserves.

You may obtain these permits at the offices of the Nature Parks or at the local DARP branch offices:

- Sabino Arana, 22-24. 08028-BARCELONA.
- Sant Francesc, 29. 17001-GIRONA.